A COURSE IN
RUSSIAN
HISTORY

The Time of
Catherine the Great

Also from M.E. Sharpe

A Course in Russian History
The Seventeenth Century
Translated by Natalie Duddington
With an introduction by Alfred J. Rieber

From the New Russian History Series

The Emperors and Empresses of Russia
Rediscovering the Romanovs
Compiled by A.A. Iskenderov
Edited by Donald J. Raleigh

Women in Russian History
From the Tenth to the Twentieth Century
Natalia Pushkareva
Translated and Edited by Eve Levin

The Reforms of Peter the Great
Progress Through Coercion in Russia
Evgenii V. Anisimov
Translated and Edited by John T. Alexander

The Russian Empire in the Eighteenth Century
Searching for a Place in the World
Alexander B. Kamenskii
Translated and Edited by David Griffiths

A COURSE IN RUSSIAN HISTORY

The Time of
Catherine the Great

V.O. Kliuchevsky

Translated and Edited by
Marshall S. Shatz

M.E. Sharpe
Armonk, New York
London, England

Library of Congress Cataloging-in-Publication Data

Kliuchevskii, V. O. (Vasili Osipovich), 1841–1911.
[Kurs russkoi istorii. Chast′ 4–5. English]
A course in Russian history—the time of Catherine the Great / by
Vasily O. Kliuchevsky : translated and edited by Marshall S. Shatz.
p.   cm.
Includes bibliographical references and index.
ISBN 1-56324-526-4 (alk. paper). —
ISBN 1-56324-527-2 (pbk. : alk. paper)
1. Russia—History—Catherine II, 1762–1796.
I. Shatz, Marshall.   II. Title.
DK170.K4513   1997
947′.06—dc21   97-8080
CIP
Printed in the United States of America

The paper used in this publication meets the minimum requirements of
American National Standard for Information Sciences—
Permanence of Paper for Printed Library Materials,
ANSI Z 39.48-1984.

∞

BM (c)	10	9	8	7	6	5	4	3	2	1
BM (p)	10	9	8	7	6	5	4	3	2	1

∼ Contents ∼

Translator's Note		vii
Introduction: Vasily Kliuchevsky and Catherine the Great		ix
I	The Russian State in the Mid-Eighteenth Century: Elizabeth and Peter III	3
II	The Coup d'État of June 28, 1762	21
III	Catherine II: Upbringing and Character	31
IV	Foreign Policy	58
V	Domestic Policy	88
VI	The Commission of 1767	105
VII	Reform of Provincial Government	132
VIII	Serfdom	148
IX	The Gentry and the Impact of Western Culture	174
Glossary of Names		197
Glossary of Terms		209
Bibliography		213
Index		217

Illustrations follow page 104.

～ Translator's Note ～

This volume is a translation of Lectures 73–81 of Kliuchevsky's *Course in Russian History*, comprising the last two lectures of Part 4 and the first seven lectures of Part 5. The Russian text used for this translation is *Kurs russkoi istorii*, edited by V.A. Aleksandrov and A.A. Zimin, in the fourth and fifth volumes of V.O. Kliuchevskii, *Sochineniia v vos'mi tomakh* (Moscow: Gos. Izdat. Politicheskoi Literatury/Izdat. Sotsial'no-ekonomicheskoi Literatury, 1956–59).

The illustrations are from Volume 12 of *Sochineniia Imperatritsy Ekateriny II*, edited by A.N. Pypin (St. Petersburg: Imperial Academy of Sciences, 1907).

The transliteration system employed is a simplified version of the Library of Congress system, but with some additional changes to facilitate pronunciation.

Dates are given according to the Julian calendar in use in Russia both in Catherine's and in Kliuchevsky's time. It was eleven days behind the Western calendar in the eighteenth century and twelve days behind in the nineteenth.

I have taken some minor liberties with the text, adding chapter titles, dividing excessively long paragraphs, and rendering names according to American usage (first name and last name), with patronymics given in the Glossary of Names. All footnotes are those of the translator.

The preparation of this volume was made possible in part by a grant from the National Endowment for the Humanities, an independent federal agency. I am grateful to the Endowment for its generous support. I also wish to thank Professors Marc Raeff and John Alexander, who kindly read the Introduction and shared with me their expert knowledge of the reign of Catherine the Great.

～ Introduction ～

Vasily Kliuchevsky and Catherine the Great

A mong the outstanding works of literature generated by the bur-geoning culture of imperial Russia in the late nineteenth and early twentieth centuries was a historical work, Vasily Kliuchevsky's *A Course in Russian History*. It may seem odd to speak of a work of history—and in five volumes, no less—in the same breath as the great novels, stories, and plays that arose alongside it, but it is not inappropriate. In its cultural significance for Russia and even in its artistic qualities, Kliuchevsky's *Course* is worthy of comparison with its fictional contemporaries. It constitutes a grand synthesis of ten centuries of Russian history, from the rise of the Kievan state in the ninth century to the emancipation of the serfs in 1861. More than any other single work, for much of the twentieth century Kliuchevsky's *Course* has shaped the conception of Russia's history in the minds of educated Russians and even, to a considerable degree, of non-Russians.

From its inception, the impact of the *Course* grew in ever widening circles, like a stone cast into a pond. At first its influence was confined to the students at Moscow University, where Kliuchevsky taught for over thirty years. Even there, it reached well beyond Kliuchevsky's own lecture hall (which was the largest at the university). Given the scarcity of printed textbooks, professors' lectures were frequently transcribed by students and disseminated in lithographed form. Sometimes the lithographed versions were authorized and corrected by the professor, sometimes they were unauthorized. Numerous lithographed editions of Kliuchevsky's lectures, some approved by him and some illicit, appeared over the years and circulated widely. The *Course* reached a much broader public when Kliuchevsky began to publish it, to great acclaim, in book form in 1904. Four parts, or volumes, had appeared by the time of his death in 1911.[1] In an article appropriately entitled "Kliuchevsky's Russia," the historian of religion George Fedotov, who was educated before the Russian Revolution, wrote that "whenever any of us think of historical Russia, what comes to mind is the Russia Kliuchevsky visualized."[2]

Kliuchevsky's impact on Russian historical scholarship continued unabated even after his death. As the occupant of the chair in Russian history at Moscow University, he contributed to the formation of much of the next generation of Russian historians. Some of them helped build the historical profession in the Soviet Union after 1917, while others, in emigration, became influential interpreters of Russia to the West. Meanwhile, the *Course* was taking on a life of its own. Unlike many other products of prerevolutionary Russian culture and scholarship, which were passed over in silence or, at best, led a shadowy existence in the Soviet years, Kliuchevsky's *Course* enjoyed virtually official recognition, despite its suspect status as an artifact of non-Marxist "bourgeois" historiography. It was first reprinted in 1921 and then a second time, astonishingly, in 1937, at the height of the Stalinist terror. In the late 1950s it was reprinted yet again, this time in a meticulously edited and annotated eight-volume collection of Kliuchevsky's works. This edition of the *Course* included a revised and enlarged version of the fifth volume (containing chapters III-IX of the present translation), on which Kliuchevsky had been working at the time of his death. Based on the drafts and manuscripts preserved in Kliuchevsky's archives, the result was a considerably expanded account of Catherine's reign, a major improvement over the version first published in the 1921 edition and widely regarded as inadequate.[3] In the late 1980s, the *Course* was reprinted once more, this time in a nine-volume edition of Kliuchevsky's writings. Meanwhile, a number of Kliuchevsky's previously unpublished lectures, letters, and other writings were being issued in the Soviet Union. As one Western scholar observed, given the immense editorial care lavished on the publication of Kliuchevsky's manuscripts, it was difficult to tell whether he was still merely a "bourgeois historian" in Soviet eyes or had become a national treasure.[4]

Finally, since the collapse of the Soviet Union, a veritable flood of new editions of Kliuchevsky's works, including the *Course*, has appeared in Russia.[5] At a time when previous ideological certainties have melted away, "Kliuchevsky's Russia" provides an attractive alternative for Russians seeking a new understanding of their past and a new sense of national identity. Well over a century since it first began to take shape, the astonishing career of Kliuchevsky's *Course in Russian History* shows no sign of coming to an end.

At first glance, Kliuchevsky would seem to have been a most unpromising candidate for such an enduring role in his country's intellectual history. He was born in 1841 in the village of Voskresenskoe, in Penza Gubernia, several hundred miles southeast of Moscow. Not only his birthplace but his social origins placed him far from the centers of Russian cultural life. He was born into the family of an Orthodox parish priest, a milieu steeped in native tradition and relatively untouched by European intellectual influences. (It has often been noted that despite—or possibly because of—this background, the church, and religious life in general, plays a minor role in the *Course*; Kliuchevsky did deal with religious themes in some of his essays, however, and he remained personally religious.) Like other sons of parish priests, he was originally trained for the priesthood himself, receiving his early education in church schools in the gubernia seat, Penza, and then in the Penza Ecclesiastical Seminary. His brilliance as a student and his growing intellectual curiosity, however, impelled him to leave the seminary and enter Moscow University to study history in 1861. He remained there until his death, taking his undergraduate, master's, and doctoral degrees and then, in 1879, succeeding his principal teacher, Sergei Solovyov, in the chair of Russian history.

When Kliuchevsky began his study of Russian history, the prevailing approach to the subject was that of the so-called "state school," exemplified by Solovyov and Boris Chicherin, who was also one of Kliuchevsky's teachers at Moscow University. Influenced by Hegel, this approach to history viewed the logical process of the evolution of the state and the actions of its rulers as the primary forces of historical development and focused attention on them. Kliuchevsky, though he always paid homage to his teachers, especially Solovyov, and was certainly influenced by the state school, soon struck off in a different direction. This was made clear in his doctoral dissertation, *The Boyar Council of Old Rus*, which traced the changing position of the boyars, the aristocracy of pre-imperial Russia, over some eight centuries of Russian history. Published in book form in 1882, it was his most significant work of original research, and in it he declared his intention to investigate "classes and interests," that is, the social groups and economic forces hidden behind the laws and institutions of the state. Kliuchevsky began to develop a sociological perspective on Russian history, one that paid particular attention to social forces and the economic, material, and institutional developments that shaped them. This represented an innovation in the historical methodology of his time, and it proved highly influential in the development of Russian historiography.

Not coincidentally, Kliuchevsky arrived in Moscow to begin his university studies in the year of the emancipation of the serfs, a time of great intellectual ferment in Russia associated with the general reform spirit of the period. New sociological and economic concepts drawn from the West were being applied to the study of Russian conditions, and socialist and populist ideological currents were generating an interest in the material life of the peasantry as well as a strong sense of social commitment on the part of many educated Russians. Kliuchevsky was never a radical, much less a socialist, but he was familiar with these intellectual and social tendencies and regarded them with a good deal of sympathy.[6] This early experience may well have contributed to the development of his interest in the history of society. It is an interest that gives him a distinct affinity with historiographical trends of the latter twentieth century. To be sure, he did not practice social history "from the bottom up," as we call it today, that is, the autonomous internal development of social groups, nor did he concentrate his attention on the laboring classes or marginalized elements of society. To the extent that he studied social groups and classes in his work, he took as his starting point their juridical relationship to the state, and for all his sympathy with the peasantry he tended to focus on the elite classes, the boyars and the gentry. Thus, rather than repudiating the political and legal approach of the state school, he infused it with a fruitful sociological perspective, investigating the social content of the historical institutions shaped by state law and governmental action.

In the end, it is difficult to pigeonhole Kliuchevsky as a historian. Although he looked for the structural materials and long-term continuities that generated the broad flow of Russian history, he avoided abstract philosophical theories and laws of historical development on the one hand and any monocausal interpretation of history on the other. Geographical and economic factors, rulers and people, material forces and cultural influences, all solidly grounded in historical fact, found their way into his approach to history. This eclecticism and concreteness have doubtless contributed to the remarkably fresh and modern quality the *Course* retains; parts of it may have been superseded by later research, but it does not read like a musty relic of a bygone era. Nevertheless, Kliuchevsky did help to give Russian historiography a new turn toward social and economic themes and, it has been argued, thereby made it receptive to the Marxist historical outlook. Certainly his concern with "classes and interests" helps to account for the respect in which he was held in the Soviet period and the status that was accorded to his *Course*.[7]

The special qualities of the *Course* did not derive from Kliuchevsky's scholarly insights alone. Throughout his career as a scholar, Kliuchevsky was also a highly gifted and dedicated teacher. His sheer appetite for teaching was prodigious: in addition to his thirty-one years at Moscow University, he taught Russian history for thirty-six years at the Moscow Ecclesiastical Academy, one of the senior seminaries of the Russian Orthodox Church, and for a number of years at the Third Aleksandrovskoe Military Academy and at Gerye's Higher Courses for Women, a college-level program for female students, who were not admitted to Russian universities. Later on he taught at the School of Painting, Sculpture, and Architecture. At one point he was teaching at four different institutions while also completing his major scholarly work, *The Boyar Council*. Besides the energy required, it must have taken enormous skill to communicate with such disparate groups of students while at the same time satisfying the authorities at such an array of institutions. The *Course* had its origins in the 1870s, which means that when it finally appeared in printed form it had been augmented, tested, and polished over some four decades of teaching. It incorporated not only the latest scholarship, both Kliuchevsky's and that of others, but many years of pedagogical experience. It is worth noting that when Kliuchevsky revised the *Course* for publication he retained the elements of direct discourse between a speaker and his audience. Readers are periodically reminded that a living voice is addressing them, actively engaged in a reconstruction of Russian history and intent on sharing it with them. So persuasive was Kliuchevsky's

voice that his students claimed to have felt they were listening to a
traveler just returned from the Russia of the past who was recounting
his personal impressions of what he had seen and heard.[8]

In addition to his teaching duties, Kliuchevsky found time to give
public lectures and speeches, from which many of his essays and articles originated, and his fame as a lecturer spread beyond the walls of
the institutions where he taught. Michael Karpovich, who attended
Kliuchevsky's lectures at Moscow University (and, as a professor at
Harvard, helped to educate much of the post–World War II generation
of Russian historians in the United States), testified that "people went
to hear his lectures as they went to hear [Chaliapin] or to see the plays
of the Moscow Art Theater."[9] Even Chaliapin went to Kliuchevsky:
when the celebrated bass was preparing for the role of Boris Godunov
in Musorgsky's opera, he consulted Kliuchevsky for historical pointers
on his portrayal of the Muscovite tsar.[10] Kliuchevsky's accomplishments as a teacher and public speaker were all the more remarkable in
that he had had to overcome a severe stutter that afflicted him in his
childhood. It left him with a slight hesitation in his speech, but he put it
to use to achieve expressive pauses that gave his lectures even greater
vividness.[11]

Finally, the literary form in which he cast his carefully crafted lectures played a particularly important role in elevating the *Course in
Russian History* to the status of a cultural monument. The almost an-
thropological descriptiveness and psychological depth of his historical
portraits—most notably, in the present volume, the chapter-length portrayal of Catherine—bring some of the pages of Tolstoy to mind, and
his characterizations of eighteenth-century sovereigns and landowners
are worthy of a Saltykov-Shchedrin or a Gogol. Not just the cadences
of Russia's nineteenth-century novelists but literary devices even a
modernist might envy found their way into his writing. He enjoyed
comical lists, for example, and occasionally his prose lapses into mim-
icry of the thought process or manner of speaking of his historical
subjects. The aphoristic wit and sharp irony that were integral elements
of his style help to offset his unabashed Great Russian patriotism
(though he was not guilty of aggressive chauvinism). To be sure,
Kliuchevsky's lifetime virtually spanned both the golden and the silver
ages of Russian literature. To live among great writers is one thing,
however; to be able to emulate some of their best qualities and apply
them to a work of history is quite another.[12] As one of his students said

of him, Kliuchevsky was both a scholar and a poet.[13] Somehow, scholarly and poetic qualities—a rare combination in any time or place—came together in an unusually harmonious fashion in this scion of the impoverished provincial clergy.

Scholarship, teaching, and artistry were the materials of which "Kliuchevsky's Russia" was built. The completed structure proved so well-proportioned, and so sturdy, that even after more than a century of existence Kliuchevsky's account of the Russian past remains in many respects the accepted wisdom against which new interpretations test their strength. The same materials went into the making of what might be called "Kliuchevsky's Catherine," that part of the *Course in Russian History* in which Kliuchevsky developed his image of the empress and interpretation of her deeds.

* * *

Catherine the Great has presented different faces to historians over the years, just as she did to her contemporaries. Kliuchevsky's image of Catherine must be placed in a broad historiographical context in order to bring its distinctive features into relief. Though only a brief overview can be given here, it is clear that a considerable evolution has occurred in Catherinian scholarship from Kliuchevsky's time to our own.

Kliuchevsky was not a specialist on the eighteenth century, and he devoted most of his original research to earlier periods of Russian history. He was nevertheless familiar with the basic historical sources on Catherine's reign: laws and government documents, the materials of the Legislative Commission of 1767, memoirs of the period, Catherine's own writings. In fact, the series of ten public lectures on Western influence after Peter the Great, which he gave in 1890–91, was something of an innovation, for until that time the eighteenth century had been little studied by Russian historians.[14] Soon, however, a number of important works began to appear. The last years of the nineteenth century and the early years of the twentieth saw a growing interest in Catherine's reign among Russian historians. As a result, pioneering studies came to be published that have proved of enduring value. To name just three historians of the period who produced major works: Alexander Kizevetter published extensively on urban reform and self-government in the second half of the eighteenth century; Paul Miliukov's *Outlines of Russian Culture* included detailed accounts of educational and cultural developments under Catherine; and V.I. Semevsky published massive studies of the condition of the peasantry in Catherine's reign and of the history of proposals for the reform of serfdom. These historians and others created a solid foundation of Catherinian scholarship, on which Kliuchevsky was able to draw. Nor did the influence necessarily flow in one direction only: Kizevetter and Miliukov, for example, had both been graduate students of Kliuchevsky's at Moscow University.

The scholars who produced these works tended to be of a liberal or populist bent. Miliukov, for one, became the head of the Kadet Party, the main liberal party of Russia, and Kizevetter was a leading member of it. Even those who were not so politically active were deeply concerned with the political and social issues of turn-of-the-century Russia, and this was undoubtedly a factor in stimulating their scholarly interest in Catherine's reign. Committed to the contemporary movement to foster the rule of law, popular participation in government, relief of the peasantry, and in general the "Europeanization" of Russian politics and society—the movement that in Kliuchevsky's lifetime culminated in the revolution of 1905—they were drawn to the study of Catherine's reign. For it was in Catherine's time that these objectives first presented themselves as real possibilities for Russia, which had lately experienced the Westernizing reforms of Peter the Great and was now ruled by a self-professed adherent of the Enlightenment. Approaching Catherine's reign as the seedtime of political and social modernization in Russia, they found its actual accomplishments highly disappointing, and their assessments of the empress were by and large negative.[15]

These historians focused particularly on the gap they perceived between Catherine's well-publicized commitment to the ideals of the Enlightenment and her failure to implement significant reforms in the two Russian institutions that so glaringly contradicted those ideals, autocracy and serfdom. As they saw it, her stated intentions to improve and streamline the Russian government notwithstanding, her foremost consideration lay in keeping her autocratic powers intact, an insistence that undermined her efforts to draw social forces into local administration; and her recognition of the unjust and inhumane features of Russian serfdom notwithstanding, she shrank from alienating the nobility, on whom her position on the throne depended, and failed to curb the landowners' arbitrary powers over the serfs and exploitation of them. Hence, at the end of this most "enlightened" monarch's thirty-four

years on the throne, autocracy and serfdom remained the foundations
of Russian political and social life, just as they had been at the beginning of the reign. Kizevetter, using a metaphor that typified this interpretation, compared the Russian state at the end of Catherine's reign to
a building whose facade had been remodeled and redecorated while
everything within it remained largely unchanged.[16]

Although they acknowledged the backwardness of Russian society
and the limitations of the country's resources, these historians tended
to blame the outcome chiefly on Catherine's own failings, on defects
in her character. Two explanatory threads ran through their writings.
One was hypocrisy, a charge with a long lineage extending at least as
far back as Pushkin's famous description of Catherine as "a Tartuffe in
skirts and a crown." In this view, Catherine's sole commitment, from
the very outset, was to her own power and glory, and her professed
adherence to progressive ideas was only for show. She found it expedi-
ent for "public-relations" purposes to correspond with Voltaire and
entertain Diderot, thus establishing her credentials as an enlightened
reformer. This gave her a positive image in Europe, enhancing her
prestige and making her territorial acquisitions more palatable.

An alternative explanation accepted the sincerity, if not the firmness, of her ideals and viewed her as more naive than hypocritical, at
least at the beginning of her reign. Having steeped herself in the
thought of the Enlightenment, she had set out to apply to her adopted
country the ideas she gleaned from Western books, only to be rudely
awakened by Russian reality: the general backwardness of the country,
the selfishness of the nobility, the volatility of the masses. The Commission of 1767, and especially the Pugachev Rebellion of 1773–74,
dispelled any remaining illusions; she quickly backtracked from her initial
reformist ambitions, accepted things as they were, and limited herself to
piecemeal and relatively minor improvements of the existing order.

Thus the dominant tone of the scholarly literature of Kliuchevsky's
day was highly critical of Catherine, in regard both to her character and
to the accomplishments of her reign. Liberal historians of the early
twentieth century, like the educated segment of Russian society of
which they were a part, were deeply committed to the struggle against
the arbitrariness of governmental power and the economic and social
inequities of their time. Consequently, they found it hard to forgive the
monarch who, it appeared, had advertised her solidarity with these
objectives and propagated them in Russia but dismally failed to pursue

them when she had the opportunity. This historical experience confirmed their own disillusionment with the ability of Russia's autocratic government and bureaucracy to solve the country's pressing problems and supported their belief that autocracy must yield to a more liberal and productive political structure.

Kliuchevsky shared his fellow historians' civic concerns and liberal ethos, and he shared their critical assessment of Catherine. It may even be that he helped to inject the element of civic engagement into the historiography of his time, an enduring legacy of the spirit of the 1860s to which he had been exposed in his student days.[17] If so, it is yet another way in which his influence has lived on long after him. There are indications of a revival of interest in Catherine's reign among post-Soviet Russian historians today. In a spirit similar to that of their counterparts in Kliuchevsky's day, these historians are searching in the Russian past for precedents for a legal order, a civil society, and state-led reform that might be retrieved and built upon in the present.[18]

In the 1960s and 1970s, a new image of Catherine the Great and her reign, quite different from the hitherto prevailing one, began to form. This was the work of Western rather than Soviet historiography. The latter on the whole perpetuated the negative appraisal of Catherine's reign it had inherited from the prerevolutionary historians, though from a different ideological standpoint. In the Soviet perspective, Catherine was merely an instrument of the class interests of the nobility, and she consistently defended those interests because her own power depended on them; all her actions had to be understood in that light and "unmasked" accordingly. On the whole, the Soviet preoccupation with class struggle and the transition from "feudalism" to "capitalism" tended to diminish interest in Catherine as a historical actor, although useful research was done on certain aspects of the reign that were of particular ideological relevance. Western scholars, meanwhile, were beginning to utilize the new opportunities opening up for research in the Soviet Union to examine government and society in Catherine's reign more deeply than had previously been possible. Western researchers, of course, could approach the subject without the kind of personal engagement that motivated the historians of Kliuchevsky's day. At the same time, from the vantage point of the late twentieth century, they were perhaps more aware of the pitfalls and difficulties of attempting to modernize a backward, underdeveloped society and therefore more willing to recognize incremental progress.[19]

The picture of Catherine that began to emerge from this new scholarship featured neither hypocrisy nor naivete but realism.[20] Catherine was now credited with a genuine commitment throughout her reign to reforms intended to strengthen and improve Russia; in implementing those reforms, however, she carefully tailored her efforts to the limited social and administrative resources at the country's disposal. New studies ranging from the center of Russian politics, society, and culture (the court and the capitals) to the hinterland (local administration, the provincial gentry) emphasized how meager those resources were.[21] The exigencies of court politics, the paucity of able and honest officials, the difficulty of policing the vast rural spaces beyond the towns, and general economic and educational backwardness all imposed severe constraints on how far and how quickly even the most enlightened monarch could proceed. Given these limitations, it would have been virtually impossible for any eighteenth-century Russian ruler to dispense with the institutions of autocracy and serfdom; even aside from the selfish interests of ruler and elite in their preservation, they were administrative necessities.

Hence, in recent historiography the emphasis has shifted from criticism of Catherine for what she failed to accomplish to recognition of how much she actually did accomplish. The Commission of 1767, the provincial reform of 1775, the charters to the nobility and the towns, and numerous cultural and educational initiatives all formed a consistent effort on the empress' part to govern her realm more efficiently and justly and to raise her subjects to "civilized," European standards. In this view, Catherine's reformist spirit flagged only in the last years of her life, when the French Revolution, as well as age and fatigue, turned her in a more repressive direction. The two most comprehensive works on Catherine the Great that have appeared in English in recent years, Isabel de Madariaga's masterly survey of the reign and John Alexander's thorough and sensitive biography, both reflect the generally positive appraisal to be found in the new historiography.[22]

One does find useful reminders in recent works that Catherine *was* an autocrat and highly jealous of her powers and prerogatives, and that many of her actions *were* done for show and prestige, though that does not necessarily preclude other motives. By and large, however, the general tone of current scholarship on Catherine is quite different from the one that prevailed in Kliuchevsky's time. It can be summed up in the following words of Marc Raeff: "When all is said and done, she did leave Russia with a stronger institutional and legal framework, with a more rational and better-ordered—and hence more efficient—central administration and, most important perhaps, with the elements of corporate self-government for the upper classes and the idea of directed social and economic development, a development which would be led by the most dynamic and successful members of the recognized estates of the realm."[23] Or, in Isabel de Madariaga's even more favorable assessment: "Perhaps her main service to Russia was that she created a framework for government and society more civilized, more tolerant, more free than ever before or after."[24]

* * *

The general framework of Kliuchevsky's analysis of Catherine and her reign is firmly grounded in the liberal historiography of his time. Kliuchevsky himself was a moderate liberal. It is difficult to tell precisely where he stood on the Russian political spectrum of the early twentieth century, for he held aloof from overt political activity and stuck closely to his scholarship and teaching. In the last few years of his life—the years in which he was preparing the *Course* for publication—he seems to have grown increasingly critical of the government and associated himself to some degree with the Kadet Party. The appraisal of Catherine he expressed in the *Course* was of long standing, however, and did not differ substantially from his earlier works on the subject.[25] He criticizes Catherine for failing to institutionalize the rule of law in Russia, despite her recognition of the harmful effects of uncurbed arbitrariness in earlier reigns; he sees her reforms as advancing the power of the central government and the interests of the nobility rather than as promoting social participation and civic initiative; and, most of all, he sharply reproaches her for her failure to mitigate the conditions of serfdom, even though she had condemned the institution's seamier sides in the early years of her reign. In the end, appetite for power and ambition for glory won out over her humane impulses and Enlightenment-inspired ideals—though Kliuchevsky does not deny the genuineness of those impulses and ideals.

Within that overall framework, Kliuchevsky provides a highly informative and highly readable introduction to the reign of Catherine the Great. He ends Part 4 of the *Course* with a colorful description of Russian court life under Elizabeth and Peter III and a dramatic narrative of the coup d'état that brought Catherine to power (chapters I–II). The first seven lectures of Part 5 (chapters III–IX) are devoted to Catherine's reign. They begin with a portrait of the empress herself and then adopt a topical approach, analyzing her foreign conquests and her major internal initiatives and evaluating their consequences. They amply display Kliuchevsky's remarkable talent for clarity of exposition and incisive detail.

Inevitably, there are some omissions and shortcomings in his analysis. He barely mentions the Pugachev Rebellion, for example, which convulsed large parts of the empire in 1773–74. (It should be pointed out that at least until the 1905 revolution governmental censorship was an ever-present consideration.) Although the origin of serfdom is not of direct relevance to Catherine's reign, Kliuchevsky's references to it reflect his view that it was primarily a result of private peasant indebtedness to landowners. Most historians today attribute serfdom to direct action by the state to bind the peasants to the land in order to protect the economic interests of the military service class. Surprisingly for a historian who was so adept at puncturing the self-serving statements of historical figures, Kliuchevsky's famous characterizations of Empress Elizabeth, and especially of Peter III, draw heavily on Catherine's memoirs, which naturally played up the defects of her predecessors. Recent historians have found more merit, if not in Peter himself, then in his brief reign, pointing out that Catherine continued many of the policies he had initiated.[26]

These are minor lapses compared to the dazzling insights Kliuchevsky's account achieves, not only into the person of this highly complex sovereign but into some of the salient features of modern Russian history as a whole. Kliuchevsky may have been critical of Catherine, but the picture of her that he presents in chapter III is not one-dimensional; it uses her memoirs and other writings and the accounts of her contemporaries to achieve a well-rounded and deeply human analysis of her character and personality. Even while concluding that ambition and cold calculation were her dominant traits, he pays due respect to her intelligence, capacity for hard work, and sheer charm. It is an extraordinary act of historical re-creation of the sort that brought Kliuchevsky such renown in his own time, and it remains so lifelike that it fairly leaps off the page.

This word portrait of the empress serves a broader purpose, however, for it introduces the central theme that runs throughout

Kliuchevsky's treatment of Catherine's reign: the impact of Western thought on Russian minds and institutions. This was a central preoccupation of Kliuchevsky's when he came to the seventeenth and eighteenth centuries of Russian history, not only in the *Course* but in some of his other works as well: his lengthy article on the seventeenth-century religious schism; his cycle of lectures on Western influence in Russia after Peter the Great; his essay on the historical "ancestry" of Pushkin's Eugene Onegin.[27] In the *Course*, Catherine encapsulates this theme in her own person. A German-born princess, raised in Lutheranism and steeped in the writings of the Enlightenment—the only Russian sovereign of significance who was born and brought up in the West—she encounters upon her arrival in Russia the "local facts" of Russian life: the court, the governmental administration, the nobility, and serfdom. The complex interplay between European ideas and native institutions and ways of thinking forms the central thread that runs through Kliuchevsky's analysis of Catherine's actions after ascending the throne. In the end, Kliuchevsky concludes that in order to preserve her prerogatives and pursue her ambitions Catherine reduced the progressive ideas of her time to a mere intellectual embellishment of her reign. He recognizes the strong pedagogical urge that was one of Catherine's chief characteristics, the persistent desire to educate and uplift her subjects, but he sees little effective realization of her progressive ideas in Russian institutions. As he puts it in a typically double-edged comment in another work, "Having decided not to become the radical reformer of the state, she wanted to remain the teacher of the nation."[28]

The structure of Kliuchevsky's discussion of Catherine's reign reflects not only the theme of Western influence in Russia but his general historical method. Taking the reader in ever-widening circles from the monarch to the institutions of the state and the principal elements of society, he moves from political to social history, ending with a consideration of serfdom and, especially, of the nobility. The gentry class as Kliuchevsky depicts it was in a sense the obverse of Catherine herself: it was a "local fact" experiencing an encounter with Western ideas and values, including, by Catherine's time, the ideas and values of the Enlightenment. Kliuchevsky criticizes the nobility even more harshly than Catherine for using its Western cultural acquisitions not to improve Russian conditions and institutions but merely to decorate its social life. He bluntly depicts the landed nobility as a parasitic class after its emancipation from compulsory state service in 1762, living a frivolous existence on the unpaid labor of its serfs while failing to exercise the leadership that might have justified its privileges. He ends his account of Catherine's reign by sketching some of the forerunners of those "superfluous men" who would haunt the pages of Russian literature in the nineteenth century. If the effort to make Russia a less oppressive, more humane, and more civilized society fell short, Kliuchevsky implies, it was not entirely the fault of the empress or of her Western-inspired ideas but of a social elite that was largely incapable of responding to them. As he had written in an earlier essay on Catherine, seemingly in reference to his own time as much as to the eighteenth century, "Catherine did not give the nation freedom and enlightenment because such things are not given out as an award but are acquired by maturity and awareness; they are earned by one's own labor and are not received gratis, like alms."[29]

Kliuchevsky does not present a fair or comprehensive image of the Westernized nobility of the eighteenth century. As a number of recent studies have made clear, it included not just disoriented Voltaireans but also talented statesmen and administrators of the sort who assisted Catherine in her reform endeavors. Nevertheless, Kliuchevsky's satirical character sketches vividly illustrate two elements of Russia's social and intellectual life that would have a profound impact on Russian history from Catherine's time onward. One was the cultural cleavage between the Westernized elite and the rest of the population, a division that exacerbated social conflict and served to equate Western culture with class interest. The other was the radicalization Western ideas might undergo when they were plucked from the historical context in which they had developed and were replanted in a very different cultural soil. Kliuchevsky's description of the way in which slogans and generalities could turn into dogmatic ideologies seems almost uncannily prophetic of the three-quarters of a century of domination by Marxist dogmas that was soon to come. His examination of Western influence in Catherine's reign led him to questions that were of urgent significance for Russia's development in his own day and have remained so ever since: how to use Western ideas and practices to improve and enrich Russian life without turning them into idle fashions or political bludgeons, and where to find the social leadership capable of performing such a delicate task.

In sum, Kliuchevsky's analysis of Catherine the Great and her time is a classic work of history. For many decades it dominated historiography on the subject both at home and abroad, and many of its insights as well as its literary delights remain undimmed by age. It is the creation of a masterful teacher and writer, one who successfully combined high scholarly standards and humane values. "Kliuchevsky's Catherine" is not the last word on this monarch, but it remains an outstanding contribution to our understanding of a historical figure who would doubtless have savored the fascination she continues to hold for posterity.

Notes

1. Biographical information on Kliuchevsky has been drawn from M.V. Nechkina, *Vasilii Osipovich Kliuchevskii: Istoriia zhizni i tvorchestva* (Moscow: Nauka, 1974), and Robert F. Byrnes, *V.O. Kliuchevskii, Historian of Russia* (Bloomington and Indianapolis: Indiana University Press, 1995). On the development and publication history of the *Course*, see also Robert Byrnes, "The Survey Course That Became a Classic Set: Kliuchevskii's *Course of Russian History*," *Journal of Modern History* 66, no. 4 (1994): 737–54. A wide-ranging collection of recent assessments and reassessments of Kliuchevsky's work and significance as a historian can be found in Marc Raeff, ed., "Kliuchevskii's Russia: Critical Studies," special issue of *Canadian-American Slavic Studies* 20, nos. 3–4 (1986).

2. George P. Fedotov, "Kliuchevskii's Russia," trans. and ed. Marshall S. Shatz, *Canadian-American Slavic Studies* 20, nos. 3–4 (1986): 204; first published 1932.

3. V.O. Kliuchevskii, *Sochineniia v vos'mi tomakh* (Moscow: Gos. izd. politicheskoi literatury/Izd. sotsial'no-ekonomicheskoi literatury, 1956–59), vol. 5; on the compilation of Part 5 of the *Course*, see "Commentary" by the editors, V.A. Aleksandrov and A.A. Zimin, pp. 403–8. The present volume is the first translation into English using this revised and expanded text. Serviceable translations of earlier sections of the *Course*, on the seventeenth century and on the reign of Peter the Great, are available: V.O. Kliuchevsky, *A Course in Russian History: The Seventeenth Century*, trans. Natalie Duddington (Chicago: Quadrangle Books, 1968; reprinted Armonk, NY, and London: M.E. Sharpe, 1994); Vasili Klyuchevsky, *Peter the Great*, trans. Liliana Archibald (London: Macmillan, 1958; reprinted Boston: Beacon Books, 1984). The only attempt at an English translation of the entire *Course*, however, is V.O. Kliuchevsky, *A History of Russia*, trans. C.J. Hogarth, 5 vols. (London: J.M. Dent & Sons, 1911–31; reprinted 1960). Not only is this translation so faulty and misleading as to be virtually unreadable, but it used the 1921 edition of Part 5 of the *Course*, which relied mainly on an early lithographed version of the text dating from 1883–84.

4. Nicholas V. Riasanovsky, "Kliuchevskii in Recent Soviet Historiography," *Canadian-American Slavic Studies* 20, nos. 3–4 (1986): 457.

5. For a thorough bibliography of publications by and about Kliuchevsky, see Byrnes, *V.O. Kliuchevskii*, pp. 261–86.

6. Soviet historians have particularly emphasized the formative influence of the 1860s on Kliuchevsky, though they have not been alone. See, for example, A.A. Zimin, "Formirovanie istoricheskikh vzgliadov V.O. Kliuchevskogo v 60–e gody XIX v.," *Istoricheskie zapiski* 69 (1961): 178–96.

7. There was much agonizing in Soviet historiography over whether, and to what degree, Kliuchevsky could be considered a precursor of Marxist history. For an account of the evolving assessment of Kliuchevsky by Soviet historians, see Nechkina, *Kliuchevskii*, pp. 20–53.

8. Ibid., p. 309.

9. Quoted in Philip E. Mosely, "Professor Michael Karpovich," in *Russian Thought and Politics*, ed. Hugh McLean et al. (Cambridge, MA: Harvard University Press, 1957), p. 3.

10. Nechkina, *Kliuchevskii*, pp. 312–14.

11. A. Kizevetter, *Istoricheskie otkliki* (Moscow: Izd. K.F. Nekrasova, 1915), p. 365.

12. A stimulating discussion of Kliuchevsky's relationship to the literature of his time is Il'ia Serman, "Kliuchevskii i russkaia literatura," *Canadian-American Slavic Studies* 20, nos. 3–4 (1986): 417–36.

13. Quoted in T. Emmons [Terence Emmons], "Kliuchevskii i ego ucheniki," *Voprosy istorii* (October 1990): 53; in English, in slightly different form, as "Kliuchevskii's Pupils," in *California Slavic Studies* 14, ed. Henrik Birnbaum et al. (Berkeley, Los Angeles, and Oxford: University of California Press, 1992), pp. 68–98.

14. Nechkina, *Kliuchevskii*, p. 301. Kliuchevsky himself did not publish the lectures, but much of their content was incorporated into the *Course in Russian History*. They were published in V.O. Kliuchevskii, *Neopublikovannye pro-izvedeniia* (Moscow: Nauka, 1983, pp. 11–112), and have been translated and edited by Marshall S. Shatz: V.O. Kliuchevskii, "Western Influence in Russia after Peter the Great," *Canadian-American Slavic Studies* 20, nos. 3–4 (1986): 467–84; 24, no. 4 (1990): 431–55; 28, no. 1 (1994): 67–98; 28, no. 4 (1994): 419–44.

15. Marc Raeff, ed., *Catherine the Great: A Profile* (New York: Hill and Wang, 1972), contains excerpts from the writings of some of these historians. For discussions of this historiography, see Raeff, *Catherine the Great*, pp. 301–21; David M. Griffiths, "Catherine II: The Republican Empress," *Jahrbücher für Geschichte Osteuropas* 21 (1973): 323–24; Gary Marker, "Who Rules the Word? Public School Education and the Fate of Universality in Russia, 1782–1803," *Russian History* 20, nos. 1–4 (1993): 15–19.

16. A.A. Kizevetter, "Imperatritsa Ekaterina II, kak zakonodatel'nitsa," *Istoricheskie ocherki* (Moscow, 1912; reprinted The Hague: Europe Printing, 1967), p. 283.

17. Emmons, "Kliuchevskii i ego ucheniki," p. 58.

18. For excerpts from some of these works, see Gary Marker, ed., "Catherine the Great and the Search for a Usable Past," *Russian Studies in History: A Journal of Translations* 33, no. 4 (Spring 1995).

19. Robert E. Jones, *Provincial Development in Russia: Catherine II and Jakob Sievers* (New Brunswick, NJ: Rutgers University Press, 1984), pp. 5–6.

20. For some of the early fruits of this research, see the broad range of articles

in "The Reign of Catherine the Great," special issue of *Canadian Slavic Studies* 4, no. 3 (1970), and the comments on these articles and related literature by Marc Raeff, "Random Notes on the Reign of Catherine II in the Light of Recent Literature," *Jahrbücher für Geschichte Osteuropas* 19 (1971): 541–56.

21. To illustrate the changing perspective, one might compare the following statements: "Much more was done in Catherine's reign to strengthen and even to spread serfdom than to limit it." V.I. Semevskii, *Krest'ianskii vopros v Rossii v XVIII i pervoi polovine XIX veka*, 2 vols. (St. Petersburg: Obshchestvennaia pol'za, 1888), vol. 1, p. 228; "A state that lacked the means to govern the serfs without the pomeshchik also lacked the means to govern the serfs against him." Jones, *Provincial Development in Russia*, p. 113.

22. Isabel de Madariaga, *Russia in the Age of Catherine the Great* (New Haven and London: Yale University Press, 1981), and *Catherine the Great: A Short History* (New Haven and London: Yale University Press, 1990); John T. Alexander, *Catherine the Great: Life and Legend* (New York and Oxford: Oxford University Press, 1989). For a post-Soviet revisionist view, see Aleksandr Borisovich Kamenskii, "Catherine the Great," in *The Emperors and Empresses of Russia: Rediscovering the Romanovs*, ed. Donald J. Raleigh (Armonk, NY, and London: M.E. Sharpe, 1996), pp. 135–76, as well as his *"Pod seniiu Ekateriny": Vtoraia polovina XVIII veka* (St. Petersburg: Lenizdat, 1992), an excerpt from which is included in *Russian Studies in History* 33, no. 4: 35–65.

23. Marc Raeff, "The Empress and the Vinerian Professor: Catherine II's Projects of Government Reforms and Blackstone's *Commentaries*" (first published 1976), in *Political Ideas and Institutions in Imperial Russia* (Boulder, San Francisco, and Oxford: Westview Press, 1994), pp. 228–29. For a detailed discussion of Catherine's eighteenth-century conception of a well-ordered society based on an estate structure, see the Introduction by David Griffiths to David Griffiths and George E. Munro, trans. and eds., *Catherine II's Charters of 1785 to the Nobility and the Towns* (Bakersfield, CA: Charles Schlacks Jr., Publisher, 1991), pp. xvii–lxix.

24. Isabel de Madariaga, "Catherine the Great," in H.M. Scott, ed., *Enlightened Absolutism: Reform and Reformers in Later Eighteenth-Century Europe* (Ann Arbor: University of Michigan Press, 1990), p. 311.

25. Particularly the lecture series he gave in 1890–91, "Western Influence in Russia after Peter the Great." It appears also in his 1896 article "Imperatritsa Ekaterina II (1729–1796)," in Kliuchevskii, *Sochineniia*, vol. 5, pp. 309–71.

26. See Marc Raeff, "The Domestic Policies of Peter III and His Overthrow" (first published 1970), in Raeff, *Political Ideas and Institutions in Imperial Russia*, pp. 188–212; Carol S. Leonard, *Reform and Regicide: The Reign of Peter III of Russia* (Bloomington and Indianapolis: Indiana University Press, 1993); Aleksandr Sergeevich Mylnikov, "Peter III," in *Emperors and Empresses of Russia*, ed. Raleigh, pp. 102–33. Elizabeth seems to have proved more resistant to revisionism, however. See, for example, Viktor Petrovich Naumov, "Elizabeth I," in *Emperors and Empresses of Russia*, ed. Raleigh, pp. 67–100, but also E.V. Anisimov, *Rossiia v seredine XVIII veka* (Moscow: Mysl', 1986). The latter is available in an English translation: Evgeny V. Anisimov, *Empress Elizabeth. Her Reign and Her Russia, 1741–1761*, trans. and ed. John T. Alexander (Gulf Breeze, FL: Academic International Press, 1996).

27. "Zapadnoe vliianie i tserkovnyi raskol v Rossii XVII v." (first published 1897), in V.O. Kliuchevskii, *Ocherki i rechi: vtoroi sbornik statei* (Petrograd: Komissariat Narodnogo Prosveshcheniia, 1918), pp. 373–453; "Western Influence in Russia after Peter the Great"; "Evgenii Onegin and His Ancestors" (first published 1897), trans. and ed. Marshall S. Shatz, *Canadian-American Slavic Studies* 16, no. 2 (1982): 227–46.

28. "Imperatritsa Ekaterina II," p. 370.

29. Ibid., p. 370.

A COURSE IN
RUSSIAN
HISTORY
The Time of
Catherine the Great

~ I ~

The Russian State in the Mid-Eighteenth Century: Elizabeth and Peter III

Six reigns in the space of thirty-seven years made the fate of Peter the Great's reforms after the Reformer's death sufficiently clear. Peter would scarcely have recognized his work in its posthumous continuation. He had acted despotically, but as the embodiment of the state he had identified his will with that of the people, recognizing more clearly than any of his predecessors that the good of the people is the true and only objective of the state. After Peter the bonds of the state, juridical and moral, began to snap, one after the other, and as they did so the idea of the state faded away, leaving behind a mere word in government documents. The most autocratic empire in the world found itself without an established dynasty, just displaced remnants of an expiring imperial house; the hereditary throne lacked a legal order of succession; the state was shut up in a palace with accidental and rapidly changing proprietors; the ruling class, of variegated composition, possessed high birth or high rank but no rights whatsoever and was constantly reshuffled; political life consisted entirely of court intrigues, Guards uprisings, and police investigations; and a general fear of arbitrariness stifled any sense of law. Those were the phenomena that struck the gaze of foreign diplomats at the Russian court. They wrote that everything here changed from one minute to the next, everyone grew frightened of his own shadow at the slightest word concerning the government, no one was certain of anything or knew to which saint he should pray.

Thoughtful people, of whom there were extremely few in the ruling circles of the day, understood the dangerous position of a state held together not by law but by incidental fact and mechanical cohesion—until the first blow should strike it from within or without. They felt a need to place the system on firm legal foundations and to bring the government closer to the society it ruled. Ivan Shuvalov submitted to Empress Elizabeth a proposal "concerning fundamental laws." Count Peter Shuvalov presented to the Senate the notion that "unimpeded knowledge of the opinion of society" is useful to the state. These proposals found eternal rest in the Senate's archives. Not only the difficult constitutional task of creating fundamental laws but even the simple matter of putting existing statutes and decrees in order, a task that had somehow been managed under Tsar Alexis,[1] proved beyond the powers of the government in the following century, when it could have made use of the methods of West European science. From 1700 on, it strove impotently for a new Code of Laws, appointing interdepartmental commissions and departmental commissions, commissions consisting solely of officials and commissions including representatives of the social estates. At the suggestion of Andrei Ostermann, a single German was even entrusted with the entire codification of the Russian laws.

Once, on March 11, 1754, a solemn session of the Senate, with the participation of members of the Colleges and chanceries and in the presence of the empress, discussed the appalling disorder in the administration of justice. The ever resourceful Peter Shuvalov explained that only a code of laws could relieve the affliction, but there was nothing from which to compile such a code, for although many decrees existed, there were no actual laws that would be clear and comprehensible to everyone. Expressing pity for her subjects who were unable to obtain justice, Elizabeth declared that, first of all, clear laws had to be drawn up; then she reasoned that manners and customs change in the course of time, requiring changes in the laws as well; and in conclusion she remarked that no individual could have detailed knowledge of all the decrees "unless he had angelic gifts." Having spoken, she arose and left, and the Senate resolved to undertake the formulation of clear and

---

[1]The Code of Laws (*Ulozhenie*) of 1649, drawn up under Tsar Alexis, was still operative in eighteenth-century Russia.

comprehensible laws. It worked on their formulation for eighty years without completing the task. At the same time, the Senate formed a commission for this purpose that included a "*de-sciences-académie* professor." In somewhat over a year the commission drew up two parts of a code but demonstrated so little juridical sense and training that it was decided not to put its work into effect. Timid impotence in regard to regular procedures, the unlimited power over individuals distinguishing all our governments in this period notwithstanding, is the usual characteristic of states of an East Asiatic type, even if they are embellished with a European-style facade.

The same characteristic manifested itself in another task whose completion Peter left to his successors: the determination of class relations. Peter had not been devoid of egalitarian tendencies when it came to state obligations. He extended some obligations of a particular class to several classes, such as the tax he imposed on all forms of bondage, and military service became an obligation of all the estates. With time, this process of generalizing obligations should have laid the foundations for the legal equality of the social classes. It would have started from below, with the legislative regulation of peasant obligations, especially the dues and services the serfs owed to their masters. This issue was already fermenting among the people in Peter's time, as is evident from Ivan Pososhkov's book. It was discussed in the Supreme Privy Council under Catherine I and in the Cabinet of Ministers under Anna; it found an indefatigable spokesman for peasant needs in Anisim Maslov, the senior procurator of the Senate; it agitated the minds of dignitaries—and it faded away, as all issues of fundamental social reform faded away after Peter. "Most people," Paul Yaguzhinsky wrote to Catherine I, "merely engage in talk about one or another need with regret and lamentation, but no one actually devotes his enthusiastic labor to it."

In view of the government's impotence, the task proceeded in a spontaneous fashion, directed by prevailing force. Absolute power, in the absence of personal qualities on the part of its bearer that justify it, usually becomes the servant either of those around it or of a social class that it fears and in which it seeks support. Circumstances in Russia made the gentry, headed by the Guards regiments, the prevailing force. Once it received its freedom,[2] the gentry by and large settled

---

[2]Peter III's decree of February 18, 1762, freed the nobility from the compulsory state service Peter the Great had imposed on it.

down in its rural "nests" with the right, or opportunity, to dispose of the persons and labor of the serf population without restraint. The close proximity of gentry and peasantry on the country estate injected a highly corrosive element into the process of moral alienation of the masters from the common people that had begun on a juridical basis in the seventeenth century and gradually intensified, eating away at the vigor of our social life. It has come down to us and will survive all those now living.

In addition, the balance that existed among the constituent elements of the social structure was lost. According to the second "revision" (1742–47), there were approximately 6,660,000 tax-paying "souls" in the gubernias of Russia and Siberia, which then numbered twelve. The secretary of the Prussian embassy at the Russian court, Johann Vockerodt, in the description of Russia that he composed thirteen years after Peter's death, provides statistics on the untaxed classes of Russian society dating from the end of Anna's reign and apparently derived from official sources. According to his figures, in the core territories of the empire, without the newly annexed provinces, there were approximately half a million hereditary nobles of both sexes, 200,000 government officials and personal nobles, and 300,000 "white" and "black" clergy, including the families of the former. (These figures, of course, have the value only of approximations and are far from precise.) If we compare these statistics for the untaxed classes with the total population subject to the "soul tax" listed in the second revision, we find that every 100 taxpayers, urban and rural, directly or indirectly supported 15 nontaxpayers of both sexes.

The weight of this privileged burden lying on the taxpayers' shoulders will become more palpable if we compare it with the quantitative relationship of the same classes 127 years later, in the forty-three gubernias of European Russia with a predominantly Russian population (excluding the Baltic, Polish, and Lithuanian provinces; Finland; and Bessarabia). For every 100 male taxpayers, there was the following number of nontaxpayers of both sexes:

	1740s	1867
Hereditary nobles	7.5	1.5
Personal nobles and officials	3.0	1.0
Clergy	4.5	2.3

Nineteenth-century Russia could not be ranked among the countries meagerly endowed with privileged classes. For example, the clergy in the Orthodox Russian gubernias in 1867 was six times as large as in the Catholic gubernias of Poland and almost six times as large as in the Protestant Baltic gubernias. The natural increase of popular life, however, counteracting the forcible social efforts of the state, had reduced by two-thirds the privileged multitude that lived on taxed labor. We can understand, and even feel, why so little in the way of cultural capital accumulated in a working population that labored so long and so excessively for the select classes.

As a result of the law of February 18, 1762, the burden on the serfs was made even greater by the injustice of an unequal distribution of obligations. Previously, the serfs and the other taxed classes had footed the bill for the army, government officials, and clergy on the pretext that they provided external defense, internal order, and spiritual pastorship. On top of that, the serfs made special payments to the landlords for their compulsory service, and those landlords, with their families, numbered no fewer than 14 per 100 male serfs (500,000 nobles of both sexes to 3,449,000 privately owned serf souls according to the second revision, without St. Petersburg Gubernia). But on what pretext did the gentry's serfs continue to support them with their compulsory labor even after the gentry's compulsory service had been abolished, while continuing to share with the rest of the taxpayers the cost of maintaining the beneficiaries in the three other untaxed classes?

Two signs of the overburdening of the landlords' serfs appeared. First, the taxed population in the interval between the first two revisions grew more than 18 percent, but this increase was distributed extremely unevenly among the taxed classes. While the urban population grew more than 24 percent and the state peasantry no less than 46 percent, the growth of the serf population was only about 12 percent. The principal reason could only be increased flight from the burdens of serfdom. Second, there was an increase in peasant disturbances. The people were very sensitive to the social injustice of which they had become the victims. During Elizabeth's reign, minor outbursts had not flared up among the serfs in view of their relative contentment. Immediately after the publication of the manifesto of February 18, however, they grew to such proportions that upon her accession to the throne Catherine had to pacify some 100,000 agricultural and 50,000 factory serfs.

Peter had brought to his reform activity not just personal energy but

a set of ideas—for example, a concept of the state and a view of
science as a state resource—and a set of tasks, some of which he
inherited and some of which he was the first to define. Those ideas and
tasks in themselves formed quite a broad program. Peter wanted to
make his people prosperous and competent. To that end, he sought to
raise their labor to the level of the state's needs—even, if possible, to a
Western European level—with the aid of knowledge; to give the products of that labor a free and direct route to Western markets by acquiring the Baltic coast; and to secure his country's communication with
the West and the uninterrupted inflow of the West's technical and
cultural resources by obtaining an influential international position.

He was well aware that he had not completed this program. He
made the state stronger and richer but did not enrich and enlighten the
people, and at the celebration of the conclusion of peace with Sweden
in 1721,[3] he told the Senate that his next task was to introduce measures for the people's relief. A reform of military finances was carried out
and was to have been expanded into a socioeconomic reform aimed at
strengthening the country's productive forces with the aid of independent
social initiative. He even began to prepare that expansion. He had already
vested responsibility for political, military, and financial affairs in a central administrative bureaucracy composed of knowledgeable specialists of
various social and even ethnic origins. Now he tried to transfer care of the
national economy and well-being to the local administration, giving it a
social character by calling on two estates to take independent initiative:
the gentry and the upper stratum of the merchants.

His effort was unsuccessful, however. Industry made no appreciable
progress after Peter, and foreign trade continued to show an unfavor-
able balance and remained, as before, in the hands of foreigners. Domestic trade fell, undermined by the absurd device of exacting tax
arrears by seizing merchants' houses and goods; many gave up trade
altogether in order to discharge their arrears. According to the second
revision, the towns had stagnated at 3 percent of the total taxed population. Nor had the administration been reorganized in the spirit of the
dual task Peter imposed on it. It did receive armed reinforcement: the
military forces guarding against external danger now began to turn
inward, to the domestic front, with the Guards supporting governments

---

[3]The Treaty of Nystadt of 1721 ended the Northern War with Sweden, which
had begun in 1700.

that viewed their own power as a usurpation and the army collecting taxes and combating banditry as well as peasant disturbances and flight. The central administration became neither aristocratic in its social composition nor bureaucratic in its training. It was led by individuals drawn from the gentry elite intermingled with men promoted from various other classes. Both the former and the latter, however, with rare exceptions, were makeshift administrators who, according to contemporary testimony, understood their work as well as they understood blacksmithing. The Senate itself more than once received imperial reprimands for ignorance and carelessness. The supreme supervisor of the administration, it organized the departments subordinate to it in such a way that it was totally unable to obtain from them a detailed list of receipts and expenditures, balances and arrears, for the twenty-seven years from 1730 to 1756.

Provincial administration was also reorganized. The town magistracies, which had been subordinated to the governors and commandants[4] under Catherine I, were restored to their former significance by Elizabeth. But the councils of gentry *landrat*s under the governors had already disappeared in Peter's reign, replaced by "commissars from the land" elected by the gentry of each district. After Peter the gentry's participation in provincial administration was localized still further: it was dispersed to the gentry estates, which became the centers of serf judicial and police precincts. Thus the gubernia associations and then the district associations of the gentry, instead of being strengthened, broke up into manorial clusters. While the aristocratic and high-ranking gentry held sway at the top, at the center the lower and middle gentry took root in the provinces, in the soil of serfdom. There was some thought, however, of bringing these manorial chiefs into class associations once again and extending their powers beyond the confines of the serf village: in 1761 the Senate allowed landlords to elect from their ranks commandants for the towns near which those elected had villages. Thus an elected representative of the gentry took the place of a crown official, governing with an elected gentry board. Around the same time, the codification commission drawing up the new Code of Laws proposed gentry "congresses of the land" of some kind for each province but did not succeed in drawing up a statute for them.

Meanwhile, a plan was already circulating in governmental circles

---

[4]*Voevody*. Originally a military governor, a *voevoda* in the eighteenth century, before 1775, was the administrative head of a province, a district, or a town.

for the general participation of the gentry in the administration, with the object of eliminating the shortage of trained administrators and judges. Peter Shuvalov realized better than many others the harm done by "incapable administrators," as he called the makeshift officials who were then running things in government offices. In an extensive memorandum of 1754 on the preservation of the nation, he explained to the Senate how to organize "the preparation of personnel for the administration of the gubernias, provinces, and towns, and thereby the preparation of personnel for the main government." Provincial administration should become "a school for young men being trained in Russian jurisprudence." It was therefore necessary to bring into provincial institutions "cadets" from the gentry, who would begin their study of affairs in the lowest ranks, gradually progress to become secretaries, commandants, gubernia councillors, and even governors, and then rise to the highest levels of the central administration.

Shuvalov's plan is represented merely as a development of the ideas of Peter I, who also brought young gentry cadets into the administrative Colleges for training and directed that only nobles be promoted to the rank of secretary. To Peter the gentry was handy administrative material, but he had no intention of giving it a monopoly on civil service. On the contrary, he wanted to fill the gentry itself with individuals promoted from other social ranks. Shuvalov's gentry mandarinate restored the old Muscovite class-bureaucratic type of administration, creating an inexhaustible breeding ground of officials out of the gentry and adding to its income from land a new source of support from office holding. The roots of Shuvalov's plan must be sought not in Peter's policies but in the petitions of the gentry, when it restored the autocracy of Anna,[5] that it be granted appointment to the highest offices in the central and provincial administration. In those separate measures, plans, and proposals concerning the gentry, one major fact emerged from all the disorder of the period and sought appropriate legal form: the beginnings of a *gentocracy*. And this fact was one of the indications of the sharp turn away from Peter's reforms after his death. The effort to raise the productivity of the people's labor with the

---

[5]A reference to the events of 1730, when Empress Anna came to the throne. An attempt by the Supreme Privy Council to impose limitations on the powers of the new empress was thwarted by the gentry, which preferred the preservation of autocracy to what it regarded as a bid for power by an oligarchic clique.

resources of European culture turned into an effort to intensify the people's financial exploitation and police enslavement.

The instrument of this turn away from Peter's reforms was the estate that Peter had intended to make the transmitter of European culture to Russian society. It is difficult to say whether the men of Elizabeth's time felt that they were straying from the path the Reformer had shown them. A bit later on, however, Count Kirill Razumovsky, the brother of Elizabeth's favorite and an educated man, took the opportunity to express this feeling. In 1770, when the renowned ecclesiastical orator Platon was delivering a sermon in the Peter-Paul Cathedral in the presence of the empress and the court on the occasion of the victory at Chesme, he descended theatrically from the pulpit and struck the tomb of Peter the Great with his staff, summoning him to arise and behold his beloved invention, the fleet. Razumovsky, amid the general rapture, amiably whispered to those around him: Why is he calling him? If he does arise, we'll all be in trouble. As it happened, it was Elizabeth—who so often proclaimed the sacred precepts of her father—who helped create the circumstances under which the estate that until now had been the customary instrument by which the government ruled society conceived a desire to rule society by means of the government.

* * *

Empress Elizabeth reigned for twenty years, from November 25, 1741, to December 25, 1761. Her reign was not without glory, nor even without benefit. Her youth had been unedifying. The tsarevna could derive neither rigorous principles nor pleasant memories from Peter's homeless second family, where the first words a child learned to pronounce were "daddy," "mama," and "soldier" and the mother hastened to marry off her daughters as quickly as possible in order not to have them as rivals for the throne in the event of their father's death. As she grew up, Elizabeth gave the appearance of a young gentlewoman who had received her upbringing in the maids' quarters. Throughout her life she did not want to know when it was time to get up, get dressed, eat, or go to sleep. Her servants' weddings afforded her great amusement: she would dress the bride herself and then, from behind the door, would feast her eyes on how the wedding guests disported themselves. In her behavior she was at times extremely simple and affectionate and at times would fly into a rage over trifles and berate whoever happened to be at hand, servant or courtier, with the most unfortunate expressions, while her ladies-in-waiting caught it even worse.

Elizabeth fell between two contrary cultural tendencies, having been brought up amid the new European currents and the traditions of pious native antiquity. Each influence left its mark on her, and she was able to combine the ideas and tastes of both. She would go from vespers to a ball and return from the ball in time for matins; she reverently honored the holy places and rituals of the Russian church and ordered descriptions from Paris of court banquets and festivals at Versailles; she had a passionate love for French plays and a fine knowledge of all the gastronomical secrets of the Russian kitchen. A dutiful daughter of her confessor, Father Dubiansky, and a pupil of the French dancing-master Rambour, she strictly observed fasts at her court, so that it was only with the permission of the patriarch of Constantinople that Alexis Bestuzhev-Riumin, her gourmet chancellor, was allowed not to eat mushrooms during Lent, and no one in the entire empire could perform the minuet or a Russian dance better than the empress.

Her religious sentiments were kindled by esthetic feeling. The prospective bride of every conceivable bridegroom on earth, from the king of France to her own nephew, saved by Biron during Anna's reign from a convent or the backwoods of the Duchy of Saxe-Coburg-Meiningen, she gave her heart to a court chorister from the Chernigov Cossacks,[6] and the palace was turned into an academy of music: Ukrainian choristers and Italian singers were engaged, and in order not to violate the integrity of the artistic effect, jointly they sang both mass and opera.

The duality of her educational influences explains the pleasant, or unexpected, contradictions in Elizabeth's character and mode of life. Vivacious and cheerful, but never taking her eyes off herself, large and shapely, with a beautiful, round, and ever-blooming face, she loved to create an impression. Knowing that men's clothes were particularly becoming to her, she held masquerades without masks at court, which the men were required to attend in full female attire, in vast skirts, and the women in male court dress. The most legitimate of all the male and female heirs of Peter I but raised to the throne by the bayonets of mutinous Guards, she inherited the energy of her great father: she built

---

[6]A reference to Elizabeth's favorite, Alexis Razumovsky.

palaces in twenty-four hours and traveled from Moscow to Petersburg in two days, scrupulously paying for each exhausted horse. Peaceable and lighthearted, she was forced to wage war for nearly half her reign, defeated the paramount strategist of the day, Frederick the Great, took Berlin, and placed masses of soldiers on the fields of Zorndorf and Kunersdorf; but Russia had not led such an easy life since the rule of Tsarevna Sophia, and no reign up to 1762 left behind such a pleasant memory. With Western Europe exhausted by two great coalition wars, it seemed that Elizabeth, with her 300,000-man army, might become the master of Europe's fate. The map of Europe lay before her, at her disposal, but she glanced at it so rarely that to the end of her life she was convinced that England could be reached by land—and it was she who founded Moscow University, the first real university in Russia.

Lazy and capricious, frightened of any serious idea, averse to work of any kind, Elizabeth was unable to fathom the complex international relations of contemporary Europe or comprehend the diplomatic stratagems of her chancellor, Bestuzhev-Riumin. In her inner chambers, however, she created for herself a peculiar political entourage of hangers-on, talebearers, and gossips, headed by an intimate collective cabinet. Its prime minister was Mavra Shuvalova, the wife of that inventive deviser of impractical projects Peter Shuvalov, and its members were Anna Vorontsova, née Skavronskaia,[7] a relative of the empress, and a certain Elizabeth Ivanovna, who was called the minister of foreign affairs: "Through her all matters were forwarded to the sovereign," a contemporary remarks. The subjects that occupied this cabinet were tale-telling, scandalmongering, informing, and various sorts of chicanery and mutual backbiting among the members of the court, which gave Elizabeth great pleasure. These were the "high circles" of the time; here important ranks and lucrative posts were given out and great affairs of state were decided.

These cabinet occupations alternated with festivities. From her youth Elizabeth had been a daydreamer, and while still a grand duchess had once in spellbound oblivion signed a document concerning an economic matter with the words Flames of Fire instead of her name. When she came to the throne, she wanted to turn the dreams of her youth into a magical reality. There was an unending series of theatrical performances, pleasure jaunts, receptions, balls, and masquerades, as-

---

[7]The family name of Elizabeth's mother, Catherine I.

tonishing in their dazzling splendor and nauseating extravagance. At times, the entire court turned into a theater lobby: from one day to the next people talked only of the French comedy, of the Italian comic opera and its proprietor Locatelli, of intermezzos, and so on. But the living quarters to which the inhabitants of the court repaired from the magnificent halls were strikingly cramped, sparsely decorated, and slovenly. Doors failed to close, and drafts came through the windows; water trickled down the wall panels, and the rooms were extremely damp; huge cracks gaped in the heating stove in Grand Duchess Catherine's bedroom, and nearby, seventeen servants were squeezed into a small storeroom. There was such scant furniture that mirrors, beds, tables, and chairs had to be moved from palace to palace, even from Petersburg to Moscow, and installed, battered and broken, in their temporary locations.

Elizabeth lived and reigned in gilded penury. At her death she left a wardrobe of over 15,000 dresses; two trunksful of silk stockings; a pile of unpaid bills; and the huge, unfinished Winter Palace, which from 1755 to 1761 had already consumed more than 10,000,000 rubles in our money.[8] Not long before her death, she had very much wanted to live in this palace and tried to get the architect, Rastrelli, to hasten the completion of at least her own living quarters, but to no avail. French fancy-goods shops sometimes refused to remit their fashionable wares to the palace on credit.

For all that, within her, unlike her Courland predecessor, somewhere deep beneath the thick crust of prejudices, bad habits, and corrupted tastes, there still dwelt a human being that manifested itself from time to time: when she vowed before seizing the throne not to execute anyone, and when she fulfilled that vow with the decree of May 17, 1744, which in practice abolished the death penalty in Russia; when she refused to confirm the savage criminal section of the Code of Laws, which had been drafted by the Commission of 1754 and already approved by the Senate, with its refined methods of capital punishment; when she refused to grant the Synod's indecent petitions urging the necessity of renouncing her vow; and, finally, when she was capable of weeping at an unjust decision extracted by the intrigues of that same Synod. Elizabeth was an intelligent and good but undisciplined

---

[8]From 1897, when the Russian Empire went on the gold standard, to the First World War, the Russian ruble was worth about fifty American cents.

and willful Russian lady of the eighteenth century. Following Russian custom, many people cursed her in her lifetime, and, also following Russian custom, everyone wept for her at her death.

One individual alone failed to weep for her, because he was not Russian and did not know how to weep. That was the heir to the throne whom she herself had appointed, the most unpleasant of all the unpleasant things Empress Elizabeth left after her. This heir, the son of Elizabeth's older sister, who died soon after his birth, was the Duke of Holstein, known in our history under the name of Peter III. By a strange play of chance, a posthumous reconciliation of the two greatest rivals of the beginning of the eighteenth century took place in the person of this prince: Peter III was the son of Peter I's daughter and the grandson of Charles XII's sister. As a result, the ruler of the little Duchy of Holstein was in grave danger of becoming the heir to two great thrones, the Swedish and the Russian. At first he underwent preparations for the former and was forced to learn the Lutheran catechism, the Swedish language, and Latin grammar. But Elizabeth, having come to the Russian throne and wishing to secure it for her father's line, despatched Major Korff with instructions to extract her nephew from Kiel and convey him to Petersburg at all costs. There, Duke Charles Peter Ulrich of Holstein was transformed into the Grand Duke Peter Fyodorovich and was forced to learn the Russian language and the Orthodox catechism.

Nature, however, was not as gracious to him as fate: the probable heir of two great foreign thrones, he was unsuited by virtue of his gifts even for his own little throne. He was born and grew up a sickly child, meagerly endowed with abilities. What ungracious nature had neglected to deny him, his absurd Holstein education removed. Orphaned early in life, Peter received in Holstein a thoroughly worthless upbringing under the direction of an ignorant courtier who treated him rudely, subjected him to punishments that were degrading and bad for his health, and even flogged him. Humiliated and constrained at every turn, he acquired bad habits and tastes, became irritable, quarrelsome, stubborn, and false, developed a deplorable tendency to lie while believing his own fabrications with artless passion—and, to add to it, in Russia he accustomed himself to getting drunk. He was so badly taught in Holstein that he came to Russia at the age of fourteen a complete ignoramus, and even Elizabeth was astonished at his lack of knowledge. The rapid change of circumstances and educational curricula totally confused a mind that was not robust in any case. Forced to study first one thing and then another without rhyme or reason, Peter ended up learning nothing, and the disparity between his Holstein and Russian circumstances, the senselessness of his Kiel and Petersburg impressions, rendered him incapable of understanding his surroundings at all. His development stopped before his growth did; as a man he remained just what he had been as a child—he grew up but did not mature. His way of thinking and acting created the striking impression that he never thought anything out or followed anything through. He viewed serious things childishly and approached childish enterprises with the seriousness of a grown man. He resembled a child who imagined himself an adult; in fact, he was an adult who always remained a child. Even after his marriage, in Russia, he could not part with his favorite dolls, and visitors at court more than once found him playing with them.

He was Prussia's neighbor in his hereditary domain and was enthralled by the military glory and strategic genius of Frederick II. Since no great ideal could fit into his miniature intellect unless broken up into tiny pieces, however, this martial rapture made Peter just a comical parody of his Prussian hero, someone who merely played soldier. He did not know and did not want to know the Russian army, and since real live soldiers were too big for him, he had soldiers made of wax, lead, and wood and arranged them in his study on tables outfitted in such a way that when he tugged wires stretched over them they emitted sounds that seemed to him like volleys of rifle fire. On appointed days he would gather his servants together, don an elegant general's uniform, and conduct a full-dress review of his toy troops, tugging the wires and harking with delight to the sounds of battle. On one occasion, Catherine was astonished at the spectacle that greeted her when she entered her husband's rooms. On a rope suspended from the ceiling hung a large rat. When Catherine asked what this was all about, Peter replied that the rat had committed a criminal offense and had been given the severest punishment in accordance with military law: it had gotten into a cardboard fortress on a table and eaten two sentries made of starch. The criminal had been apprehended, court-martialed, and sentenced to death by hanging.

Elizabeth was reduced to despair at the character and behavior of her nephew and could not spend a quarter of an hour with him without experiencing distress, anger, and even revulsion. In private, the empress would burst into tears when the subject of Peter came up and lament that God had given her such an heir. Her pious tongue would issue opinions of him that were not pious in the least: "that damned nephew," "my nephew is a monster, the devil take him!" So Catherine relates in her memoirs. According to her, it was thought likely at court that at the end of her life Elizabeth would have consented if it had been proposed that she deport her nephew from Russia and name his six-year-old son Paul as her heir. But her favorites, after contemplating such a step, lacked the courage to take it, and, in the typical fashion of courtiers, turned around and sought to ingratiate themselves with the future emperor.

With no suspicion of the misfortunes that threatened him, admonished by his aunt's inauspicious opinions, this man who was turned inside out, his concepts of good and evil muddled, came to the Russian throne. There he preserved in full the narrowness and pettiness of the ideas and interests in which he had been raised and educated. His cramped Holsteinian intellect was incapable of expanding to the geographical scale of the boundless empire he had unexpectedly obtained. On the contrary, on the Russian throne Peter became even more of a Holsteiner than he had been at home. The one quality with which nature, so stingy otherwise, had endowed him with merciless generosity now expressed itself with particular force: cowardice, combined with a frivolous heedlessness. He was afraid of everything in Russia, called it an accursed country, and expressed the conviction that he would inevitably perish there, but he made no effort to familiarize himself with it and establish close relations with it; he learned nothing about it and shunned everything in it. It frightened him, the way children are frightened when they are left alone in a large empty room.

Guided by his tastes and fears, he surrounded himself with an entourage of a kind that had not been seen even under Peter I, who was so indiscriminate in this regard. He created a little world of his own in which he tried to hide from the Russia that terrified him. He set up a special Holstein Guards regiment composed of every sort of international riffraff (but not of his Russian subjects), for the most part sergeants and corporals of the Prussian army—"a rabble," in the words of Princess Catherine Dashkova, "consisting of the sons of German cobblers." Taking as his model the army of Frederick II, Peter tried to imitate the manners and habits of a Prussian soldier. He began to smoke an inordinate amount of tobacco and drink an excessive number of bottles of beer, believing that otherwise it was impossible to become "a real manly officer." Once he came to the throne, Peter rarely remained sober until evening and was usually tipsy when he sat down to table. Binges took place every day in this Holsteinian entourage, which was joined from time to time by passing comets—touring singers and actresses. In this company, according to the testimony of Andrei Bolotov, who saw him at close hand, the emperor talked "such nonsense and such foolishness" that the hearts of his subjects bled with shame in the presence of foreign envoys. He would suddenly begin to elaborate impossible reform plans, would take up with epic fervor the story of his unprecedented conquest of a gypsy camp near Kiel, or would simply blab some important diplomatic secret. Unfortunately, the emperor felt an inclination to play the violin and was entirely serious in considering himself a virtuoso. He suspected that he harbored a great comic talent, for he was quite adept at making faces, mimicked the priests in church, and at court deliberately replaced the ancient Russian bow with the French manner of greeting in order to reproduce the awkward curtsies of the elderly ladies of the court. One intelligent lady whom he amused with his faces said of him that he was not like a sovereign at all.

During his reign, several important and sensible decrees were issued, for example, the decree abolishing the Secret Chancery and the decree allowing Old Believers who had fled abroad to return to Russia and prohibiting persecution of the Old Belief. These decrees were inspired not by abstract principles of religious toleration or protection of the individual from denunciations but by the practical calculations of men close to Peter—the Vorontsovs, the Shuvalovs, and others—who, to save their own situation, wanted to use the tsar's mercy to secure the emperor's popularity. The decree on the freedom of the nobility also originated from such considerations. Peter himself, however, had little concern for his position, and by his behavior he soon succeeded in provoking a unanimous murmuring within society. It was as though he were deliberately trying to set all classes against him, and the clergy above all. He did not hide his contempt for the rites of the Orthodox Church—on the contrary, he provocatively flaunted it and publicly mocked Russian religious sentiment. During services in the court chapel, he would receive ambassadors while walking back and forth as though he were alone in his study, would converse loudly, and would stick out his tongue at the priests. Once, on Pentecost, when all had gone down on their knees, he gave a loud guffaw and left the church. The archbishop of Novgorod, Dimitry Sechenov, the president of the Synod, was given an order to "purge the Russian churches," that is, to leave in them only the icons of the Savior and the Mother of God while removing the rest, and for the Russian priests to shave their beards and dress like Lutheran pastors. The implementation of these orders was postponed, but the clergy and society took alarm: the Lutherans were coming! The black clergy was especially irritated at the secularization of the church's real estate, which Peter undertook. The College of Economy, which administered the church's property and had previously been under the jurisdiction of the Synod, was now directly subordinated to the Senate and was instructed to give out to the peasants all the church lands, including those they tilled for the monasteries and the hierarchy, and out of the income collected from them to allocate limited fixed sums for the maintenance of church institutions. Peter did not succeed in implementing this measure, but it made an impression.

Much more dangerous was his irritation of the Guards, that touchy and self-confident part of Russian society. From the moment he came to the throne, Peter tried in every way to advertise his unbounded worship of Frederick II. In front of everybody he would piously kiss a bust of the king, and once, at a banquet in the palace, he went down on his knees before his portrait. Immediately after his coronation, he donned a Prussian uniform and began wearing a Prussian decoration more often. The multicolored and classically close-fitting Prussian uniform was introduced into the Russian Guards regiments, replacing the roomy old dark-green caftan Peter I had given them. Regarding himself as Frederick's military apprentice, Peter tried to introduce the strictest discipline into the rather relaxed Russian army. Exercises took place every day. Neither rank nor age freed anyone from marching. Dignitaries who had not seen a parade ground for years, and in addition had succeeded in arming themselves with gout, had to undergo the military-ballet-like drills of Prussian officers and perform all the firearms exercises. Old Prince Nikita Trubetskoi, a field marshal and former procurator-general of the Senate, because of his rank of lieutenant colonel in the Guards, had to appear for training and march along with the soldiers. Contemporaries could not get over how times had changed—how, as Bolotov put it, the sick and the healthy and even the old-timers were now lifting their legs and marching alongside the young, and marking time and wading through the mud just as nicely as the soldiers.

What was most offensive was that Peter gave preference in every respect to his motley Holsteiners over the Russian Guards, referring to the latter as janissaries. Meanwhile, the Prussian ambassador was running Russia's foreign policy and managing everything at Peter's court. Before his coronation, Peter had been a Prussian informant and had sent Frederick II information on the Russian army during the Seven Years' War; once on the Russian throne, he became a loyal subject of the Prussian envoy. An indignant feeling of wounded national dignity began to grow, and the hateful specter arose of a repetition of the evil days of Biron; the indignation was intensified by fear that the Russian Guards would be dispersed to the army regiments, as Biron had previously threatened to do. Moreover, the entire society sensed the vacillation and arbitrariness of the government's actions, the absence of any unity of thought or definite direction. The disarray of the governmental mechanism was clear to everyone. All these things provoked a simultaneous murmuring, which seeped down from the highest circles and became nationwide. Tongues were loosened, seemingly without fear of the police; in the streets, dissatisfaction was expressed openly and loudly, with no apprehension about blaming the sovereign. The murmuring imperceptibly developed into a military conspiracy, and the conspiracy led to a new coup d'état.

～ II ～

The Coup d'État of June 28, 1762

The person in whose name the movement came to be undertaken was the empress, who had acquired wide popularity, especially in the Guards regiments. The emperor was on bad terms with his wife, threatening to divorce her; even to shut her up in a convent; and to replace her with an individual close to him, the niece of the chancellor Count Michael Vorontsov. For a long time Catherine remained aloof, patiently enduring her situation and refraining from direct relations with the malcontents. Peter himself, however, goaded her to action. To fill the cup of Russia's sorrows to overflowing and bring the nationwide murmuring to an open outburst, the emperor concluded peace (on April 24, 1762) with that same Frederick who had been reduced to despair by Russia's victories under Elizabeth. Now Peter not only renounced the gains from those victories—even the ones Frederick himself had conceded, in East Prussia—and not only concluded peace with him but joined forces with Prussia against the Austrians, Russia's recent allies. The Russians gritted their teeth in vexation, Bolotov remarks.

At a gala dinner on June 9, on the occasion of the confirmation of the peace treaty, the emperor proposed a toast to the imperial family. Catherine drank the toast sitting down. To Peter's question as to why she had not stood, she replied that she did not deem it necessary, since the entire imperial family consisted of the emperor, herself, and their son, the heir to the throne. "And what about my uncles, the princes of Holstein?" Peter objected and ordered Adjutant General Gudovich, who was standing behind his chair, to go over to Catherine and convey a word of abuse to her. Fearing, however, that Gudovich in delivering the impolite word might soften it, Peter shouted it across the table himself for all to hear. The empress burst into tears. That same evening an order was issued to arrest her. It was not carried out, however, at the entreaty of one of Peter's uncles, the unwitting culprits of the scene.

Henceforth, Catherine began to lend a more attentive ear to the suggestions her friends had been making to her from the moment Elizabeth died. The enterprise had the sympathy of a number of individuals in the highest ranks of Petersburg society, in large part people who had been personally offended by Peter. One was Count Nikita Panin, the Elizabethan diplomat and tutor of the heir to the throne, Grand Duke Paul. Another was the nineteen-year-old Princess Dashkova, the sister of Peter's favorite, who had strong connections in the Guards through her husband. The archbishop of Novgorod, Dimitry Sechenov, who because of his office could not, of course, take a direct part in the conspiracy, was also sympathetically inclined. Most of all, however, the affair was assisted on the quiet by Count Kirill Razumovsky, hetman of Ukraine and president of the Academy of Sciences, a rich man who was extremely well liked in his Izmailovsky Guards Regiment on account of his generosity. The actual agents of the enterprise were young Guards officers: Passek and Bredikhin of the Preobrazhensky Regiment, Lasunsky and the Roslavlev brothers of the Izmailovsky, and Khitrovo and the noncommissioned officer Potemkin of the Horse Guards.

Serving as the center around which these officers came together was the whole nest of Orlov brothers, two of whom, Gregory and Alexis, particularly stood out: strong, tall, and handsome, empty-headed and desperately brave, masters at organizing drinking bouts and fist fights to the death in the outskirts of Petersburg, they were famous in all the regiments as idols of the young guardsmen. The elder of them, Gregory, an artillery officer, had long had relations with the empress, which were skillfully concealed. The conspirators were divided into four sections, headed by separate leaders who met to confer. There were none of the usual conspiratorial rituals, however, neither regular meetings nor deliberate methods of propaganda, and there is no indication of a detailed plan of action. Nor was there a need for any. The Guards had been schooled for so long by a whole series of palace coups that they needed no special preparation for such an enterprise as long as they had a popular figure, in whose name it was always possible to raise the regiments. On the eve of the coup, Catherine counted on her side some 40 officers and 10,000 soldiers of the Guards.

The coup was not a surprise; everyone was expecting it. For a whole week beforehand, amid growing agitation, crowds of people, especially guardsmen, thronged the streets of the capital, almost openly "cursing" the sovereign. Impressionable observers were counting the hours in anticipation of an outburst. Denunciations reached Peter, of course, but, cheerful and unconcerned, failing to understand the seriousness of the situation, he paid no attention to anything and continued his empty-headed ways at Oranienbaum. He took no precautionary measures and even fanned the smoldering flames himself, like an active conspirator. Having terminated one war without benefit to Russia, Peter ventured on another of even less benefit, breaking with Denmark in order to retrieve Schleswig, which Denmark had taken from Holstein. While mobilizing the forces of the Russian Empire in bellicose fashion against little Denmark to restore the integrity of his native Holstein, Peter at the same time took a stand for freedom of conscience in Russia. On June 25 a decree was issued to the Synod enjoining the equality of the Christian creeds and directing that fasts be nonobligatory, that sins against the seventh commandment not be condemned, "for even Christ did not condemn them," and that all peasants belonging to the monasteries be taken over by the state. In conclusion, the decree demanded of the Synod the unquestioning implementation of all the emperor's measures. Peter's wild orders prompted belief in the most improbable rumors. Thus it was said that he wanted to divorce all the ladies of the court from their husbands and remarry them to others of his choice, and to set the example by divorcing his own wife and marrying Elizabeth Vorontsova (though that could have happened). The general unspoken agreement to get rid of such an autocrat at all costs becomes understandable.

Only a propitious occasion was awaited, and Peter prepared the ground for it himself with his Danish war. The Guards were waiting in distress for the order to begin their march abroad, and Panin regarded the sovereign's arrival in Petersburg to see them off as the appropriate moment for a coup. But its outbreak was accelerated by a chance circumstance. An agitated Preobrazhensky corporal came to Passek to ask whether the emperor would be overthrown soon and to inform him that the empress had died. The soldiers' anxiety had been aroused by rumors about Catherine that the conspirators themselves had spread. Passek sent the soldier away, assuring him that nothing of the sort had happened. The latter hastened to another officer, who was not a party to the conspiracy, and told him the same thing, adding that he had already been to see Passek. This officer informed his superiors of what he had heard, and on June 27 Passek was arrested. His arrest brought all the conspirators to their feet, in fear that the arrested man might give them away under torture.

That night it was decided to send Alexis Orlov for Catherine, who was living at Peterhof while awaiting the emperor's name day (June 29). Early on the morning of June 28, Orlov burst into Catherine's bedroom and told her that Passek had been arrested. Hastily dressing, the empress and one of her ladies-in-waiting got into Orlov's carriage, with Orlov on the coachbox, and were driven directly to the Izmailovsky Regiment. At the sound of drumbeats, the long-prepared soldiers ran out into the square and immediately took the oath, kissing the empress's hands, feet, and dress. The colonel himself, Count Razumovsky, appeared. Then, preceded by a priest with cross in hand to administer the oath, they moved on to the Semyonovsky Regiment, where the same scene was repeated. At the head of both regiments and accompanied by a crowd of people, Catherine went to the Kazan Cathedral, where in a service she was proclaimed autocratic empress. From there she set out for the newly built Winter Palace, where she found the already assembled Senate and Synod, which adhered to her unquestioningly and took the oath. The Horse Guards and the Preobrazhensky Regiment joined the movement, along with several army units, and a crowd of more than 14,000 surrounded the palace, enthusiastically hailing Catherine, who was making the rounds of the regiments; the crowds echoed the troops. With no objections or hesitations, both officials and commoners took the oath—whoever could get into the palace, which was opened to all comers. Everything happened as though of its own accord, as if some unseen hand had arranged it all beforehand, getting everyone's agreement and notifying them at the appropriate time. Catherine, seeing how heartily everyone greeted her and tried to catch her hand, explained this unanimity on the grounds of the popular character of the movement: all had taken part in it voluntarily, feeling themselves to be independent actors rather than puppets of the police or curious spectators. Meanwhile, a brief manifesto was hastily composed and distributed to the populace, announcing that the empress, in accordance with the manifest and unfeigned wishes of all her faithful subjects, had ascended the throne to defend the Orthodox Russian Church, Russia's triumphant glory, and the country's domestic institutions, which had been completely subverted.

On the evening of June 28, at the head of several regiments, Catherine—on horseback, in a Guards uniform of the old Petrine cut and a hat adorned with a green oak twig, her long hair loose—alongside Princess Dashkova, also on horseback and in a Guards uniform, advanced on Peterhof. The emperor, with his suite, was to have gone there that day from Oranienbaum to dine at Monplaisir, the Peterhof pavilion where Catherine was installed. With a large company of courtiers, Peter had arrived at Monplaisir—it was empty. The whole garden was searched—she was nowhere to be found! It was learned that early in the morning the empress had secretly left for Petersburg. Everyone was plunged into confusion. Three dignitaries, including Chancellor Vorontsov, sensing what was up, offered to ride to Petersburg to find out what was happening there and to appeal to the empress's conscience. Afterward, Catherine publicly asserted that they had even been ordered to kill her if necessary. Upon their arrival in Petersburg, the intelligence gatherers took the oath to the empress and did not return. Having received some news from Petersburg, those at Peterhof set to work dispatching adjutants and hussars along all the roads to the capital, writing orders, and giving advice as to how to proceed. It was decided to seize Kronstadt and from there to move on the capital with the use of naval forces. When the emperor and his entourage approached the fortress, however, he was informed that he would be fired on if he did not leave. Peter did not have the heart to take Field Marshal Münnich's advice to leap ashore, or to sail to Revel and from there to Pomerania and place himself at the head of the Russian army abroad. He hid in the very bottom of the galley and, amid the sobs of the court ladies who had accompanied the expedition, sailed back to Oranienbaum.

An attempt to enter into negotiations with the empress failed; a proposal to reconcile and share power went unanswered. Peter was then forced to write out in his own hand and sign a proclamation sent to him by Catherine, according to which "of his own accord" he swore to renounce the throne. When Catherine and her regiments reached Peterhof on the morning of June 29, Peter, who had let himself be brought there from Oranienbaum, was with difficulty protected from the inflamed soldiers. He fell into a faint at the Peterhof palace from excessive shock. A little while later, when Panin arrived, Peter threw himself upon him and clutched his hands, pleading to be allowed to keep the four things that were especially dear to him: his violin, his favorite dog, a negro, and Elizabeth Vorontsova. He was allowed to keep the first three, but the fourth was dispatched to Moscow and married to Alexander Poliansky.

A chance guest of the Russian throne, Peter flashed across the Russian political horizon like a shooting star, leaving everyone bewildered as to why he had appeared there. The former emperor was taken to Ropsha, a country house that had been given to him by Empress Elizabeth, and the next day Catherine triumphantly entered Petersburg.

So ended this revolution, the most lighthearted and delicate of all those known to us, which cost not a single drop of blood—a real ladies' revolution. It did cost a great deal of wine, however: on the day of Catherine's entry into the capital, June 30, all the drinking establishments were opened to the troops. In a mad ecstasy, soldiers and their wives hauled out the vodka, beer, mead, and champagne, pouring it into tubs, kegs, or whatever came to hand. Three years later the matter of compensation for the Petersburg wine merchants "for wines pilfered by soldiers and other people during Her Majesty's happy accession to the imperial throne" was still being processed in the Senate.

The affair of June 28, though it was the culmination of a series of eighteenth-century palace coups, was not like them in every respect. It, too, was carried out by the Guards, but it was supported by the openly expressed sympathy of the capital's population, which gave it a popular cast. Moreover, it bore an entirely different political character. In 1725, 1730, and 1741, the Guards had installed, or restored, the customary supreme power in the person of one or another individual whom the Guards' leaders represented to them as the legitimate heir of that power. In 1762, the Guards emerged as an independent political force—and not a conservative one, as before, but a revolutionary force—overthrowing the legitimate bearer of the supreme power to whom they themselves had taken the oath not long before. Their indignant national feelings were mingled with a self-satisfied awareness that they were creating and giving to the fatherland their own government, one that was illegitimate but would understand and pursue the country's interests better than the legitimate one. In explanation of the enthusiasm the Guards displayed in the coup, Catherine wrote shortly afterward that the lowest Guards soldier regarded her as the work of his own hands. And in reply to the revolutionary loyalty of her Guards, Catherine hastened to declare that usurpation could be a reliable pledge of state order and popular well-being.

When the agitation stirred up in Petersburg by the coup had subsided, the excesses of the patriotic rejoicing in the streets were glossed over in a solemn document that explained the meaning of the events that had taken place. A second, "detailed" manifesto was issued on July 6. This was both a justification of the seizure of power and a confession, both a denunciation of the fallen ruler and an entire political program. With merciless candor, it exposed the criminal or shameful actions and evil intentions of the former emperor, which, according to the assurances of the manifesto, would have led to rebellion, regicide, and the ruin of the state. Seeing the fatherland perishing and heeding "the loyal subjects chosen and sent by the people," the empress had dedicated herself either to becoming a sacrifice for the dear fatherland or to rescuing it from the perils that threatened it. The manifesto denounced and castigated, in the person of the overthrown emperor, not an ill-fated accident but the very structure of the Russian state. "Absolute power," the manifesto stated, "unrestrained by good and philanthropic qualities in the sovereign who rules autocratically, is such an evil as to be the direct cause of many pernicious consequences." Never had the Russian government so openly proclaimed from the height of the throne to its people the sad truth that the capstone of the state edifice in which they dwelt, by its unsound construction, constantly threatened to destroy the edifice itself. To stave off this calamity, the empress "most solemnly" gave her imperial word to legitimate such state institutions as would preserve "even to our descendants" the integrity of the empire and of the autocratic government and would deliver faithful servants of the fatherland "from despondency and insult."

Even this coup, however, so lightheartedly and harmoniously carried out, had its doleful and unnecessary epilogue. At Ropsha, Peter was lodged in one room and barred not only from the garden but even from the terrace. The palace was surrounded by sentries from the Guards. Those assigned to look after the prisoner treated him rudely, but his chief supervisor, Alexis Orlov, was affectionate with him, kept him occupied, played cards with him, and loaned him money. From the moment of his arrival at Ropsha, Peter had felt unwell. In the evening of July 6, the day on which the manifesto was signed, Catherine received a note from Orlov written by a frightened and scarcely sober hand. One thing only could be understood: on that day, at table, Peter had started an argument with one of the company; Orlov and the others had hastened to separate them but had done so in such an awkward fashion that the ailing prisoner wound up dead. "We did not separate them in time, and he had already passed away; we ourselves do not remember what we did." Catherine, in her own words, was touched and even stunned by this death. But, she wrote a month later, "we have to go right on—suspicion must not fall on me." Following the solemn manifesto of July 6, another, sad one was read in the churches on July 7, announcing the death of the former emperor, who had succumbed to a severe colic, and inviting prayers "without rancor" for the salvation of the deceased's soul. He was taken directly to the Alexander Nevsky Monastery and modestly interred there next to the former ruler Anna Leopoldovna. The entire Senate asked Catherine not to attend the burial.

When we read the manifesto of July 6, we sense that we are standing at an important turning point in Russian life. It promised something new, or hitherto unattained, namely, a state based on law. Let us look back a bit so as to see how little preparation there was for such a state, how the idea of it, flaring up from time to time, had quickly died out. Up to the end of the sixteenth century, we observed the Russian state still resting on the foundations of the patrimonial order, in which the state was considered not a union of the people but the family property of the sovereign, and the subject knew only his obligations, having no rights guaranteed by law. The Time of Troubles, it would seem, should have purged the state of the last remnants of that patrimonial order: the people had emerged from the chaos by their own efforts and elected a new dynasty that had not built the state, as its predecessor had, and could not consider it its patrimony. They had shown themselves capable of becoming active participants in the building of the state and had ceased to serve as mere construction material. Indeed, after the Troubles we observe two currents in Muscovite political life: one was carving out a new channel, that of initiative by the "land," while the other was drawn back to the abandoned riverbed of officialdom. As the new stream grew more distant from its source, however, it gradually bent toward the old one and by the end of the seventeenth century had merged with it. Old patrimonial concepts and habits revived along with the new dynasty. In his governmental decrees, the new dynasty's founder[1] tried to show the people that he saw himself not as someone elected by the people but as the nephew of Tsar Fyodor and regarded this kinship as the true source of his power. The independent popular initiative called forth by the Troubles was, to be sure, consolidated in the all-estate Assembly of the Land. At the same time, however, its natural foundation, local self-government, declined, and the Assembly of the Land failed to mold itself into a stable, permanent institution. It soon lost its original all-estate composition and in the end died out, swept away by the maelstrom of Peter's reforms.

In his ideas and aspirations, Peter I came close to the concept of a state based on law. He considered the objective of the state to be the *common good*, the people's well-being, not dynastic interest, and the means of attaining it to be legality, the firm preservation of "civil and political rights." He regarded his power not as his hereditary property but as belonging to the office of tsar and his activity as service to the state. Circumstances and habits, however, prevented him from bringing his deeds into full accord with his ideas and intentions. Circumstances forced him to work more in the realm of politics than of law, and from his predecessors he inherited two harmful political prejudices: belief in the creative force of state power, and confidence in the inexhaustible nature of the people's strength and patience. He did not stop at anyone's rights or at any popular sacrifice. Though he became a reformer in the European spirit, he preserved within himself too much of the pre-Petrine, Muscovite tsar. He took into account neither the people's sense of justice nor their psychology, and he hoped to uproot age-old custom and introduce new ideas as easily as he changed styles of dress or the width of manufactured cloth. Implementing everything by force, trying to elicit even independent social activity by means of coercion, he built a law-based system on general arbitrariness; hence his law-based state lacked the element that, alongside state power and legal rules, would have given it life—the free individual, the citizen.

Peter did not succeed in implanting his idea of the state in the popular consciousness, and after him it expired even in governmental minds. It was beyond the comprehension of his legitimate successors, his grandson and daughter. Other successions brought to the throne

---

[1]Tsar Michael, the first ruler of the Romanov dynasty, who was elected to the throne by an Assembly of the Land in 1613.

accidental rulers, even foreigners, who could not view Russia as their patrimony or even as their fatherland. The state shut itself up in the palace. Governments that were defending their power not even as dynastic property but simply as a usurpation they could not justify to the people needed military and political, not popular, support.

But the muddy wave of palace coups, of favor and disgrace, gradually deposited around the throne the semblance of a ruling class, with a variegated social composition but a uniform cast of mind and manners. This was merely a new formation of the military service class that had long functioned at the court of the patrimonial Muscovite sovereigns under the command of the boyars. In the *oprichnina* of Ivan the Terrible, this class had taken on a vivid political coloration as a police security corps directed against the sedition of the boyars and the "land." In the seventeenth century, its upper stratum, the gentry of the capital, absorbed the remnants of the boyar class and took its place in the administration. Under Peter the Great, transformed into the Guards and infused with an admixture of foreigners, it was also destined to become the transmitter of Western culture and military technology. The state was not stingy in rewarding the gentry for its administrative and military services: it increased the tax burden on the people for the gentry's maintenance, gave it a huge quantity of state lands, and even enserfed some two-thirds of the rural population for its benefit. Finally, after Peter the gentry as a whole, through the Guards, created accidental governments, freed itself from compulsory service, and with new rights became the dominant estate, holding in its hands both the administration and the national economy.

Thus this estate took shape from century to century, remaking itself in accordance with the needs of the state and the influences it absorbed along the way. At the moment of Catherine's accession, it constituted the *nation* in the political sense of the word, and with its assistance the palace state of Peter I's successors took on the aspect of a gentry state. A popular state based on law was still in the future, and not an immediate prospect.

～ III ～

Catherine II:
Upbringing and Character

Catherine II's manifesto of July 6, 1762, announced a new force that was henceforth to direct the life of the Russian state. Until now its sole mover—recognized in the empire's one fundamental law, Peter the Great's statute on succession to the throne[1]—had been the all-powerful will of the sovereign, personal discretion. Catherine declared in her manifesto that autocratic power by itself, without the accidental, nonobligatory restraint of good and philanthropic qualities, is an evil harmful to the state. Laws were solemnly promised that would indicate to all state institutions the limits of their activity. How the principle of legality proclaimed here was introduced into the life of the state is what interests us about the reign of Catherine and her successors; how it happened that Catherine II proclaimed this principle is what interests us about her personality, her fate, and her character.

The June coup d'état of 1762 made Catherine II the autocratic empress of Russia. From the very beginning of the eighteenth century, those who held supreme power in Russia had been either extraordinary individuals, like Peter the Great, or accidental ones, like his successors—even those among them who, by virtue of Peter's law, had been named to the throne by the previous accident, as were the infant Ivan VI and Peter III. Catherine II brought to a close this series of excep-

---

[1]Peter the Great's law of 1722 left it to the reigning sovereign to name his or her successor.

tional phenomena in our wholly irregular eighteenth century: she was the last accident on the Russian throne and had a long and unusual reign that formed an entire era of our history. Subsequent reigns would start out on a legal basis and in a spirit of established custom.

On her mother's side, Catherine belonged to the Holstein-Gottorp family, one of the numerous princely clans of north Germany, and on her father's side to another, even more petty sovereign family of the same region, that of Anhalt-Zerbst. Catherine's father, Christian August, of the Zerbst-Dornburg line of the House of Anhalt, was in service to the king of Prussia, like many of his neighbors among the petty north-German princes. He served as the regimental commander, commandant, and then governor of the city of Stettin, was an unsuccessful candidate for duke of Courland, and ended his extraterritorial service as a Prussian field marshal, elevated to that rank under the patronage of Russia's Empress Elizabeth. It was in Stettin that his daughter Sophie Augusta, our Catherine, was born on April 21, 1729. This princess thus united in her person two of the petty princely houses of northwestern Germany.

Northwestern Germany in the eighteenth century was in many respects a curious little corner of Europe. Here, medieval German feudalism was wearing itself out and was down to its last dynastic regalia and genealogical traditions. With its endless family divisions and subdivisions—its princes of Brunswick-Luneburg and Brunswick-Wolfenbüttel; of Saxe-Romburg, Saxe-Coburg, Saxe-Gotha, and Saxe-Coburg-Gotha; of Mecklenburg-Schwerin and Mecklenburg-Strelitz; of Schleswig-Holstein, Holstein-Gottorp, and Gottorp-Eutin; of Anhalt-Dessau, Anhalt-Zerbst, and Zerbst-Dornburg—it was an archaic feudal anthill, bustling and for the most part poor, highly inbred and quarrelsome, swarming in cramped condition and on tight budgets, and with an imagination that readily soared beyond the narrow confines of the ancestral nest. Within this circle, everyone lived in hopes of a happy accident, counting on kinship ties and foreign conjunctures, on desirable combinations of unexpected circumstances. Hence it always had a requisite supply of petty bridegrooms looking for great brides, poor brides pining for rich bridegrooms, and, finally, heirs and heiresses waiting for vacant thrones. Understandably, such tastes bred political cosmopolitans whose thoughts were not of their homeland but of a career and whose homeland was wherever their careers were successful. Here, living among foreigners was a family business, serving at a foreign court and inheriting what belonged to someone else a dynastic imperative. That is why this little world of petty princes acquired considerable international importance in the eighteenth century: more than once, minor princes issued from it who played a major role in the fate of great European powers, including Russia. Mecklenburg, Brunswick, Holstein, Anhalt-Zerbst—each in turn sent us political wayfarers in the form of princes, princesses, and mere salaried campaigners.

Thanks to the fact that one of Peter the Great's daughters married the duke of Holstein, this house acquired significance in our history. From the very beginning of the eighteenth century, Catherine's relations on her mother's side, lineal and collateral, had either served abroad or sought thrones elsewhere by marriage. Her grandfather (in a collateral line), Frederick Charles, who was married to the sister of the Swedish king Charles XII, laid down his life in a single battle at the beginning of the Northern War, fighting in his brother-in-law's army. A cousin of hers once removed, Frederick Charles's son, Duke Charles Frederick, married Peter the Great's elder daughter Anna and had prospects for the Swedish throne, which were unsuccessful. To make up for it, the Swedes in 1742, at the conclusion of an unsuccessful war with Russia, elected his son, Charles Peter Ulrich, who was born in 1728 and whose mother died at his birth, the heir to the Swedish throne, in order by this courtesy to ingratiate themselves with his aunt, the empress of Russia, and soften the terms of peace. Elizabeth had already snared her nephew for her own throne, however, and in his stead thrust upon the Swedes—not without detriment to Russian interests—another Holsteiner prince, Adolph Frederick, Catherine's uncle, whom the Russian government had previously installed as duke of Courland. Another of Catherine's Holsteiner uncles, Charles, had been declared the fiancé of Elizabeth herself when she was still a tsarevna, and only the prince's death shortly thereafter prevented him from becoming her husband. In view of these family events, an elderly canon of Brunswick could tell Catherine's mother, without straining his gift of prophecy: "On your daughter's brow I see at least three crowns." In this petty German princedom, the world had already grown accustomed to seeing heads that foreign crowns awaited, having been left without heads of their own.

Catherine was born into the modest circumstances of a petty German prince who had become a Prussian general. She grew into a lively, mischievous, even daredevil girl, who loved to play pranks on her elders, especially her governesses, and to show off her courage to other children, and who was able to keep from flinching when she was afraid. Her parents did not burden her with their educational concerns. Her father was a diligent campaigner, while her mother, Johanna Eliza-beth, a contentious and restless woman who was simply drawn to quarrels and scandal, was intrigue personified, shadiness incarnate. She liked being anywhere but at home. In her time she traveled over almost all of Europe, visited every capital, and served Frederick the Great on diplomatic business of the sort that real diplomats were shy about taking on themselves, thereby earning much respect from the great king; not long before her daughter's coronation she died in Paris in highly straitened circumstances, because Frederick was stingy about paying for the services of his agents. Catherine could only thank fate for the fact that her mother was rarely at home: in the upbringing of her children the Stettin commandant's wife adhered to the simplest precepts, and Catherine later acknowledged that she was inured to expecting a maternal slap for any blunder she made.

She was not yet fifteen when one of her Holsteiner uncles, who was in the Saxon and later the Prussian service, fell in love with her and even obtained his niece's consent to marry him. But a purely Holstein-ian conjunction of favorable circumstances destroyed this early idyll and delivered the princess of Anhalt-Zerbst from the modest fate of a Prussian colonel's or general's wife, vindicating the Brunswick canon's prophecy by affording her only one crown, not three—but one that was worth ten German crowns. First, Empress Elizabeth, despite more recent passions of her fickle heart, preserved to the end of her life a tender memory of her Holsteiner fiancé, who had died so prema-turely, and turned her attention to his niece Catherine and her mother, sending them knickknacks such as her portrait set in diamonds, worth 18,000 rubles (no less than 100,000 in today's rubles). Such gifts were no small source of support for the family of the Stettin governor and later Prussian field marshal in the less fortunate days of their lives. Then, too, the insignificance of Catherine's family was of great assis-tance to her. The Petersburg court at this time was seeking a bride for the heir to the Russian throne, and farsighted Petersburg politicians advised Elizabeth to direct the search toward a modest ruling house, for a bride of prominent dynastic origin might not show proper obedi-ence and respect to her husband or the empress. Finally, among the matchmakers trying to set Catherine up in Petersburg was one quite significant figure in Europe of the time—the Prussian king Frederick II. After his bandit-like seizure of Silesia from Austria, he needed the friendship of Sweden and Russia and intended to secure it through the marriages of the heirs of those two powers. Elizabeth very much wanted to marry her nephew to the princess of Prussia, but Frederick begrudged the expenditure of his sister on the Russian barbarians and designated her for the Swedish heir, Elizabeth's aforementioned Holsteiner protégé Adolph Frederick, in order to reinforce his diplomatic agents in Stockholm. To the Russian heir he wanted to consign the daughter of his faithful field marshal, the former governor of Stettin, calculating that he would make of her, too, a reliable agent in the capital of an empire he feared. He acknowledges in his memoirs with great self-satisfaction that the marriage of Peter and Catherine was his doing, his idea, that he considered it essential for the state interests of Prussia and saw in Catherine the individual most suitable for securing them as far as Petersburg was concerned.

All these factors determined Elizabeth's choice, despite the fact that—or, rather, among other considerations, because—the bride on her mother's side was her fiancé's second cousin. Elizabeth considered the Holstein clan her own family and regarded this marriage as a family affair. All that remained was to reassure the father, a strict Lutheran of the old orthodox school, who could not tolerate the idea of his daughter's conversion to the Greek heresy, but he was persuaded that the religion of the Russians was almost Lutheran and that they did not even accept veneration of the saints.

The designs of the fourteen-year-old Catherine converged with the subtle calculations of the great king. The family instinct had awakened in her early in life. By her own admission, at the age of seven the idea of a crown had already begun to ferment in her mind, a foreign crown, of course, and when Prince Peter of Holstein became the heir to the Russian throne, "in the depths of my heart I destined myself for him," because she considered that the most significant of all possible matches. Later, she candidly admitted in her memoirs that after her arrival in Russia the Russian crown pleased her more than the person of her fiancé. When in January 1744 the invitation from Petersburg reached her mother in Zerbst to come immediately to Russia with her daughter, Catherine persuaded her parents to accept it. Her mother was actually offended for her lovelorn brother, to whom Catherine had already given her word. "And my brother George, what will he say?" her mother asked reproachfully. "He can only want my happiness," the daughter answered, blushing. And so, shrouded in deep secrecy, under an assumed name, as though preparing for some evil deed, mother and daughter hastily set out for Russia and in February presented themselves to Elizabeth in Moscow.

The whole political world of Europe marveled when it learned of the Russian empress's choice. Immediately after her arrival, Catherine was assigned teachers of Scripture, the Russian language, and dancing—the three basic subjects of higher education at Elizabeth's national-Orthodox and terpsichorean court. Without yet having mastered Russian and knowing just a few scattered phrases, Catherine memorized "like a parrot" the confession of faith drawn up for her, and some five months after her arrival in Russia, at the rite of adherence to Orthodoxy, pronounced it in the court chapel loudly and clearly, without stumbling. She was given the Orthodox name Catherine Alekseyevna, in honor of the empress's mother. This was her first ceremonial appearance on the court stage, and it evoked general approval and even tears of emotion from the spectators, but she herself, a foreign ambassador remarked, did not shed a single tear and bore herself like a real heroine. The empress bestowed on the new convert a folding icon with a diamond clasp worth several hundred thousand rubles. The next day, June 29, 1744, Peter and Catherine were betrothed, and in August 1745 they were married, celebrating their wedding with ten days of festivities before which the fairy tales of the Orient paled by comparison.

Catherine came to Russia an utterly destitute bride. She later acknowledged that she brought with her a total of a dozen shifts and three or four dresses, and those were paid for by a bill of exchange sent from Petersburg for her traveling expenses. She did not even have bed linen. That was very little to live on respectably at the Russian court, where a palace fire, which burned only a part of Elizabeth's wardrobe, once consumed some 4,000 dresses. Catherine subsequently recalled her observations and impressions of the court in those years with the self-satisfied equanimity of someone looking back from a distance over a muddy road she has just crossed. At times the palace resembled a costume party, at times a gambling casino. Ladies changed their clothes two or three times a day, the empress as many as five times, hardly ever wearing the same dress twice. Games of chance for large

sums went on from morning to night amid gossip, subterranean intrigue, scandalmongering, informing, and flirtation, endless flirtation.
In the evenings the empress herself took an active part in the gambling.
Cards saved the social life of the court: there was no other common
interest to reconcile these people, who met daily at the palace while
cordially detesting each other. They had nothing about which to make
polite conversation; they were capable of displaying their wit only in
mutual backbiting; and since they were complete ignoramuses, they
were wary of turning the conversation to science, art, or anything of
that sort. According to Catherine, probably half of this society could
barely read, and scarcely a third knew how to write. They were uni-
formed court lackeys, differing little in their manners and ideas from
the liveried ones, despite the presence among them of eminent old
family names, titled and untitled. When Elizabeth's favorite, Count
Alexis Razumovsky, played faro,[2] holding the bank himself and deliberately losing in order to maintain the glory of an open-handed lord,
the ladies-in-waiting and other courtiers stole money from him. Prince
Ivan Odoevsky, an actual privy councillor and president of the College
of Hereditary Estates, a government minister of sorts, once filched
1,500 rubles in his hat, handing over the stolen money to his servant in
the vestibule.

These dignitaries were treated like lackeys. The wife of Count Peter
Shuvalov, the boldest statesman under Elizabeth, would hold church
services when her husband returned from that same Razumovsky's
hunting party without having been beaten by the good-natured favorite,
who tended to be violent when drunk. Catherine relates that once,
during a festivity at Oranienbaum, Peter III, in front of the diplomatic
corps and a hundred Russian guests, beat his favorites, Master of the
Horse Lev Naryshkin, Lieutenant-General Alexis Melgunov, and privy
councillor Dmitry Volkov. The half-witted autocratic emperor treated
his exalted favorites the way the drunken favorite of the intelligent
autocratic empress could treat any court dignitary. The empress herself
set the tone of court life. Symbolizing the dimensions and wealth of
her empire, she made public appearances dressed in enormous crino-
lines and covered with diamonds, and went to the Trinity Monastery to
pray wearing all the Russian decorations then in existence. Slovenli-
ness and caprice held sway in the everyday practices of the palace.

---

[2]The word "faro," which is called for here, was omitted from the text.

Neither the order of court life, nor the rooms, nor the palace's entrances were sensibly or comfortably arranged. A foreign ambassador arriving at the palace for an audience would be met by all sorts of garbage being taken from the inner rooms. The ladies of the court had to imitate the empress in everything but surpass her in nothing. Those who had the audacity to be born more beautiful than she, or to dress more elegantly, inevitably came in for her wrath. For these qualities on one occasion, before the entire court, she cut off with scissors "a charming ornament of ribbons" on the head of the wife of the master of the horse, Naryshkin. Once she had to shave off her own blonde hair, which she had dyed black. Immediately the order went out to all the ladies of the court to shave their heads. Weeping, they parted with their coiffures and replaced them with ugly black wigs. And one time, irritated at the discord of her four favorites, on the first day of Easter she berated all forty of her maids, gave a scolding to the choir and the priest, and ruined everybody's paschal mood. Loving gaiety, she wanted everyone to amuse her with cheerful conversation, but woe to anyone who uttered even a single word in her presence about illnesses, deaths, the Prussian king, Voltaire, beautiful women, or the sciences, so for the most part everyone cautiously kept silent. In vexation, Elizabeth would fling her napkin on the table and leave the room.

Catherine went to Russia with thoughts of a crown, not of family happiness. But at first after her arrival she nearly succumbed to the illusion of a happy future. It seemed to her that the grand duke loved her, even passionately. The empress said that she loved her almost more than she loved the grand duke and showered her with endearments and gifts, the smallest of which amounted to ten or fifteen thousand rubles. But she soon sobered up, having sensed the dangers that threatened her at the court, where the mode of thought—to translate her expression as mildly as possible—was base and corrupt (*lâche et corrompue*). The ground shook under her feet. Once at the Trinity Monastery she and her fiancé were sitting by a window and laughing. Suddenly the empress's personal physician Armand Lestocq burst from her rooms and declared to the young couple: "Your gaiety will soon be over." Then, turning to Catherine, he continued: "Start packing your things; you will soon be on your way back home!" It turned out that Catherine's mother had quarreled with the courtiers and meddled in the intrigues of the French plenipotentiary, Marquis de la Chétardie, and Elizabeth had resolved to deport the irrepressible governor's wife along with her daughter. The mother was in fact subsequently deported, though without her daughter. At this threat of an unexpected separation, the fiancé gave his betrothed to understand that he would part with her without regret. "For my part," she adds, as though in revenge, "knowing his character, I would have had no regrets about him, but I was not so indifferent to the Russian crown."

Not long before the wedding, she pondered her future. Her heart foretold no happiness for her; her marriage promised her only unpleasantness. "Ambition alone sustained me," she adds, remembering those days much later in her memoirs. "In the depths of my soul there was something, I know not what, that left me in no doubt for a moment that sooner or later I would achieve my goal, I would become the autocratic empress of Russia." This premonition helped her to overlook, or patiently to endure, the many thorns with which her life's path was strewn. After the wedding, the sixteen-year-old prophetic dreamer embarked on a prolonged education by ordeal. Her family life with a seventeen-year-old perpetual adolescent started off grey and hard. The hardest lessons, however, were not those she learned from her husband. She managed to get along with him more or less. He played with his dolls and his soldiers, did stupid things, and turned to his wife for advice; and she came to his aid. He betrayed her in her difficulties, now offering to instruct her in rifle drill and sentry duty, now cursing her when he lost to her at cards. He confided to her his amorous affairs with her ladies-in-waiting and her maids, was not the least bit interested in her thoughts and feelings, and left her to occupy herself to her heart's content with her tears and her books. So their married life went, day after day, over a long stretch of years. A complete indifference to one another reigned over their marriage, the almost amicable mutual apathy of a couple who had nothing in common and even detested each other, though they lived under one roof and were called husband and wife—not the highest sort of family happiness, but fairly common in those circles.

The real tyrant over Catherine was "dear auntie." Elizabeth kept her like a wild bird in a cage, not allowing her to go out for a walk without permission, or even to go to the bathhouse, to rearrange the furniture in her rooms, or to have pen and ink. Those around her did not dare to speak to her in a low voice, and she could send her parents only letters composed in the College of Foreign Affairs. Her every step was followed; eavesdroppers listened to her every word and reported it to the empress with slander and fabrication; what she did alone in her rooms was observed through the keyholes. Those of her servants to whom she showed trust or attention were immediately expelled from the palace. Once, as the result of an insulting denunciation, she was forced to fast at an inopportune time solely in order to clarify through the priest her relations with a handsome servant with whom she had exchanged a few words across a room in the presence of workers. To give her a keener appreciation of the fact that nothing was sacred for this pious court, she was forbidden in the name of the empress to weep very long for her deceased father on the grounds that he was not a king: it was not such a great loss. Until late in her life, Catherine could not recall this callousness without heartfelt indignation. Endearments and insanely lavish gifts alternated with more frequent rude reprimands, all the more offensive in that they were often transmitted through servants; when she delivered them personally, Elizabeth would fly into a frenzy that threatened to come to blows. "Not a day passed," Catherine writes, "that I was not scolded and tales were not told about me." After one of these indecent scenes, when Elizabeth spoke at length of her "thousand acts of vileness," Catherine nearly succumbed to a terrible impulse: a maid found her with a large knife in her hand, which fortunately turned out to be so dull that it did not even penetrate her corset.

This was a momentary loss of heart in the face of life's adversities. But Catherine came to Russia with considerable preparation for any such adversities. In early youth she had seen a great deal. Born in Stettin, she lived for a long time in the care of her grandmother in Hamburg and frequented Brunswick, Kiel, and Berlin itself, where she saw the court of the Prussian king. All this helped her to amass an abundant store of observations and experiences, developed in her a worldly knack and habit of sizing up people, and stimulated her thoughts. Perhaps this observant and pensive quality, together with her innate vitality, was the cause of her early development: at fourteen she seemed an already full-grown young woman, striking everyone with her tallness and a maturity beyond her years.

Catherine received an education that freed her early in life from any excessive prejudices that might have impeded her worldly success. At this time Germany was inundated with French Huguenots fleeing their homeland after Louis XIV's revocation of the Edict of Nantes. These émigrés belonged in large part to the industrious French bourgeoisie.

They soon took the urban professions in Germany into their hands and began to dominate the education of children in the upper circles of German society. Catherine was taught Scripture and other subjects by a French court chaplain, Father Pérard, a zealous servant of the pope; by the Lutheran pastors Dowe and Wagner, who scorned the pope; and by a Calvinist schoolteacher, Loran, who scorned both Luther and the pope. When she came to Petersburg, she was assigned as her instructor in the Greco-Russian faith the Orthodox archimandrite Simon Todorsky, who had completed his theological education at a German university and could only regard all three, the pope, Luther, and Calvin alike, as dogmatists who had divided a single Christian truth. One can imagine what a diverse stock of religious views and outlooks on life might be garnered from such an encyclopedic array of teachers. This diversity, which merged in Catherine's lively fifteen-year-old mind into a chaotic indifference to religion, proved very useful to her when her Anhalt-Zerbst-Holstein fate and her own ambition took her to the Petersburg court. In her words, amid uninterrupted afflictions, "only the hope or prospect not of a heavenly crown but of an earthly one sustained my spirit and courage."

The realization of that prospect required all the available means that her nature and education had bestowed on her and that she had acquired by her own efforts. In childhood she had been told repeatedly, and she herself had known since the age of seven, that she was very unattractive, even thoroughly plain, but she also knew that she was very intelligent. Therefore an intensive development of her mental qualities had to compensate for the shortcomings of her outward appearance. The objective with which she went to Russia gave a distinctive direction to that effort. She decided that in order to fulfill the ambitious dream that was deeply engraved in her soul she had to please everyone, above all her husband, the empress, and the nation. In her fifteen-year-old mind, this project had already formed into an entire plan, and she speaks of it in an elevated tone, not devoid of religious animation, as one of the most important tasks of her life, which was accomplished not without the will of Providence. The plan was drawn up, she acknowledges, without anyone else's participation; it was the fruit of her mind and soul, and she never lost sight of it. "Whatever I did always led toward it, and my whole life was a search for the means to achieve it." She spared neither her intellect nor her heart, putting every means into play, from sincere affection to sheer obsequiousness. Her task was made easier by the fact that she wanted to please the people she needed regardless either of their merits or of her own inner attitude toward them. Those who were intelligent and good were grateful to her for understanding and appreciating them, while those who were evil and stupid noted with satisfaction that she considered them intelligent and good; she forced both to think better of her than she thought of them. Guided by these tactics, she treated everyone as well as possible and tried to win everyone's favor, the great and the small, or at least to assuage the hostility of those who were not well disposed toward her. She made it a rule to believe that she needed everyone, adhered to no party, meddled in nothing, and always displayed a cheerful countenance; and she was obliging, attentive, and courteous to all while giving preference to none. She showed great respect for her mother, whom she did not love, boundless obedience to the empress, whom she laughed at, and marked consideration for her husband, whom she scorned—"in a word, I tried by every means to win the approval of the public," among whom she counted her mother, the empress, and her husband equally.

Taking it as her precept to please the people with whom she had to live, she assimilated their mode of action, their manners, and their morals and overlooked nothing in order to familiarize herself thoroughly with the society into which her fate had thrust her. In her words, she completely transformed herself into an observer—very passive, very modest, and even seemingly indifferent. Meanwhile, she resorted to questioning the servants; she listened with both ears to the tales of her garrulous lady-in-waiting, who knew the alluring chronicles of all the Russian court families from the time of Peter the Great and even earlier and supplied Catherine with a number of anecdotes that she found highly useful for getting to know the society around her; she was not even squeamish about eavesdropping. During a prolonged and dangerous illness soon after her arrival in Russia, Catherine became used to lying with her eyes closed; thinking that she was asleep, the court ladies assigned to look after her uninhibitedly shared tales with each other, and by not destroying their illusion she found out a great deal that she would never have learned without such a subterfuge.

"I wanted to be Russian so the Russians would like me." In accordance with the method she had adopted of pleasing others, this meant even living in the Russian manner, that is, the way the Russian courtiers passing before her lived. At first, in her words, she "plunged headlong" into all the petty squabbles of the court, where gambling and dressing filled the day. She began to concern herself a great deal with her attire, to delve into court gossip, to gamble feverishly and lose heavily. Finally, having noticed that everyone at court loved gifts, from the lowest servant to the grand duke, the heir to the throne, she started to throw money left and right; something need only be praised in her presence and it seemed shameful to her not to make a gift of it. The 30,000 rubles allotted to her for her personal expenses were insufficient, and she fell into debt, for which she received painful reprimands from the empress. She even borrowed tens of thousands with the aid of the English ambassador, which came close to a political bribe, and by the end of Elizabeth's life, she had so exhausted her credit that she lacked the funds to have a dress made for Christmas. By this time, according to her estimate, not counting her mother's debts, which she had assumed, she owed more than half a million rubles—no less than three and a half million in our money—"a terrible sum, which I repaid in installments only after I came to the throne."

She applied her rule also to another peculiarity of Elizabeth's court of which she made good note: religious sentiment here was reduced entirely to church obligations, fulfilled out of fear or for the sake of propriety, at times not without feeling, but also without anxiety in regard to one's conscience. From the moment she arrived in Russia, she assiduously studied the rituals of the Russian church, strictly observed the fasts, and prayed long and ardently, especially when other people were present, sometimes even exceeding the wishes of the pious Elizabeth but making her husband terribly angry. In the first year of her marriage, Catherine fasted for the first week of Lent. The empress expressed her wish that she fast the second week also. Catherine responded with a request that she be allowed to eat Lenten fare for the whole seven weeks. More than once she was found before the icons with a prayer book in her hands.

However flexible she was, however much she adapted to the Russian court's mores and tastes, those around her felt, and gave her to understand, that she was not part of the court, not one of their own. Neither the court's diversions, nor cautious flirtations with court cavaliers, nor long sessions before her mirror, nor all-day horseback rides, nor summertime hunts along the coast near Peterhof and Oranienbaum with a rifle on her shoulder stifled the feeling of boredom and loneliness that arose within her in moments of reflection. To abandon her birthplace for a distant country where she hoped to find a second fatherland and to wind up among wild and hostile people, where there was no one with whom she could have a heart-to-heart talk, and she could not tame anyone no matter how agreeable she was—in such a situation there were moments when the bright dream of ambition, which had brought her to such an unsociable wilderness, began to fade. At first, Catherine cried by herself a good deal. Always ready for battle and self-defense, however, she refused to surrender, and she made of her despair an instrument of self-education, a spiritual mirror. Most of all, she was afraid of appearing to be a pitiful, defenseless victim. The empress's attacks aroused her indignation as a human being; her husband's scorn insulted her as a wife and a woman; her self-esteem suffered, but out of pride she refused to show her suffering or complain of her humiliation so as not to become an object of offensive pity. Alone, she would shed tears, but then she would quietly dry her eyes and with a cheerful countenance go out to her ladies-in-waiting.

It was in books that Catherine encountered a true and reliable ally in the struggle against boredom. She did not immediately find her own kind of literature, however. In Germany, and when she first came to Russia, she showed no particular inclination for reading. Not long before her marriage, an educated foreigner whom she respected, fearing the pernicious influence of the Russian court on her intellect, advised her to read serious books, among them *The Life of Cicero* and Montesquieu on the causes of the greatness and decline of the Roman Republic.[3] With great difficulty she obtained these books in Petersburg. She read two pages about Cicero, then took up Montesquieu, which made her think a bit, but as she was not in a position to read consistently, she began to yawn and, saying that it was a good book, put it aside to return to her dresses. But the unbearably senseless life that Elizabeth had arranged for her niece, the dull company ("*l'insipide compagnie*") with which Catherine was surrounded, and the mindless conversations she heard around her every day taught her to read more attentively and made books her refuge from depression and boredom. After her marriage, in her words, all she did was read. "Never without a book and never without grief, but always without amusement"—that is how Catherine describes the way she spent her time. In a mock

---

[3]A reference to Plutarch's *Life of Cicero* and to Montesquieu's *Considerations on the Causes of the Greatness of the Romans and Their Decadence*, published in 1734.

epitaph she wrote for herself in 1778, she admits that in the course of eighteen years of boredom and solitude (marriage) she had sufficient time to read a good many books. At first she read novels indiscriminately. Then the works of Voltaire came into her hands and proved a decisive turning point in her choice of reading: she could not tear herself away from them and had no desire, she adds in a letter to Voltaire himself, to read anything that was less well written and from which less benefit could be derived.

Reading was not merely a diversion for her, however. She subsequently took up a history of Germany, published in 1748 by a French canon, Barre, in ten ponderous volumes, painstakingly reading one volume every eight days, and with the same regularity she studied the enormous philosophical dictionary of Bayle, in four bulky volumes, reading a volume every six months.[4] It is hard even to imagine how she coped with this dictionary, forcing her way through a thicket of learned citations and theological and philosophical doctrines, not understanding all of it, and how she produced in her own mind a logical arrangement of the knowledge drawn from a source in alphabetical disorder. At the same time she read a number of Russian books, whatever she could get hold of, unafraid of those whose awkward exposition made them very difficult. Catherine transformed her sport into regular work, and she liked to work with extreme intensity, patiently whiling away long hours in her room over Barre or Bayle, just as in summer at Oranienbaum she spent entire mornings roaming with a rifle on her shoulder or rode horseback for thirteen hours a day. She was not afraid of overexertion. It was as if she were testing herself, making a review of her powers, both physical and intellectual. In a sense, what engaged her in her reading was not so much the content of what she read as the way it exercised her attention, the intellectual gymnastics it provided. And she trained her attention and broadened the scope of her thinking. Without difficulty she read even Montesquieu's *Spirit of the Laws*, which also came out in 1748; she did not fling it aside with a yawn and the comment that it was a good book, as she had done previously with another book by the same

---

[4]Joseph Barre, canon of St. Genevieve and chancellor of the University of Paris, was the author of *A General History of Germany*, published in 1748. Pierre Bayle was a French Huguenot philosopher whose writings had a strong influence on the Enlightenment. His chief work was the *Historical and Critical Dictionary* of 1697.

writer. Tacitus's *Annals*, with its deep political melancholy, produced an unusual revolution in her mind, forcing her to see many things in a dark light and to delve deeply into the interests behind the events taking place before her eyes.

But Catherine could not pore over her learned books as a tranquil academic recluse: court politics, from which she was jealously and rudely thrust aside, touched her to the quick, impinging directly on her feeling of personal safety. She had been summoned from Germany with the sole objective of procuring for the Russian throne a reserve heir, in case of emergency, given the physical and mental unreliability of the present appointee. For a long time, a full nine years, she was unable to fulfill that commission, and as a result of the delay she suffered no little grief. Even the birth of Grand Duke Paul on September 20, 1754, however, did not win her decent treatment. On the contrary, she began to be treated as someone who had carried out her assigned task and was not needed for anything further. Her newborn son, as state property, was immediately taken from his mother and was shown to her for the first time only forty days later. Ill, moaning, and dissolved in tears, she was cast alone and unattended into a squalid room between doors and badly closing windows; her linen went unchanged, and she was given nothing to drink. At this time the grand duke was carousing in celebration with his entourage, barely stopping by to tell his wife that he had no time to stay with her. The empress bestowed 100,000 rubles on Catherine for the birth of her son. "And why am I given nothing?" asked a terribly irate Peter. Elizabeth ordered that he be given the same amount. But there was not a kopeck in her study, and her secretary begged Catherine, for the love of God, to loan him the money she had been granted in order to give it to the grand duke. She tried to strengthen her shaky position and, by all the measures she took, with well-deserved success acquired sympathy within society. She spoke Russian well and even wrote it decently; the illiteracy that prevailed at court excused her lapses in syntax and especially in spelling, where in a three-letter Russian word she made four mistakes.[5] It was noted that she knew a great deal about the Russian state, something rarely encountered amid the ignorance of the court and government of the time. In Catherine's words, she finally succeeded in getting

---

[5]*Ischo* for *eshche*. The word *eshche*, meaning "still," or "again," is spelled with three letters in Cyrillic; Catherine used four letters, all of them wrong.

people to regard her as an interesting and far from stupid young person, and not long before the Seven Years' War foreign ambassadors were writing of her that now she was not only loved but feared, and many people, even those who were on the best of terms with the empress, still sought an opportunity to ingratiate themselves with the grand duchess as well.

But public opinion even then, as always in Russia, was poor support for any political position. Catherine sought a more reliable ally. The chancellor, Count Alexis Bestuzhev-Riumin—extremely sly and suspicious, inflexible in his opinions, stubborn, despotic, and vengeful, quarrelsome and often petty, as Catherine characterizes him—stood out sharply from the crowd of court nonentities with whom Elizabeth surrounded herself. A disciple abroad of Peter the Great, Bestuzhev-Riumin had held foreign diplomatic posts for many years and knew well the relations of the European cabinets. Then, as a creature of Biron's in Empress Anna's cabinet of ministers, he was sentenced to be quartered but was pardoned after the fall of the regent and recalled to office from exile by Empress Elizabeth. He acquired masterful skill in maintaining his position at the Petersburg court, in a milieu devoid of any moral or political stability. His mind, woven entirely out of court chicanery and diplomatic conjunctures, was accustomed to pursuing every thought to the end, spinning out every intrigue to the last knot and conceivable consequence. Once he formed an opinion, he implemented it no matter what, regretting nothing and sparing no one. He had decided that the aggressive Prussian king was dangerous to Russia, and he refused to enter into any dealings with a bandit state, which was Prussia's reputation in Europe at the time. He greeted Catherine, too, with hostility, regarding her as a Prussian agent. And to this enemy, from whom she expected every evil, she was the first to extend her hand, which was grasped with undiplomatic trustfulness. They became friends, as people who tacitly understood each other and knew how to forget at the right moment what it was inappropriate to remember, but still harbored a grudge against one another.

Common enemies and dangers drew them together. The empress began to have attacks of illness. In the event of her death, under Emperor Peter III—a real Prussian agent—Bestuzhev was threatened with exile on account of Prussia, Catherine with divorce and a convent on account of Vorontsova. Personal and party enmities intensified the danger. In the female reigns of the eighteenth century, favorites occupied the role of tsars' wives in earlier times, bringing their relatives to court and thereby roiling court life. The latest young favorite of the decrepit Elizabeth was Ivan Shuvalov, who elevated the court career of his family and its adherents. These additions to the court increased the number of the fierce and hated chancellor's enemies, with whom the court was replete in any case; they became Catherine's foes as well because of her friendship with Bestuzhev. Both friends were on guard and began to make preparations. Bestuzhev drew up and communicated to Catherine a plan according to which, in the event of Elizabeth's death, she would be proclaimed co-ruler with her husband, and the chancellor, while remaining in charge of foreign policy, would become the head of the Guards regiments and the whole military administration, army and navy. Co-rulership with her husband, however, promised Catherine no greater success than wedlock had. She wanted full, not shared, power and decided, in her words, to reign or perish. "Either I shall die or I shall reign," she wrote to her friends. She began to amass resources and adherents. She borrowed ten thousand pounds sterling from the English king for gifts and bribes, pledging on her word of honor to act in the common interests of England and Russia. She began to think about winning over the Guards to her cause in the event of Elizabeth's death and entered into a secret agreement on this matter with Hetman Kirill Razumovsky, the commander of one of the Guards regiments. With the assistance of the chancellor, she intervened on the quiet in ongoing political matters.

But the Seven Years' War swept like a whirlwind over both conspirators; the chancellor fell, Catherine remained on her feet. Bestuzhev-Riumin was accustomed to combining Prussia and France in his hostility while remaining friends with England, and an English pension of 12,000 rubles, which augmented the Russian chancellor's 7,000-ruble salary, added warmth to his conviction, which had not cooled in any case, of the unity of interests of Russia and England. Now international relations were turned upside down: France found itself on the side of Prussia's enemies, while England befriended Frederick II. Bestuzhev was unable to take evasive action; the Shuvalovs undermined Elizabeth's trust in him, and in February 1758 he was arrested. He and Catherine succeeded in burning their dangerous papers, but the investigation revealed their secret relations and her correspondence with the commander in chief of the Russian army in the field against Frederick, a strictly forbidden interference in politics. The empress was terribly angry. Rumors began to circulate that Catherine was about to be banished from Russia. "The serpent must be crushed," Catherine's enemies whispered to Peter. Courtiers were afraid to speak with her as a person in disgrace. An indecent trick on the part of the grand duke made her position even shakier. Around this time she was again preparing to become a mother, and her wild husband expressed his extreme bewilderment in this regard to those around him.

Catherine drew herself up to her full height and prepared to defend herself. She responded to the threat of banishment with a counterattack, writing the empress a resolute letter in Russian requesting that she be allowed to return home to Germany, as it had become unbearable for her to live in Russia with the hatred of her husband and the disfavor of the empress. Elizabeth promised to have a talk with her, but the conversation was put off for an agonizingly long time. Catherine wore herself out crying, grew thin, and finally declared that she was ill and required a priest. The alarmed marshal of the court, Count Alexander Shuvalov, called in the doctors, but she told them that since she was dying she needed spiritual assistance, that her soul was in danger and her body no longer needed physicians. Dubiansky, her confessor as well as the empress's, after listening to her detailed account of her situation, arranged matters in a trice. Within a day, after midnight, Catherine was summoned. The favorite advised her that in order to succeed she should show the empress at least a little humility. Catherine began with a lot, throwing herself on her knees before Elizabeth and refusing to get up when the latter tried to raise her. "You want me to send you back to your family?" Elizabeth asked with tears in her eyes. "But you have children." "They are in your hands, and nothing could be better for them." "But how will this banishment be explained to society?" Elizabeth objected. "Your Majesty will announce, if you find it suitable, in what way I incurred your disfavor and the hatred of the grand duke." "And what will you live on with your family?" "What I lived on before it pleased you to bring me here." Elizabeth was thrown off balance, and, ordering Catherine a second time to arise, she drew aside to consider what to do next. Remembering that she had come to have it out with the grand duchess, she began to scold her for interfering in political matters that were none of her business, reproached her for her excessive pride, reminded her that four years ago she had refused to bow properly to her, the empress, and added, "You fancy that no one is as smart as you are." Catherine replied to everything clearly and respectfully, but to the last reproach she objected that if she had thought that of herself she would not have let herself get into her present stupid situation.

All this time the grand duke was standing a little way off, whispering to Count Shuvalov. Confident that Catherine would not regain her health, he had that very day joyfully promised his Vorontsova to marry her as soon as he became a widower. Now, drawn into the conversation and vexed that Catherine was not in fact about to die, he began to attack her. She replied firmly and with restraint to his embittered and absurd statements. Walking back and forth across the room, Elizabeth grew mollified, and going up to Catherine she said benevolently, in a low voice, "I have much more to say to you," and with that gave her to understand that she did not wish to speak before witnesses. "I also cannot speak, however much I might wish to open my heart and soul to you," Catherine managed to say, barely audibly. This heartfelt whisper achieved its purpose, and Elizabeth was touched. Her tears welled up, and to hide her agitation "she dismissed us," on the pretext of the late hour.

This is how Catherine herself describes this hour-and-a-half–long agonizing conversation. Two usurpers of the throne grappled with each other, and the future one triumphed: she was subsequently begged not to do what she herself had been threatened with and to give up the idea of returning to her homeland, which would greatly sadden the empress and all honest people. Elizabeth indicated the impression this conversation made on her when she expressed to her entourage the opinion that her nephew was a fool but the grand duchess was very intelligent.

Thus Catherine took her position by force and by the end of Elizabeth's reign had fortified it so well that she came safely through all the vicissitudes at court. Knowing how to yield to dismal circumstances, she reconciled herself to the unenviable position of an abandoned young wife and even drew advantages from it. Marital discord furthered the parting of the couple's political destinies: the wife began to follow her own road. Toward the end of her life, Elizabeth went completely to pieces. Her daily occupations, in Catherine's words, became an unbroken string of caprices, hypocrisy, and dissipation. Her nerves, unstrung by the petty irritations of envy and vanity, gave her no peace; she was tormented by fear that she would suffer the fate she herself had arranged for Anna Leopoldovna. A woman without firm principles and without any serious occupation but sufficiently intelligent to understand the absurdity of her situation, she fell into a state of interminable boredom, from which she was saved only by the fact that she slept as much as possible. In such circumstances she might have yielded to the insistence of those close to her that it was essential to alter the succession to the throne. Some at court were thinking of the six-year-old Tsarevich Paul, with both of his parents to be sent out of Russia, while others wanted to banish only his father, regarding his mother as a support of order. Both parties anxiously awaited Elizabeth's death, expecting nothing for Russia from her nephew but grief. At moments even for Elizabeth this anxiety turned to terror, but as she was not in the habit of thinking seriously about anything she vacillated, and her favorites did not inspire her with resolve.

Peter III came to the throne. From the first days of his reign, Catherine began to be treated with contempt. The role of victim was already familiar to her, however. The French ambassador Breteuil in his dispatches kept a diary of how she played that role. At the beginning of April 1762, he wrote, "The empress tries to arm herself with philosophy, though it is contrary to her character." In another dispatch he wrote, "People who see the empress say that she is unrecognizable, is withering away, and probably will soon go to her grave." But she did not go to her grave; the whole time, with a firm though inaudible tread, she was advancing along the path she had marked out, stealthily drawing closer to the throne. All Petersburg, coming to the palace to pay its respects to Elizabeth's remains, saw Catherine, in deep mourning, standing reverently beside the coffin of the deceased. At the funeral she was the most zealous of all in fulfilling the burial rites of the Russian church; both the clergy and the people were very touched by this, and their confidence in her became all the stronger amid the growing murmuring at the mad behavior of the emperor. In the words of the same ambassador, she strictly observed all the feasts and fasts, everything that the emperor treated so flippantly and that the Russians took so seriously. The ambassador, despite his April prophecy of the empress's imminent death, at the beginning of June was obliged to write that the empress was displaying courage and that all loved and respected her to the same degree as they hated the emperor. We have already seen how Catherine made use of the general discontent, especially among the Guards, and with her confederates carried out the coup d'état that put an end to the six-month reign of Peter III.

She had been born to a bleak lot and early in life became acquainted with the privations and anxieties inseparable from a precarious status. In early youth, however, fate plucked her out of the poor and constricted circumstances of her birth and thrust her onto broad and noisy political stages where important people acted and important deeds were done. Here Catherine saw a great deal of glory and power, an abundance of brilliance and wealth. She encountered people who risked everything to acquire these things, such as Frederick II, and she saw people who, by taking risks, had obtained them all, such as Empress Elizabeth. These examples tempted her, they whetted her appetite for ambition and impelled her to exert all her efforts in this direction; and Catherine by nature was not devoid of the qualities from which, with appropriate refinement, the talents necessary for success in such an enticing and slippery walk of life can be developed.

Catherine grew up with the idea that she had to break her own path, make a career, and develop the qualities she needed in order to do so, and her marriage afforded her excellent practical experience in this endeavor; it not only gave her ambition an object, but it made the attainment of that object a matter of personal safety. She did her work ably. From childhood she had been told that she was ugly, and early in life this made her learn the art of pleasing, of seeking within her soul what was lacking in her outward appearance. In order to be something in the world, she wrote, recalling her childhood thoughts, we have to have the necessary qualities; so let us look carefully within ourselves to see whether we have them, and if not, then let us call them forth. She discovered or developed within herself characteristics of high worldly value, a precise knowledge of her spiritual inventory: composure without coldness, liveliness without excitability, flexibility without flightiness, decisiveness without rashness. It was hard to take her by surprise: she was always fully mustered. Frequent reviews kept her forces at the ready, in a state of mobilization, and in life's conflicts she easily deployed them against people and circumstances.

In dealing with people she displayed a matchless ability to listen, to hear out any sort of nonsense patiently and attentively; to divine the mood, the timid or inarticulate thoughts of others; and to come to their assistance. This won people over, inspired their trust, and disposed them to be frank; in conversation with her a person felt at ease and unconstrained, as though he were talking to himself. Furthermore, contrary to people's usual inclination to note the weaknesses of others in order to use them to their detriment, Catherine preferred to study their strong sides, which she might have occasion to turn to her own advantage, and she was able to point them out to their possessors. People generally do not like to have others search their souls, but they do not grow angry, they are even touched, when virtues are discovered in them, especially when they can barely discern these virtues themselves. In this ability to make an individual feel that there was something better in him lay the secret of the irresistible charm that, in the words of Princess Dashkova, who experienced it herself, Catherine exerted on those whom she wanted to please—and she wanted to please everyone, always; she regarded it as her profession.

Her way of treating people rendered her inestimable service in her governmental activity. She possessed to a high degree the art, generally termed the gift, of suggestion: instead of giving orders she knew how to hint at her wishes, which, in the mind of the person being given the suggestion, imperceptibly turned into his own ideas and were the more zealously executed. An observant attitude toward people taught her to recognize their hobbyhorses, and after setting a rider on his steed she would let him run, like a child mounted on a broomstick, and he ran and ran, enthusiastically spurring himself on. She knew how to make someone else's pride an instrument of her ambition, to turn someone else's weakness into her own strength.

By her own conduct she elevated the life of the Russian court, which in previous reigns had at times resembled a gypsy camp, at times an amusement park. Order was introduced into the expenditure of time. Strict morals were not demanded, but good manners and respectable behavior were required. The polite simplicity of Catherine's own treatment even of the palace servants was a complete novelty after the customary rudeness of former times. Only in old age did she begin to weaken, to grow capricious and shout at people—always, however, apologizing to those she had offended with the admission that she was becoming impatient.

She dealt with circumstances in exactly the same way that she dealt with people. She tried to adapt to every situation in which she found herself, however much it contradicted her tastes or principles. "Like Alcibiades, I shall get along both in Sparta and in Athens," she said; she liked to compare herself with the heroes of antiquity. But that meant giving up her own local attachments, even her moral convictions. Well, what of it? She was in fact an émigré who had voluntarily exchanged the fatherland of her birth for a political fatherland, a for-

eign country that she chose as her field of activity. Love for a fatherland was for her a childhood memory, not a current sentiment or a
constant motif of her life. Her origin as a petty princess of north
Germany, the flexibility of her nature, and, finally, the spirit of the age
helped her to renounce territorial patriotism. It was not difficult for her
to rise from the little basket of Anhalt-Zerbst to the cosmopolitan
viewpoint on which the contemporary philosophical thought of Europe
rested, and Catherine herself acknowledged that she was "free of prejudices and by nature of a philosophical mind." For all that, she was too
concrete an individual, she felt her real appetites too keenly, to wander
in an ethereal cosmopolitan desert, contenting herself with the meager
concept of a universal humanity. Earthly expanses beckoned her, not
celestial heights. Justifying herself for having assimilated the way of
life of the Russian court, which she referred to in the worst possible
terms, she wrote in her memoirs that she took it as her rule to please
the people with whom she had to live. The necessity of living with
people who were not of her choosing forced her, with the help of
philosophical analysis, to supplement this rule in order to preserve at
least a vestige of moral independence: among foreign and disagreeable
people she would live their way but think her way.

To Catherine, from her youth, living had meant working, and since
her goal in life consisted of inducing people to help her break loose
from her obscure lot, it became her life's work to win over both
people and circumstances. By the very nature of this work, she needed
others much more than they needed her. Moreover, for a long time
fate compelled her to move among people who were stronger but less
far-sighted than she was, who remembered her only when they needed
her. Therefore, from an early age she acquired the idea that the best
way to make use of circumstances and people was to swim for the
time being in the current of the former and to serve as an obedient but
not blind instrument in the hands of the latter. More than once she put
herself in the hands of others, but only that they might carry her to a
place she desired but was unable to reach by herself. In this principle
of life lay the source of both the strong and the weak sides of her
character and activity. In accommodating herself to people in order to
tame them, she expected reciprocity on their part, an inclination to be
tamed. She did not care much for stubborn people who had an intractable character or were prepared to forge ahead regardless of obstacles.
They themselves avoided her or withdrew from her, so that her con-

quests of other people's souls were facilitated by the selection of sub-jects, which she failed to perceive. On the other hand, she was capable of exerted effort, of intense and even excessive labor, and therefore to herself and to others she seemed stronger than she was. But she grew more accustomed to working on her manners and her method of treat-ing people than on herself, on her own feelings and convictions; there-fore, her manners and her treatment of people were better than her feelings and convictions. Her thinking was more flexible and im-pressionable than profound and reflective; it was open to correction, but it was not creative.

A deficiency of moral consideration and independent thought de-flected Catherine from the proper path of development on which her fortunate nature had placed her. She understood early in life that for every individual, knowledge of people must begin with knowledge of oneself. Catherine was one of those rather rare people who know how to look at themselves from the side, as the saying goes, objectively, as though at an interesting passerby. She noted her weaknesses and de-fects with a certain self-satisfaction, without whitewashing them, and she called them by their real names, without the least pang of con-science or any impulse of regret or repentance. At the age of fifteen she had sketched her philosophical portrait for an educated foreigner. Thirteen years later she reread her depiction of "a philosopher of fif-teen" and was astonished that at such an age she already knew so well all the turns and inner recesses of her soul. This astonishment was also a drop of seductive poison that seeped into her consciousness of her-self. She could not remove her gaze from the interesting passerby, and in her eyes he grew into a fascinating image; innate pride and firmness of character in the midst of afflictions made the idea of being misera-ble insupportable to him; he was a knight of honor and nobility and even began to transform himself from a woman into a man. Catherine writes of herself in her memoirs that she had a mind and character incomparably more masculine than feminine, although she retained all the agreeable qualities of a woman worthy of love. The tree of self-knowledge without sufficient moral fertilization bore unwholesome fruit—conceit.

Catherine's writings reflected both her varied interests and the en-thusiasms of her lively intellect. German by birth, French by education and favorite language, she occupies a prominent place in the ranks of Russian writers of the eighteenth century. She had two passions, which over the years turned into habits or daily necessities—reading and writing. In her lifetime she read an immense number of books. Even in her declining years she admitted to her secretary, Alexander Khrapovitsky, that she read books six at a time. Her wide reading stimulated her literary productivity. She wrote a great deal in French and even in Russian, though with mistakes she joked about. It was as difficult for her to do without book and pen as it was for Peter the Great to do without ax and lathe. She confessed that she did not understand how anyone could spend a day without marking up at least one sheet of paper. Our Academy of Sciences recently published her writings in twelve bulky volumes.[6] She wrote in the most diverse genres: didactic tales for children, pedagogical instructions, political pamphlets, plays, memoirs; she contributed to magazines, translated the life of Alcibiades from Plutarch, and even composed a life of St. Sergius of Radonezh. When her grandchildren came along, she took up the Russian chronicles for their benefit; ordered extracts and information from Professor Chebotarev, Count Musin-Pushkin, and other individuals; and drew up easy-to-read notes on Russian history, in parts, with synchronic and genealogical tables. "You keep telling me that I am a rascal," she wrote to Baron Grimm, "but I tell you that I have become a regular archives mouse."

Her writings do not display any original talent. She was highly imitative, however, and assimilated other people's ideas so readily that she made them her own. Time and again, one can hear echoes and repetitions of Madame de Sévigné, Voltaire, Montesquieu, Molière, and others. This is especially noticeable in her French letters, of which she was a great devotee. Her correspondence with Voltaire and with her foreign agent, Baron Grimm, fills whole volumes. She superbly assimilated the style and manner of her models, the contemporary French writers, especially their elegant and witty jocularity. The contents are very diverse, but the tone is always the same, evidently unforced and playful in a refined way, and in this tone she writes about the mysteries of the Eucharist, politics, her court, and the health of her lapdog. In her letters the words are considerably better than the ideas.

Catherine assigned a very large place in her writing activity to dra-

---

[6]A.N. Pypin, ed., *Sochineniia Imperatritsy Ekateriny II*, [The Works of Empress Catherine II], 12 vols. (St. Petersburg: Imperial Academy of Sciences, 1901–7). Volume 6 was never published.

matic composition. She was the principal supplier of the repertoire for the theater in her Hermitage, where she gathered a select company. She wrote "proverbs," or vaudevilles, comedies, comic operas, even "historical representations from the life of Rurik and Oleg, an imitation of Shakespeare." *Oleg* was produced at the municipal theater in Petersburg on the occasion of the peace with Turkey at Jassy (1791), with extraordinary splendor: more than 700 performers and extras took the stage. Poor Khrapovitsky spent whole nights copying the empress's plays and composing arias and couplets for her operas and vaudevilles—Catherine herself could not cope with poetry.

In her plays Catherine depicted the king of Sweden, the Martinists, her own courtiers. It is difficult to say how much she revealed of herself in her "dramomania." To be sure, in her character and her mode of action there was a great deal of dramatic movement. Cheerful by nature, she could not do without company, and she acknowledged that she loved being among people. In her intimate circle she was simple, affectionate, and jocular, and everyone felt cheerful and unconstrained around her. When she entered a reception hall, however, she was transformed. She assumed a reserved and majestic air, walked slowly with small steps, and met those who were being presented to her with a stereotyped smile and a somewhat sly glance of her light-grey eyes.

The way she carried herself was reflected in all her activity and shaped the whole makeup of her character. Whatever the society in which Catherine moved, whatever she did, she always felt as though she were on stage, and therefore she did too much for show. When she contemplated some action, she thought more about what would be said of her than about what would come of the action she was contemplating; the setting and the impression were more important to her than the action itself and its consequences. Hence her weakness for publicity, sensation, and flattery, which befogged her clear mind and seduced her cold heart. She valued the attention of contemporaries more than the opinion of posterity; in return, she was esteemed more highly during her lifetime than she came to be after her death. As she herself was wholly a creature of intellect without any participation of the heart, so her activity contained more effect and brilliance than greatness and creativity. What she wanted, it seemed, was that she herself be remembered longer than her deeds.

～ IV ～

Foreign Policy

The century of our history that began with a tsar-carpenter ended with an empress-writer. The government's efforts in the material realm seemed to lead logically to work on people's minds. Such is the perspective that unfolds when we look at our eighteenth century. Let us not lose sight of it as we study the reign of Catherine II.

When she came to the throne, Catherine had a superficial knowledge of the state of affairs in the empire, of her own governmental resources, and of the difficulties that awaited her. Meanwhile, however, she had to smooth over the impression of the coup d'état by means of which she had come to the throne and justify her illegitimate appropriation of power. In the first moments after her accession, she could not refrain from ecstasy over her success in realizing her long-standing dream, which might have seemed only a childish fantasy back in Stettin or Zerbst. This ecstasy, however, was poisoned by the thought of her precarious position on the throne. Not infrequently, amid the company of the court, she would fall into a pensive mood, and for all her ability to control herself she could not hide her anxiety. The coup did not leave everyone satisfied, and even among its participants there were those who felt insufficiently rewarded. The success of some went to the heads of others, inciting them to repeat it, and encouraged grumbling, for which there was a ready pretext. Catherine had accomplished a dual usurpation: she had taken power from her husband without handing it over to her son, the natural heir of his father. In the Guards there was alarming talk of elevating "Ivanushka"—as the former emperor, Ivan VI, was called—to the throne, and questions were raised as to why Tsarevich Paul had not been crowned. In society it was even said that it would be advisable for Catherine to marry the former emperor to consolidate her position on the throne. Catherine met with him shortly after her accession and ordered that he be urged to take monastic vows. Circles, or "parties," began to form within the Guards, though without turning into a conspiracy. Catherine was particularly alarmed at the mad attempt in 1764 by an unbalanced army second lieutenant, Vasily Mirovich, to liberate Ivanushka from the Schlüsselburg Fortress and proclaim him emperor—an attempt that ended with the murder of the prisoner, who had gone insane in confinement, a ghastly victim of the lawlessness for which the Russian throne had become a breeding ground after the death of Peter the Great.

Catherine's accomplices in preparing and carrying out the June coup d'état also caused her no little trouble and distress. They sensed how much Catherine was obligated to them, and, needless to say, they wanted to take advantage of their position. Frederick II was right when he said many years later to the French ambassador Ségur, who was on his way to Petersburg, that Catherine was not so much the perpetrator as the instrument of the coup: weak, young, alone in a foreign land, on the verge of divorce and incarceration, she had placed herself in the hands of the people who wanted to rescue her, and after the coup she could not yet govern anything.

Those people, who now surrounded Catherine, headed by the quintet of Orlov brothers (all awarded the title of count), hastened to reap the fruits of the "great event," as they called the June affair. They were all, as foreigners put it, dyed-in-the-wool "Russkies," striking in their lack of education and in this respect inferior to the statesmen of Elizabeth's time, the Panins, Shuvalovs, and Vorontsovs. Having grown used to treating Catherine without ceremony during the time of the conspiracy, they did not want to give up this habit after the coup. At the moment of Elizabeth's death, a Guards captain, the husband of Princess Dashkova, had sent word to Catherine, saying, "Just give the order, and we will raise you to the throne." Now those people were prepared to tell her, "We have raised you to the throne, so you are ours." They were not content with the rewards they had received, with the fact that Catherine had given them some 18,000 peasant souls and 200,000 rubles (no less than a million in our money) in one-time grants, not counting lifetime pensions. They besieged the empress, thrust their opinions and interests on her, and sometimes bluntly asked for money. In conversation with Ambassador Breteuil, she compared herself to a rabbit that has been roused and is being hunted with might and main, so harried was she from all sides by representations that were not always reasonable or honest.

Catherine had to stay on good terms with these people. That was unpleasant and untidy, but not especially difficult. She put her usual methods into play—her inimitable ability to listen patiently and reply cordially and not be at a loss on difficult occasions. In the memoirs of Princess Dashkova, we encounter an example of the art with which the empress made use of these methods. On the fourth day after the coup, while the two ladies were chatting, Lieutenant General Ivan Betskoi burst in and, falling to his knees, practically in tears begged Catherine to say to whom she felt she owed the throne. "To God and the choice of my subjects," Catherine answered. "Then I am not worthy of this mark of distinction," Betskoi exclaimed and started to take off his Order of Alexander. "What is the meaning of this?" Catherine asked. "I will be the most wretched of mortals unless Your Majesty recognizes me as the sole architect of your accession! Was I not the one who incited the Guards? Was I not the one who threw money to the people?" Confused at first, Catherine quickly collected herself and said, "I recognize how much I owe you, and since I am obliged to you for my crown, to whom, if not to you, would I entrust the preparation of the crown and of everything that I shall wear at my coronation? I place at your disposal all the jewelers of the empire." Beside himself with delight, Betskoi took his leave of the ladies, who could not stop laughing for a long time.

Catherine needed a little time and patience for her supporters to come to their senses and put their relations with her on a proper footing. It was much harder to justify the new government in the eyes of the people. Catherine was poorly informed of the people's situation before her accession and had very few means of finding out about it: the Russian court under Elizabeth was too remote from Russia, not just geographically but, even more, morally. Once she came to the throne, Catherine quickly understood that things were in a very bad way there: she noticed "signs of a great murmuring at the form of government in recent years." Almost all the factory and monastic peasants were in open disobedience to the authorities, and in places the landowners' peasants were also beginning to join them. In 1763 a forged decree of

Catherine's circulated among the people; it was suffused with strong irritation at the gentry, "who scorn divine law and the laws of the state, who have driven out justice and banished it from Russia." The deep masses of the people far from the capital did not experience the empress's personal charm directly and contented themselves with dark rumors and the simple fact that could be understood from the public manifestos: Peter III had been emperor, but his wife, the empress, had overthrown him and put him in prison, where he soon died. Those masses, who had long been in a state of ferment, could be pacified only by palpable measures of justice and general welfare.

Thus, by her revolutionary seizure of power, Catherine had tied a complex knot of diverse interests and expectations that showed her the direction her activity should take. In order to smooth over the impression of usurpation, she had to become popular in broad circles of the population, acting contrary to her predecessor and rectifying what he had spoiled. Her predecessor had offended national sentiment, scorning everything Russian and betraying Russia to its enemy; Catherine was obliged to act earnestly in a national spirit and restore the abused honor of the nation. The previous government had incited everyone against it by its aimless arbitrariness; the new one, by rational and liberal measures, must strengthen legality in government, as had been promised in the July manifesto. Catherine had been raised to the throne by the gentry Guards, however, and the gentry was not content with the law on the freedom of the nobility: it demanded the broadening and strengthening of its rights as the dominant estate. The voice of the Guards and the gentry, of course, made the greatest impression on the supreme power created by the movement of June 28. Thus, to be popular, the activity of the new government had to follow simultaneously a *national*, *liberal*, and *gentry* course. It can easily be seen that this threefold task suffered from an irreconcilable internal contradiction. After the law of February 18, the gentry stood at cross-purposes to all the interests of the people and even to the reform requirements of the state.

Activity by the government in the spirit of that estate could be neither liberal nor national, that is, it could not be popular. Moreover, liberal reforms in the spirit of the ideas of the age could not find in the organs of the government, within the service class, sufficiently well-prepared or sympathetic agents and executors, so alien were those ideas to all the traditions, conceptions, and habits of the Russian administration. Whether drawing on her flexible intellect or on the lessons of experience and observation, Catherine found a way out of the inconveniences of her program. Since she was not in a position to reconcile its contradictory tasks and did not want to sacrifice any one of them for the sake of the others, she divided them, assigning each to a separate sphere of governmental activity. National interests and feelings were given broad scope in foreign policy, which was rapidly set in motion. An extensive reform of the local administrative and judicial systems was undertaken, following the proposals of progressive Western European writers of the time but mainly with the homegrown objective of occupying the idle gentry and strengthening its position in the state and society. The liberal ideas of the age were also allotted a sphere of their own. They served as the basis for a proposed system of legislation. They were put forward as principles in individual statutes; were introduced into the everyday exchange of opinions; were allowed to embellish governmental business and social life; and were given currency in the private conversations of the empress, in fashionable drawing rooms, in literature, and even in the schools as an educational device. The actual content of current legislation, however, reinforced indigenous facts that had taken shape well before Catherine or that fulfilled desires voiced predominantly by the gentry—facts and desires completely alien to the ideas that were being disseminated. The three-fold task developed into a practical program: a strictly national, boldly patriotic foreign policy; mildly liberal, perhaps humane methods of administration; complex and well-constructed local institutions with the participation of three estates; propagation of the enlightened ideas of the time in salons, literature, and the schools; and cautiously but consistently conservative legislation with special attention to the interests of one estate. The basic idea of this program can be expressed as follows: tolerant dissemination of *the ideas of the age* and legislative reinforcement of *local facts*.

Let us now make a survey of how this program was implemented, starting with foreign policy. I will not recount the events of Russia's international relations in this period, the wars, battles, and peace treaties, which are sufficiently well known, but will only summarize the beginnings and ends, comparing the plans that were conceived and carried out by the Russian cabinet with the results achieved.

Foreign policy is the most brilliant aspect of Catherine's governmental activity, and it made the strongest impression on her contemporaries and immediate posterity. When one wants to say the best that can be said about this reign, one speaks of the victorious wars with Turkey, the Polish partitions, Catherine's authoritative voice in Europe's international relations. On the other hand, foreign policy was the field in which Catherine could most conveniently win popular favor. Here, issues that the entire nation could understand and sympathize with were being decided—the Pole and the Tatar were Russia's most popular enemies at this time. Finally, in this sphere it was unnecessary either to devise a program or to seek ways to arouse people: the tasks were ready-made, posed directly by age-old historical circumstances, and they demanded resolution more urgently than any others. The empress therefore turned her greatest attention to this aspect of government.

After the Peace of Nystadt, when Russia acquired a firm foothold on the Baltic Sea, two immediate issues of foreign policy remained, one territorial and the other national. The first was to advance the southern boundary of the state to its natural frontiers: the northern shoreline of the Black Sea, including the Crimea, the Sea of Azov, and the Caucasus Mountains. This was the "eastern question" in its contemporary historical form. Then there was the task of completing the political unification of the Russian people by reuniting Russia with its western part, which had been separated from it. This was the "Western Russian question." Both these issues were essentially of local significance. They had arisen historically out of the mutual relations of neighboring states, and there was no historical connection between them. Therefore, in order to be resolved successfully, they needed to be *localized* and *separated*, that is, resolved without outside intervention, without the participation of third parties, and not both together but each singly. The intricacies of international relations, however, and the clumsiness or arrogance of statesmen gave a different direction to the course of affairs.

At first, Catherine was too preoccupied after her accession with strengthening her shaky position to have any desire for complications in Europe, and she shared the general thirst for peace. The Seven Years' War was coming to an end, and all its participants were utterly exhausted and financially drained. Catherine did not renounce the peace with Prussia that Peter III had concluded, she recalled her troops from the Prussian territories they had conquered, and she stopped the preparations for war with Denmark. Her initial acquaintance with the state of affairs within the empire also disposed Catherine to behave quietly. When she ascended the throne, the Russian army in Prussia had not received its pay for the eighth month. The Office of State Expenditure reckoned the treasury's unpaid debts at seventeen million—one million more than the annual sum of state revenue, as the Senate knew. The yearly deficit during the Seven Years' War had reached seven million. Russia's credit fell: Elizabeth tried to borrow two million rubles in Holland, and this loan found no takers. The navy, in Catherine's words, was in a state of neglect, the army was in disarray, the fortresses were falling down. A bit later, in 1765, Catherine made an inspection of the Baltic Fleet. Peter the Great's beloved child appeared before her as a pathetic orphan: vessels collided with each other, their rigging broke, ships of the line could not line themselves up, and when they fired they were unable to hit their target. Catherine wrote that these were boats for catching herring, not a military fleet, and she acknowledged that we had a boundless number of ships and men aboard them, but neither a navy nor sailors. In 1762 she confessed candidly and indiscreetly to the ambassador of a by no means friendly France that she needed no less than five years of peace to put her affairs in order, and meanwhile she would conduct herself with all the sovereigns of Europe like a skillful coquette. But she was mistaken in her cavaliers.

Before then, Polish affairs deflected Catherine from the path of nonintervention. The death of the Polish king Augustus III was expected imminently. This raised the question of a new royal election, which usually troubled Poland's neighbors. For Russia it was a matter of indifference who would be engaged for the Molièrean role Polish history had devised of king of a republic.[1] Under the constitution of the Republic, a king hostile to Russia was harmless, and a friendly one was useless; in either case, Russia had to achieve her objectives by bribery and arms. But Catherine had a candidate whom she wanted to promote at all costs. This was Stanislas Poniatowski, a fop born for the boudoir, not for any throne: he could not take a step without a witty word and a stupid action. Two principal reasons might be suspected for Catherine's insistence: (1) Stanislas had left her with some very pleasant memories of his stay in Petersburg during Elizabeth's reign, and

---

[1]Poland, which called itself a republic, was an elective monarchy whose king by the eighteenth century had lost most of his power.

(2) his candidacy afforded Catherine the not inconsiderable satisfaction of extracting from Frederick II a letter acknowledging that the Astrakhan melons she had sent him were infinitely precious to him coming from a hand that dispensed crowns. The reasons that were adduced publicly were no more plausible.

This candidacy brought with it a series of temptations and difficulties. First of all, hundreds of thousands of rubles had to be amassed to bribe the Polish magnates who were selling out their fatherland, headed by the Catholic primate, the chief hierarch; then, 30,000 Russian troops had to be stationed at the Polish border and another 50,000 held ready to support the freedom and independence of the Republic; and, finally, the entire course of foreign policy had to be reversed abruptly. Hitherto, Russia had maintained an alliance with Austria, which France had joined during the Seven Years' War. At first, after her accession, when she still had a poor understanding of things, Catherine had asked her advisers' opinion concerning the peace with Prussia concluded under Peter III. Her advisers did not regard this peace as useful to Russia and spoke in favor of renewing the alliance with Austria. Catherine's old friend Alexis Bestuzhev-Riumin, whom she had brought back from exile, also took this position, and at the time she especially valued his opinion. Whenever a difficult matter arose, a handwritten note would go off to him: "Little father, Alexis Petrovich! Please help me out with your advice." Close by him, however, stood a younger diplomat, his pupil and an adversary of his system, Count Nikita Panin, the tutor of Grand Duke Paul. He was not only for peace but openly for an alliance with Frederick, arguing that without his assistance nothing could be achieved in Poland. Catherine held out for some time: she did not want to continue the hated policy of her predecessor and be the ally of a king whom she had publicly proclaimed an evildoer to Russia in her July manifesto, but Panin won out and for a long time remained Catherine's closest collaborator on foreign policy.

At this point Catherine firmly believed in Panin's diplomatic talents. Later on, however, she sometimes disagreed with his opinions and grew dissatisfied with his slow mind and irresolute character, but she utilized him as a pliant interpreter of her views. The treaty of alliance with Prussia was signed on March 31, 1764, while the electoral agitation in Poland after the death of Augustus III was in progress. But this alliance was only one element of the complex system of international relations that was being devised. Panin was a diplomat of a new stamp, unlike Bestuzhev. For many years he had held the difficult post of ambassador in Stockholm and had acquired knowledge and skill in diplomatic affairs, but he did not combine his intellect with the industry his teacher had exhibited. After his death, Catherine complained that she had suffered quite a bit with this lazybones during the first Turkish war. After Bestuzhev, who was hardworking and practical to the point of cynicism, a diplomat of petty methods and immediate objectives, Panin came to diplomacy proclaiming ideas and principles. As an abstract thinker, his irresolute mode of action notwithstanding, he liked broadly conceived, bold, and complex plans, but he did not like to study the details of implementing them or the conditions that made them implementable. He was a gentleman-diplomat, and since his broad plans were built on the mirage of peace and love among the European powers, he was also, despite his diplomatic sybaritism, an idyllist-diplomat, one who was sensitive and dreamy to the point of Manilovism.[2]

Panin became the author of an international scheme unprecedented in Europe. He was not the one who first thought of it, however. In 1764, not long before the treaty of March 31, the Russian ambassador in Copenhagen, Baron Johann-Albrecht Korff, submitted a statement to the empress suggesting the possibility of forming a strong alliance of powers in the north to counteract the southern Austro-Franco-Spanish alliance. Panin promptly appropriated this idea and developed it. According to his project, the northern non-Catholic states, though with the inclusion of Catholic Poland, would unite for mutual support, for defense of the weak by the strong. The military task, direct opposition to the southern alliance, would rest on the principals of the northern alliance, its "active" members, Russia, Prussia, and England. The only demand on the second-rank states, the "passive" members, such as Sweden, Denmark, Poland, Saxony, and other minor states that might join the alliance, would be that in conflicts between the two alliances they refrain from adhering to the southern one and remain neutral. This was the Northern System, which created a sensation in its time. Its inconveniences are easy to see. To act together and in a friendly fashion was difficult for states so differently constituted as the autocracy of Russia, the constitutional aristocracy of England, the soldiers' monar-

---

[2]Manilov is a character in Gogol's *Dead Souls*, a landowner who dreams of grandiose projects but whose house and estate are slovenly and neglected.

chy of Prussia, and the republican anarchy of Poland. Moreover, the members of the alliance had too few common interests: England had nothing to do with the European continent aside from her commercial and colonial relations; Prussia was not at all disposed to defend Saxony, which inclined toward Austria, and even wanted to seize it as it had seized Silesia. The troop of passive members of the alliance, under the guardianship of England, Russia, and Prussia, was a diplomatic cart drawn by a pike, a swan, and a crab.[3] Frederick II greeted Panin's plan with irritable or sarcastic comments, affirming that the Russian alliance was enough for him—with it, he feared no one, no one would touch him, and he did not need other allies. On the whole, Frederick had a low opinion of his Russian advocate, and he wrote that Panin lacked correct conceptions of the interests, the policies, or the degree of power of the European sovereigns. Panin could not make the king change his mind, England also shunned the alliance, and the Northern System was never embodied in any international document (it died unborn, without having come into being). It remained simply an inclination on the part of the Russian cabinet, one of those simple-hearted Russian diplomatic projects about which real diplomats speak with a condescending smile.

The treaty of March 31 was not so fruitless, and it had a variety of consequences that were disadvantageous to Russia. First of all, Russia did not need it. Its main provisions were a mutual guarantee of possessions and a reciprocal obligation not to allow any changes in the Polish constitution and to obtain the restitution to the religious "dissidents" of their former rights, or at least of freedom from persecution. But on all these points Frederick, after the Seven Years' War, was either useless to Russia or, close at hand and with an alliance, would damage Russia's interests no less than he might have without an alliance. Isolated and helpless, his greatest fear was of a break with Russia, and he even came down with a new disease, the fear of war. He could not forget the visit to Berlin in 1760 of the Cossacks and Kalmucks, and he subsequently admitted that for a long time he dreamed frequently about those guests.

Moreover, this alliance, the purpose of which was to facilitate

---

[3]A reference to Ivan Krylov's fable of incompatible partners unsuccessfully trying to pull a cart. Ivan Andreyevich Krylov (1769–1844) was a popular writer of moral fables in the style of Aesop and La Fontaine.

Russia's objectives in Poland, only made them more difficult. Russia relied there on the patriotic party of the Czartoryski princes, who were trying, along with the new king, to raise their country out of anarchy by means of reforms: replacing the Sejm's *liberum veto* with a majority vote, establishing a hereditary monarchy, revoking the right of confederation, and so forth. Panin himself was not opposed to the reforms; he found it too cruel to prevent the Poles from emerging from barbarism, and he took comfort for his ambition in the dream of becoming known as the restorer of Poland. These reforms were not dangerous to Russia; there was even an advantage in Poland's growing somewhat stronger and becoming a useful ally in the struggle with their common enemy, Turkey. But Frederick did not even want to hear of awakening Poland from her political lethargy, as he put it, and he pushed Catherine into the treaty with Poland of February 13, 1768, under which Russia guaranteed the inviolability of the Polish constitution and pledged to allow no changes in it. Thus the Prussian alliance forced Catherine to repulse the reformist party of the Czartoryskis, an important support for Russian policy in Poland.

The same alliance set Austria, Russia's longstanding but now forsaken ally, against her. On the one hand, Austria, together with France, incited Turkey against Russia in 1768, and, on the other, it hammered away at a European anxiety: that a one-sided Russian guarantee would threaten the independence and existence of Poland, the interests of the neighboring powers, and the whole political system of Europe. From Vienna Frederick was invited to offer Poland a joint Austro-Prussian guarantee of its constitution to supplement the Russian one. An individual guarantee would be replaced by a collective one, and the Republic would come under the triple protectorate of its neighbors. Frederick gladly responded to the invitation, scenting spoils and a favorable rearrangement of the map: a division of influence in Poland might lay the foundation for a division of territory and turn the alliance with Russia into a means of counteracting that country. The impression Emperor Joseph II drew from his meeting with Frederick in 1769 apropos of this Viennese scheme was expressed in his opinion of the king: "He is a genius, he speaks marvelously, but every word he utters shows him to be a swindler." Frightening Austria with Russia, Russia with Austria, and both with France in the event of their alliance, he manipulated the bewilderingly complex relations of the European cabinets, making up for his lack of power with a shamelessness that embarrassed even the diplomatic conscience of that period. Relying on his alliance with Russia, he tied into a single knot the Russian-Polish and Russian-Turkish questions and drew them both out of the sphere of Russian policy, making them European issues. He thereby took away from Russian policy the means of resolving them in a historically correct way—separately and without outside participation.

These were the inconveniences and difficulties created for Russia by the Northern System and the Prussian alliance. With that system, Catherine embarked on a policy of dreams, setting herself objectives that were too remote from current needs or even unrealizable, and with that alliance she subordinated herself to someone else's policy. Finally, the system and the alliance together made it more difficult to achieve the direct and immediate objectives that history indicated. A brief survey of the course and methods of foreign policy in the reign we are studying will suffice for us to see the impact these defects had on the resolution of the two immediate tasks.

Let us begin with the eastern question. It reflected in a particularly glaring way the lack of political perspective, the tendency to look beyond immediate objectives without considering the available means. The question consisted of extending the territory of the state in the south to its natural frontiers, the Black Sea and the Sea of Azov—and at the time it consisted of nothing more. Such an objective seemed too modest, however: an uninhabited steppe, the Crimean Tatars—those were conquests that would not pay for the gunpowder expended on them. Voltaire jokingly wrote to Catherine that her war with Turkey could easily end up turning Constantinople into the capital of the Russian Empire. Epistolary compliments coincided with serious intentions in Petersburg and sounded like a prophecy. The Turkish war was an experiment for Catherine. In six years the empress had succeeded in spreading her wings wide, displaying her flight to Europe with her deeds in Poland and at home with her convening of the representative commission of 1767. Her name was already being enveloped in a bright haze of greatness. For her to descend to earth and walk like ordinary sovereigns would have meant allowing this radiance to dissipate like a will-o'-the-wisp. Then all the envy and malice frustrated by her success would erupt, and God knew what might follow.

In this elated mood Catherine greeted the Turkish war, for which she was totally unprepared. One could not be despondent. "Let us go forward boldly—that is the proverb with which I have spent the good and the bad years alike, and I have lived a full forty years now, and what do my present troubles mean compared to those of the past?" So Catherine wrote to one of her foreign friends at the very beginning of the military operations—a beginning that was not altogether successful. And she developed an amazing energy. She functioned as the real chief of the general staff, delved into the details of the military preparations, drew up plans and instructions, and hastened with all her might to build an Azov flotilla and frigates for the Black Sea. She searched every nook and cranny of the Turkish Empire in an effort to create complications, conspiracies, or uprisings against the Turks in Montenegro, in Albania, among the Mainotes,[4] and in Kabardia. She stirred up the tsars of Imeritia and Georgia—and at every step ran up against her own lack of preparedness. Having decided to send a naval expedition to the shores of the Peloponnese, she asked her ambassador in London to send her a map of the Mediterranean Sea and the Archipelago and also to procure a cannon founder more accurate than ours, "who cast a hundred cannon, only ten of which are good for much." Making efforts to incite Transcaucasia, she was at a loss as to where Tiflis was located, on the shore of the Caspian or the Black Sea or in the interior of the country. Her mood changed with her changing impressions. "We'll give them a dressing-down they didn't expect," she wrote soon after receiving news of a breach in November 1769. "We've cooked up a lot of trouble, someone will find it to his taste," she wrote in a thoughtful mood half a year later, when the war was heating up. But bold spirits like the Orlov brothers, who knew only how to be daring, not how to think, dispelled her growing pensiveness. At one of the first sessions of the council assembled to deal with the war under the chairmanship of the empress, Gregory Orlov—of whom Catherine had told Frederick II that he was a hero similar to the ancient Romans of the best times of the republic—proposed sending an expedition to the Mediterranean. A little later, his brother Alexis, who was receiving medical treatment in Italy, indicated the real objective of the expedition: if it sailed, then let it sail to Constantinople and liberate all the Orthodox from the yoke of oppression, driving the infidel Moslems, in Peter the Great's words, back to the sandy wastes of the steppe, their former dwelling place. He himself asked to be the leader of the uprising of the Turkish Christians.

---

[4]Inhabitants of the southern Peloponnese in Greece.

It took great faith in Providence to send a fleet on such a mission nearly all the way around Europe—a fleet that Catherine herself four years earlier had deemed good for nothing. It hastened to justify her opinion. Scarcely had the squadron that sailed from Kronstadt in July 1769 under the command of Gregory Spiridov entered open waters than one of the most recently built ships proved unseaworthy. The Russian ambassadors in Denmark and England, who observed the squadron as it passed, were struck by the ignorance of the officers, the dearth of good sailors and the abundance of sick ones, and the despondency of the whole crew. The squadron moved slowly. Catherine was beside herself with impatience and asked Spiridov for God's sake not to tarry, to pluck up his courage, and not to disgrace her before the whole world. Of the squadron's fifteen large and small ships, only eight reached the Mediterranean. When Alexis Orlov inspected them in Livorno, his hair stood on end and his heart bled: no provisions, no money, no doctors, no experienced officers. "If all the services were in the same state of ignorance as this navy," he reported to the empress, "our country would be the most pitiful in the world." With an insignificant Russian detachment, Orlov quickly roused the Peloponnese, but he could not give the insurgents a firm military organization, and when he sustained a defeat by an advancing Turkish force, he abandoned the Greeks to the whim of fate, vexed that he had not found a Themistocles among them.

Catherine approved all of his actions. Joining the other squadron of John Elphinstone, which had arrived in the meantime, Orlov gave chase to the Turkish fleet and, in the Strait of Chios near the fortress of Chesme, overtook an armada numbering more than twice as many ships as the Russian fleet. His bold spirit quailed at the sight of "those structures," but his horror at his situation inspired a desperate bravery, which communicated itself to the entire crew, "to fall or annihilate the enemy." When, after a four-hour battle, the Turkish admiral's ship following the Russian *Eustathius* was set on fire by it and blew up, the Turks took shelter in the Bay of Chesme (June 24, 1770). A day later, on a moonlit night, the Russians launched fireships, and by morning the Turkish fleet, crowded into the bay, had burned (June 26). Back in 1768, Catherine had written to one of her ambassadors regarding the Peloponnesian expedition that had just been undertaken: "If it pleases God, you will see miracles." Miracles had already begun, and one was at hand: a fleet turned up in the Archipelago that was even worse than the Russian one—and of the Russian ships Orlov himself had written from Livorno that "if we didn't have to deal with the Turks, we could easily sink all of them." But Orlov did not succeed in crowning the campaign by breaking through the Dardanelles to Constantinople and returning home by way of the Black Sea as he had intended.

After the astonishing naval victories in the archipelago, equally astonishing land victories followed in Bessarabia, at the Larga and the Kagul (July 1770). Moldavia and Wallachia were occupied, Bender was taken; in 1771, the lower Danube from Giurgiu onward was seized and the whole of the Crimea conquered.[5] The territorial task of Russian policy in the south seemed to have been completed; even Frederick II found the annexation of the Crimea to Russia a moderate peace term. But Petersburg's policy, too bold in its beginnings, was too timid in its calculation of the results obtained. For fear of alarming Europe with such large annexations as the Crimea and the Azov and Black Sea steppe, where the Nogai Tatars roamed between the Kuban and the Dniester, a new scheme was devised: instead of annexing all these Tatars to Russia, merely to detach them from Turkey and declare them independent or, more precisely, to force them to exchange their loose dependence on the sultan, who was of their own faith, for the protection of the menacing tsarina, who was not. The Nogai yielded to the Russian proposal, but the khan of the Crimea understood the complicated plan and bluntly called it nonsensical and foolhardy in his reply to the Russian plenipotentiary. The Crimea was conquered in 1771 in order to thrust Russian freedom upon it. The Russian peace terms also included the liberation from Turkey of Moldavia and Wallachia, which had been conquered by Russia, and Frederick considered this a possibility.

Now let us compare the end of the war with its beginning, in order to see how little they tally. Two liberations of Christians in different European outskirts of the Turkish Empire had been undertaken: the Greeks in the Peloponnese and the Romanians in Moldavia and Wallachia. The first was given up because it could not be carried out; the second had to be given up to please Austria. The end result was a third, the liberation of Moslems from Moslems, of Tatars from Turks, which had not been contemplated when the war began and which absolutely no one needed, even those who were being liberated. The

---

[5]The Larga and the Kagul were rivers in Bessarabia. Bender was a major fortress on the Dniester River.

Crimea, which Russian troops had already marched through in Anna's reign and which was now conquered again, was not worth even a single war but had been fought over twice.

The second war with Turkey was provoked by the oversights that had prepared the ground for, or accompanied, the first one. A quasi-independent Crimea under the protection of Russia caused the latter more trouble than it had previously, as a result of the bitter civil strife between the Russian and the Turkish parties and the forcible replacement of khans. Finally, it was decided to annex it to Russia, which led to a second war with Turkey. In view of this war, the Northern System and the Prussian alliance were abandoned, and the former system of an Austrian alliance was restored. Catherine's foreign-policy collaborators also changed: Potemkin and Bezborodko replaced Panin.

The new relationships and men notwithstanding, however, the old way of thinking was retained: the habitual propensity for building "Spanish castles," as Catherine called her bold plans. In view of a second war with Turkey, two castles were constructed and in 1782 were proposed to the new ally, Austria. Between the three empires of Russia, Austria, and Turkey, an independent state would be formed from Moldavia, Wallachia, and Bessarabia under the ancient name of Dacia and the rule of a sovereign of the Greek faith. In the event of a successful outcome of the war, a Greek empire would be restored, the throne of which Catherine intended for her second grandson, Constantine. Catherine wrote to Joseph II that the independent existence of these two new states on the ruins of Turkey would guarantee perpetual peace in the east. Joseph agreed without question that it certainly would, especially if Austria meanwhile annexed something from Turkey. With his minister Prince Kaunitz, he drew up a plan to procure from this "Greek project" of Russian diplomacy the Turkish fortress of Khotin on the Dniester and a wide band of territory from the Olt River, a tributary of the Danube, all the way to the Adriatic, including Little Wallachia, Serbia, Bosnia, and even Istria and Dalmatia, territories of the Venetian Republic, which would be compensated for them from the Turkish territorial fund of the Peloponnese, Crete, Cyprus, and other islands. And all that for a Dacia and a Greek empire without Greece! At this point the politics of archaeological restoration met the politics of real interests, of land-grabbing calculations. The second war (1787–91), victorious and terribly costly in men and money, ended the way the first one should have: with the retention of the Crimea and the conquest of Ochakov[6] and the steppe as far as the Dniester. This consolidated Russia's position on the northern shore of the Black Sea, without Dacia and without the second grandson on the throne of Constantinople.

The eastern question was not thereby eliminated, however. The struggle with Turkey accomplished some tasks but introduced others, thus broadening the eastern question. The appeal to the Porte's subject nationalities at first served only as an agitational device for the purpose of creating difficulties for the enemy. Inciting the Tatars, the Greeks, the Georgians, and the Kabardians would set Turkey on fire from all four corners, as Catherine put it, but no thought was given to what was to be built on the ashes. With tender emotion Alexis Orlov dreamed only of how, once the Turks had been expelled from Europe, piety would again be restored in their place. Even the creative mind of Nikita Panin, in a plan for a Russian alliance with Prussia and Austria in 1770 for the purpose of driving the Turks out of Europe, had comforted itself with the thought that, once Austria had been compensated from Turkish lands, the territories remaining with the Turks, along with Constantinople itself, would be turned into a republic. This triple alliance was a new Panin team to be harnessed to the diplomatic cart, while his Turkish Republic was a match for Orlov's restoration of piety to the places deserted by the Turks.

It was only before the second Turkish war that diplomatic delirium began to form itself into more definite plans built on historical memories or religious and national ties. But the creators of those plans understood neither religious nor national interests as the basis for political constructions, and they annexed Turkey's Slavic territories to Austria and Orthodox Greek territories to Catholic Venice. On the eve of the first Turkish war, efforts had been made in Petersburg to convince the Austrian ambassador that it would be more advantageous for Austria to rule Belgrade and its environs than Silesia, and they advised him to act along these lines. Moreover, events in fact followed not the twists and turns of the diplomatic imagination but the movements of armies, which depended on geographical distances. Hence the attempt to liberate the Greeks of the Peloponnese concluded with the liberation of the Crimean Tatars; Orthodox Georgia was roused, but the terms of the peace treaty included the annexation of Moslem Kabardia. The Treaty

---

[6]A Turkish fortress on the northern shore of the Black Sea.

of Kuchuk Kainarji of 1774 stipulated only an amnesty for the Greeks, who had arisen for their freedom, while the hospodars of Moldavia and Wallachia, who had not lifted a finger for the liberation of their principalities, received the right, under the protection of the Russian ambassador in Constantinople, to petition the Porte on matters concerning them through representatives, and this right became the basis for the autonomy of the Danubian principalities. The Russian ambassador's protection of Moldavia and Wallachia broadened into a Russian protectorate over all the Turkish Christians.

This, in turn, defined the terms of the eastern question in Russia's foreign policy at the beginning of the nineteenth century. Under cover of the Russian protectorate, one part of European Turkey after another was detached, fully or conditionally, in the order of their geographical proximity to Russia. Sometimes, though, that order was violated by the earlier or later political awakening of one or another nationality. Beginning with the Danubian principalities, the process continued with Serbia and Greece and stopped at Bulgaria.

Fewer political chimeras were permitted in the Western Russian, or Polish, question—but a good many diplomatic illusions, self-deceptions (or misunderstandings), and, most of all, contradictions. The question concerned of the reunification of Western Rus with the Russian state. It had arisen in these terms back in the fifteenth century and for a century and a half had been resolved in this direction, and it was understood in these terms in Western Russia itself in the mid-eighteenth century. From the reports of the bishop of White Russia, George Konissky, who came to her coronation in 1762, Catherine could see that it was not a matter of political parties or of guaranteeing the political constitution but of religious and ethnic instincts inflamed to the point of mutual slaughter, and no treaties or protectorates had the power to untie this religious and ethnic knot peacefully. What was needed was armed occupation, not diplomatic intervention. To Catherine's question as to what benefit the Russian state might derive from a defense of the Orthodox in Poland, one local abbot answered bluntly: the Russian state might take from the Poles 600 versts of highly fertile land with countless Orthodox folk. Catherine could not fit such a crudely straightforward statement of the issue into the patterns of her political thought, and she approached this issue of popular psychology by the roundabout path of diplomacy.

The general national and religious issue can be separated into three specific tasks: the matter of territory, the matter of protection, and the matter of policing. It was proposed to extend the northwestern frontier to the Western Dvina and the Dnieper, with the inclusion of Polotsk and Mogilev; to obtain restoration to the Orthodox of the rights that had been taken away from them by the Catholics; and to demand that the numerous Russian fugitives be returned and no new ones accepted. The program of Russian policy was originally limited to these matters.

The dissident issue, that is, protecting the Orthodox coreligionists and other "dissidents," as they were then termed, winning them rights equal to those of the Catholics, was particularly important for Catherine, since it was the most popular issue, but it was also particularly difficult, because it irritated many sensitive feelings and impassioned interests. But it was precisely in this matter that Catherine's policy displayed a particular lack of ability to adapt its mode of activity to actual circumstances. The dissident issue required a strong and authoritative hand, but King Stanislas Augustus IV, a weak-willed individual in any case, had been given neither power nor authority, having obligated himself under the treaty with Prussia not to permit any reforms in Poland that might strengthen the position of the king. As a result of his impotence, Stanislas was left, as he put it, "in a state of total inactivity and nonbeing." He lived in poverty without a Russian subsidy—at times he and his court lacked daily sustenance, and he had to make ends meet with small loans. By their guarantee the Russians supported the Polish constitution, which was legalized anarchy, and then became indignant that such anarchy made it impossible to get any sense out of Poland.

Moreover, Panin posed the issue of the dissidents in a very hypocritical fashion. Equality of rights with the Catholics, which the Russian government demanded, could mean both political and religious equality. The Orthodox expected from Russia first of all religious equality— freedom of worship; restitution of the dioceses, monasteries, and cathedrals taken from them by the Catholics and Uniates; and the right of involuntary Uniates to return to the faith of their Orthodox fathers. Political equality, the right to participate in the legislature and the administration, was not so desirable for them and was even dangerous. In the Republic, only the gentry enjoyed political rights. The upper strata of the Orthodox Russian gentry had been polonized and catholicized. What remained intact was poor and uneducated, and it was difficult to find an individual among them capable of being a deputy to the Sejm, sitting in the Senate, or occupying any state function, because, as the Russian ambassador in Warsaw wrote to his court, all the Orthodox gentry tilled the land themselves and lacked any education. Even the bishop of White Russia, George Konissky, the head of the Orthodox of Western Rus, who by virtue of his rank should have sat in the Senate, could have no place there since he was not of gentry origin. Besides, political equality threatened the weak Orthodox gentry with even greater animosity on the part of a dominant Catholic gentry forced to share its dominance with its enemies. All these considerations inhibited the dissidents' desire for political rights.

Panin, on the other hand, pressed for political equality above all. While acting in the name of freedom of conscience as the minister of an Orthodox power, he found the strengthening of Orthodoxy, as well as Protestantism, in Poland to be detrimental to Russia. The Protestant religion might draw the Poles out of their ignorance and lead to an improvement of their political structure that would be dangerous for Russia. "This inconvenience cannot arise in regard to our coreligionists," meaning that from Orthodoxy there was no reason to fear either the eradication of ignorance or an improvement of the political structure. If we strengthened the Orthodox too much, however, they would become independent of us. They must be given political rights only for the purpose of making them a reliable political party with the legal right to participate in all Polish affairs but not otherwise than under our protection, "which we confer upon ourselves *for all time*." Here the dreamy idyllist of the Northern System is a thoroughgoing Machiavellian. By means of forced confederations, that is, armed uprisings organized under pressure from Russian troops, and arrests of the most stubborn opponents, such as the bishop of Cracow, Kajetan Soltyk, the Russian government achieved what it wanted: the Sejm passed, along with the Russian guarantee of the constitution and freedom of worship for dissidents, equalization of their political rights with the Catholic gentry.

Panin miscalculated, however, and the dissidents' apprehensions were borne out. Equality for the dissidents ignited the whole of Poland. Scarcely had the Sejm dispersed after confirming the treaty of February 13 than a lawyer, Joseph Pulaski, raised a confederation against it at Bar. Following his successful example, antidissident confederations began to flare up throughout Poland. All the homeless and idle—played-out gentry, landowners' servants, townsfolk, and villagers—assembled under the banners of these confederations and spread out across the country in small bands, plundering everyone they came upon in the name of faith and fatherland. Some of their own people caught it, but most of all it was dissidents and Jews who suffered. In accordance with the customary right of confederation, wherever they operated, local authorities were abrogated and total anarchy prevailed. It was a Polish gentry version of the Pugachev Rebellion, in its morals and methods no better than that Russian peasant uprising, and it is difficult to say which of them heaped more disgrace on the state order that engendered it, although the reasons for the two movements were diametrically opposed: there, it was the oppressors pillaging for the right to oppress, here it was the oppressed pillaging for liberation from oppression.

The Russian empress stood for order and the laws of the Republic; the Polish government left it to her to suppress the uprising and remained a curious spectator of events. There were some 16,000 Russian troops in Poland. This division waged war on half of Poland, as it was said at the time. The majority of the troops served as garrisons in the towns, and only a quarter of them pursued the confederates. But, as the Russian ambassador reported, however much they pursued this wind, they could not catch it and just tormented themselves in vain. The confederates found support everywhere; the petty and middling gentry secretly supplied them with all their needs. Catholic fanaticism was inflamed by the clergy to the highest degree; under its impact all social and moral bonds snapped. The aforementioned Bishop Soltyk, facing arrest, made an offer to the Russian ambassador to persuade the Catholics to grant concessions to the dissidents if the ambassador would allow him to go on conducting himself as a selfless fighter for the faith in order to retain credit in his party—that is, would allow him to be a fraud and a provocateur. The Russian cabinet became convinced that it could not cope with the consequences of its own policy and instructed the Russian ambassador to urge the dissidents themselves to sacrifice a portion of the rights they had been granted in order to preserve the remainder and to petition the empress to allow them to make such a sacrifice. Catherine gave her permission, meaning that she was forced to renounce the admission of dissidents to the Senate and the ministries, and their right to be elected to the Sejm and their access to all governmental posts were confirmed only in 1775, after the first partition of Poland.

One of the reasons for the roundabout formulation of the dissident question was the police issue that was linked to it. The practices of Russia's autocratic/gentry government weighed so heavily on the lower classes that from time immemorial thousands of people had fled into anarchic Poland, where life was more tolerable on the lands of the self-willed gentry. Panin considered it especially harmful to endow the Orthodox in the Republic with overly broad rights because flight from Russia would intensify all the more, "given freedom of religion combined with the advantages of a people free in all things." Russian politicians regarded the Orthodox common folk of the Republic from this same lordly viewpoint: they saw them, as coreligionists, as a pretext for interference in Polish affairs, but they had no desire to use them as material for political agitation against the ruling class since they were in the position of a ruling class themselves. The dissident issue intensified the long, uninterrupted struggle in Ukraine between the Orthodox and the Uniates and Catholics, encouraging the former as much as it embittered the latter. The answer of the Orthodox to the Confederation of Bar was the "haydamak" uprising of 1768, which included not only the haydamaks, Russian fugitives who had escaped to the steppe, but the Zaporozhian Cossacks, headed by Maxim Zhelezniak, settled Cossacks, and serfs, along with the *sotnik*[7] Ivan Gonta and other leaders. A false charter of Empress Catherine even appeared, with an appeal to arise against the Poles in defense of the faith. As of old, the insurgents slaughtered Jews and gentry and massacred the inhabitants of the town of Uman. Greek and servile fanaticism, as King Stanislas termed the uprising, fought with fire and sword against Catholic and gentry fanaticism. Russian troops suppressed a Russian uprising; those insurgents who escaped impalement or the gallows returned to their former condition. In view of the ambiguity of Russian policy, the Orthodox dissidents of Western Rus could not understand what Russia wanted to do for them: whether it came to liberate them entirely from Poland or merely to give them equality; whether it wanted to rescue them from the Catholic and Uniate priests or from the Polish landowners as well.

During the six or seven years of chaos that arose in Poland with the death of King Augustus III in 1763, the idea of annexing Western Rus cannot be detected in Russian policy, which is filled with questions of

---

[7]A Cossack rank equivalent to lieutenant.

guarantees, dissidents, and confederations. Panin's concern for confer-
ring on Russia the right to protect the dissidents "for all time" suggests
rather that this idea was completely foreign to him. The Russian cabinet at first contented itself with (or thought only about) rectifying the
frontier from the Polish side and giving some territorial compensation
to Frederick for his assistance in Poland. But the Russo-Turkish war
gave matters a broader turn. Frederick at first was frightened by this
war, apprehensive that Austria, out of malice at the Russo-Prussian
alliance, would intervene by standing up for Turkey and would involve
Prussia as well. To ward off this danger, Berlin at the very start of the
war launched the idea of partitioning Poland. This idea did not belong
to anyone in particular but arose of its own accord from the whole
structure, way of life, and immediate surroundings of the Republic, and
it had long been nursed in diplomatic circles, as far back as the seventeenth century. Under Frederick II's grandfather and father, the partition of Poland had been suggested to Peter the Great three times,
always without fail including the ceding of West Prussia, an annoying
expanse of territory that separated Brandenburg from East Prussia, to
the Prussian king. What belonged to Frederick was not the idea itself
but its practical elaboration. He himself admitted that, out of fear of
Russia's growing strength, he tried to draw advantage from its success—without war, without sacrifice or risk, only by cunning. Russia's
war with Turkey gave him the desired opportunity, which, as he put it,
he seized by the hair. His plan was to draw Austria, which was hostile
to both Russia and Prussia, into the Russo-Prussian alliance for diplomatic—though not military—assistance to Russia in the war with Turkey, with all three powers to receive territorial compensation not from
Turkey but from Poland, which had provided the grounds for the war.[8]

After three years of negotiations, conducted with "feigned conscien-
tiousness," in Panin's phrase, the participants, shuffling territory and
populations like playing cards, added up the scores of the game.
Moldavia and Wallachia, Christian principalities won from the Turks
by Russian troops, were, at the insistence of Frederick—Russia's
ally—returned to the Turkish yoke, liberation from which had solemnly been promised to them. In return for this concession, the Russian cabinet, which had obligated itself to preserve the territorial

---

[8]The disorders in Poland had spilled over into Ottoman lands, provoking the
Turks to declare war on Russia.

integrity of Christian Poland from its predatory neighbors, forced Russia to participate with those neighbors in Poland's plunder. The upshot was that some Polish territories went to Russia in exchange for Turkish ones, as payment for Russia's military expenses and victories, while others went to Prussia and Austria just like that, for nothing—or, to the former as a kind of commission and for stating the issue in a new way, for style; and to the latter as a form of compensation for Austria's enmity toward Russia, evoked by its alliance with Prussia.

Finally, on July 25, 1772, an agreement among the three partitioning powers ensued, under which Austria received all of Galicia, including districts that had been seized even before the partition, Prussia received West Prussia along with certain other lands, and Russia received White Russia (the present-day gubernias of Vitebsk and Mogilev). The share going to Russia, which had borne the entire burden of the Turkish war and the struggle with the Polish chaos, was not the largest: according to the calculations Panin presented, in population it ranked second and in revenue last; the most populous share was Austria's, the most profitable Prussia's. When the Austrian ambassador announced to Frederick what Austria's share was to be, however, the king could not restrain himself from exclaiming, after a glance at the map: "The devil take it, sir, I see that you have an excellent appetite: your share is as big as mine and Russia's put together; you do indeed have an excellent appetite." But he was more satisfied with the partition than the other participants. His satisfaction reached the point of selflessness, that is, a desire to be conscientious: he acknowledged that Russia had many rights to act as it did in Poland, "which cannot be said of us and Austria." He saw how badly Russia had used its rights both in Turkey and in Poland, and he sensed how his new strength had grown out of those mistakes. Others sensed it as well. The French minister took malicious pleasure in warning the Russian plenipotentiary that Russia would in time regret the strengthening of Prussia, which it had done so much to foster. Within Russia, Panin was also accused of strengthening Prussia excessively, and he himself confessed that he went farther than he had wished. Gregory Orlov considered the treaty on the partition of Poland, which so strengthened Prussia and Austria, a crime that deserved the death penalty. Be that as it may, this is an occasion that will remain a rare fact of European history: when the Slavic state of Russia, during a reign with a national orientation, helped a German electorate with scattered territory become a great power stretching across a broad unbroken expanse, from the Elbe to the Niemen, on the ruins of another Slavic state.

Thanks to Frederick, the victories of 1770 brought Russia more glory than benefit. Catherine emerged from the first Turkish war and the first partition of Poland with independent Tatars, White Russia, and a great moral defeat, having aroused and failed to justify so many hopes in Poland, Western Rus, Moldavia and Wallachia, Montenegro, and the Peloponnese.

I will not go into the details of the two further partitions of Poland, which were an inevitable extension of the first one; they were called forth by the same causes and accompanied by similar events. The partitioners were the same, and the methods of division were the same. Poland now was paying with its lands the expenses of Austria and Prussia for the war with revolutionary France, as previously it had paid Russia's expenses for the Turkish war. The same game continued to be played, but the players had changed their seats: Russia was no longer acting in alliance with Prussia against Austria but vice versa. Nor was the current ally any better than the former opponent, but common spoils reconciled friends and foes. In the Four-Year Sejm (1788–91) the reformist party in Poland drew up a new constitution and managed to get it through by revolutionary means on May 3, 1791. It provided for hereditary kingship, a Sejm without the *liberum veto*, the admission of deputies from the town dwellers, full equality of rights for the dissidents, and the abolition of confederations. As before, however, the adherents of the old ways formed a confederation (at Targowica) and invited in Russian troops, while the Prussians appeared without an invitation. Again, half of Poland was conquered by the Russians. The old pretexts for foreign intervention were complicated by a new one: "infernal doctrines," the poison of the "democratic spirit" that had infected Poland and posed extreme danger to its neighbors. After the second partition, in 1793, the Republic of ten million, stretching "from sea to sea," was reduced to a narrow band of territory between the middle and upper Vistula and the Niemen-Viliya, with a population of three million, the old constitution, and the subjection of the king's foreign policy to Russian supervision. The uprising of 1794, with its declaration of war on Russia and Prussia and the dictatorship of Tadeusz Kosciuszko, was Poland's death agony. The country was conquered once again by Russian forces. The convention of October 13, 1795, by which the three powers divided the remnant of Poland among

themselves, confirmed by an international document the fall of the
Polish state.

Let us compare the end of the Polish question with its beginning.
The task at hand was to reunify Western Rus; instead, Poland was
partitioned. Obviously, these were essentially different actions—the
first was demanded by the vital interests of the Russian people, while
the second was an act of international violence. The solution did not
correspond to the task. To be sure, Western Rus did enter into the
partitions as far as Russia was concerned but under another political
title deed, so to speak—not as the result of Russia's individual struggle
with Poland in the name of the political unification of the Russian
people but as a share in an act of usurpation by the three neighboring
powers in the name of the right of force. Russia annexed not only
Western Rus but also Lithuania and Courland—but then not the whole
of Western Rus, having ceded Galicia to German hands. It was said
that in the first partition Catherine wept over this concession; twenty-
one years later, in the second partition, she said calmly that "in time
we'll have to barter with the emperor for Galicia; it's irrelevant to
him." Galicia, however, remained in the possession of Austria even
after the third partition.

Poland was not a superfluous member of the family of states of
northeastern Europe when it served as a weak intermediary among
three strong neighbors. Freed of Western Rus, however, which weakened it, and having reformed its political structure, as its best people
strove to do in the period of the partitions, it might have done good
service to Slavdom and to international equilibrium by standing as a
firm bulwark against Prussia, which was striking eastward with all its
might. With the fall of Poland, conflicts among the three neighboring
powers were not moderated by any international buffer and would tell
the more painfully on Russia, whose border on the Niemen became no
safer with Prussian outposts in the vicinity. In vain, Catherine joked
about how Frederick's successor, the sanctimonious Frederick William
II, "for a couple of weeks went about in his shirt with a sword in order
to see spirits and, after a meeting with Christ, refrained from declaring
war on us as a result of his prohibition." The clairvoyant raved with the
designs of the sober minded. Meanwhile, "our ranks had diminished"—there was one less Slavic state; it became part of two German
states, and this was a great loss for Slavdom.

Russia did not appropriate anything immemorially Polish; it took only its own ancient lands and part of Lithuania, which had at one time attached those lands to Poland. But with Russian participation, a spacious new grave opened in the Slavic cemetery, in which so many of our ethnic kin, the west Slavs, were already buried. History bade Catherine to retrieve from Poland what Poland held that was Russian, but it did not suggest that she divide Poland with the Germans. It was a matter of bringing Poland within its ethnographic boundaries, of making it a really Polish Poland, not of making it a German Poland. It was a rational demand of national life that Western Rus be saved from polonization, and only cabinet politics could have delivered Poland up to germanization. Without the Russian territories, within its own national frontiers, even with an improved political structure, an independent Poland would have been incomparably less dangerous to us than the same Poland in the form of Austrian and Prussian provinces. Finally, the destruction of the Polish state did not save us from conflict with the Polish people: within seventy years after the third partition, Russia had made war on the Poles three times (in 1812, 1831, and 1863).[9] The Republic's ghost, rising from its historical grave, created the impression of a living national force. Perhaps, in order to avoid hostilities with its people, their state should have been preserved.

Thus, the two immediate issues of foreign policy were resolved, though with vacillations, excessive sacrifices, and deviations from a direct path. The northern shore of the Black Sea from the Dniester to the Kuban was consolidated. The south Russian steppe, the immemorial refuge of predatory nomads, came within the Russian economic orbit and was opened to settled colonization and culture. A string of new cities arose—Yekaterinoslav, Kherson, Nikolaev, Sevastopol, and others. Before the first Turkish war, as Catherine put it, there was not a single Russian ship on the Black Sea. The treaty of 1774 gave freedom of navigation to Russian merchant vessels, and the turnover of Russian Black Sea trade, which in 1776 had not reached 400 rubles, by 1796 had grown to almost 2 million. To these economic advantages was added new political strength: the military fleet that arose in Sevastopol with the annexation of the Crimea secured the coastal possessions and served as support for Russia's protectorate over the eastern Christians. In 1791 Vice-Admiral Fyodor Ushakov successfully fought the Turk-

---

[9]A reference to the Napoleonic wars and the two Polish uprisings against Russian rule.

ish fleet in sight of the Bosporus, and the idea once again lit up in Catherine's mind that it might be possible to proceed directly to Constantinople. On the other hand, almost the whole of Western Rus was reunited, and the titular formula "of all Russia"[10] acquired a meaning that coincided with reality. The lands acquired in the west at the time had a population, for the most part indigenous Russian, of approximately 6,770,000, those in the south a population of 200,000 or so Moslems and Christians. The western annexations today form ten gubernias, the southern ones three.

The methods Catherine employed in her international policy considerably lowered the value of the successes achieved in the resolution of these two issues. At the beginning of the reign, Catherine had set herself the goal of living in friendship with all the powers so as to have the possibility of always standing at the side of the most oppressed and thereby being the arbiter of Europe (*l'arbitre de l'Europe*). It was difficult to play such a role in the political Europe of the time. It was not peoples but courts or cabinets that acted in the international European politics of the large and most of the small continental states. Popular interests were subordinated to the calculations and tastes of diplomacy or filtered into politics through the prism of diplomatic thought, which refracted and frequently dissolved them. All those cabinet masters—the Choiseuls, the Kaunitzes, the Hertzbergs—were playing their last hands before the Revolution tossed their cards out the window, where they lay until the Congress of Vienna once again turned Europe into a casino of cabinet diplomacy. Knowing the costs of their trade all too well, these gamblers sought simpletons, not judges. Catherine was familiar with this political world through its representatives in Petersburg, and she understood that one achieved success there by making an impression, not vice versa, and that modesty about one's strength was taken as a sign of weakness. Moreover, she needed to make an impression for domestic purposes as well. She entered this world with a bold tread, taking a proud and arrogant tone that elicited the complaints of foreign ambassadors. In the immediate sphere of her foreign relations, in Courland, Poland, and Sweden, she was not an arbiter but an impassioned partisan. She set up her own parties, intrigued, bribed, created enemies, and, in the end, so muddled

---

[10]That is, the designation "emperor/empress of all Russia" in the title of the country's sovereign.

her international policy that she herself compared it to a bog: scarcely did she pull one paw out of the mud than another got stuck. Instead of friendship with all the powers, in the thirty-four years of her rule she set Russia to quarreling with almost all of the major states of Western Europe and brought into our history one of its most sanguinary reigns. She conducted six wars in Europe and before her death was preparing for a seventh, with revolutionary France.

Having begun in practice with direct intervention in the affairs of others, Catherine's European arbitration, given her means and a power unrestrained by a sense of responsibility, might have caused a great deal of trouble had her policies not suffered from a lack of discernment that reduced the danger, an inability to place a task squarely within feasible limits and steadfastly bring it to a conclusion. Recognizing that a good beginning is half the task, Catherine usually began with loud declarations and a broad program, but then, after looking around and coming across obstacles, she would strike bargains, make concessions, and lower her sights, sometimes crying out to her minister "hold firm, not a step back" and backing down nevertheless. Or else she would construct a plan with an ulterior motive, cloaking it in a specious principle. When the French Revolution broke out, Catherine understood its serious import, grew indignant at the faintheartedness of Louis XVI, and as early as 1789 predicted for him the fate of Charles I of England. She appealed for unanimity and heroism on the part of the other princes, the king's brothers, saying that they needed fire in their bellies, and she beat her head against the wall, as she put it, trying to mobilize Austria and Prussia against revolutionary France in the name of the monarchical principle. On the quiet, however, she admitted to her intimates that what she wanted was to entangle the Austrians and Prussians in French affairs so as to have her own hands free: "I have a number of unfinished projects, and it is essential that they be kept occupied and not hinder me." Catherine wanted to arrange things in Poland to suit herself. But the Austrians and Prussians saw through her transparent cunning, were sluggish in mobilizing against France, remained indifferent to principle, without chagrin bore their losses on the Rhine in expectation of gains on the Vistula, and finished the division of Poland in splendid fashion with Russia's aid and participation.

In relative terms, Russia did not become stronger in the west; as much as her strength grew, at the cost of great sacrifices, she allowed her opponents to strengthen themselves just as much, without any sacrifices. But this was deemed unimportant, a mere detail: Catherine admitted that, having become used to great affairs, she did not like trifles. And great affairs were available: seven million new subjects and a strong impression at home and abroad. The political world recognized that Catherine had "a great name in Europe and a power belonging exclusively to her." In remote, out-of-the-way places in Russia, it was long remembered and said that during this reign our neighbors did not insult us and our soldiers vanquished all and won renown. Bezborodko, the most prominent diplomat after Panin, expressed this very simple general impression in a refined form when he told young diplomats at the end of his career, "I do not know how things will be in your time, but in our day not a single cannon in Europe dared to fire without our permission."

～ V ～

Domestic Policy

C atherine's domestic policy was no simpler as far as its tasks were concerned than her foreign policy. The latter had to display the power of the empire and satisfy national feeling; the former had to display the brilliance of the government, consolidate the position of its proprietor, and reconcile antagonistic social interests. Moreover, the instruments of action were of no use in domestic policy: instead of armed force, deservedly renowned, and diplomacy, with its subtle maneuvers, here one had officialdom with its hopeless inertia (or routine) and the gentry with its ignorance and "age-old laziness," of which the former chancellor Bestuzhev-Riumin had complained bitterly.

Catherine earnestly continued the study of the course of affairs in the empire that she had begun before her accession now that new, broader paths had opened to her. She often attended the Senate, listened attentively to the speeches and opinions of the senators, perused certain matters herself, made inquiries, and questioned all and sundry. In this way she formed a picture of the empire's situation at the moment of her accession—a picture that, somber in the extreme, she presents in her early and later notes and remarks. We have already seen the condition in which she found the armed forces and finances. Elizabeth and Peter III had appropriated state revenue for themselves and, when asked for money for the state's needs, would reply angrily, "Find the money wherever you like, but what we have set aside is ours." Therefore the treasury paid almost no one. The price of bread in Petersburg doubled. Almost all branches of trade were turned into wasteful private monopolies. Brutal torture and punishment for trifles had so hardened people's minds that they could not even conceive of a different, more humane system of justice. The prisons were overflowing; Elizabeth had freed some 17,000 prisoners before her death, but at Catherine's coronation in 1762 about 8,000 still remained. For all its brutality, justice was sold to the highest bidder. There was a countless multitude of laws, and they were changed time and again, but the courts were not in the least concerned about safeguarding them; they were utilized only when they were of benefit to the strongest. The judicial institutions had passed all bounds: some ceased activity, while others were overwhelmed. Everywhere the people complained of extortion and bribery, but the governors and their chancelleries subsisted on bribes because they did not receive salaries. The Senate's orders were carried out only after they were issued for the third time.

The Senate itself, the supreme guardian of legal order so cherished by Peter the Great, had turned into a thoroughly idle institution under its procurator-general, Alexander Glebov, "a swindler and a scoundrel," as Catherine termed him. The senators heard appellate cases in their entirety, not in the form of summaries, and it took six weeks just to read a case concerning the commons of the town of Masalsk. The Senate appointed commandants of all the towns, but it had no list of towns and did not know how many there were. In rendering its judgments, it never looked at a map of the empire, so that sometimes it did not know what it was judging. In fact, it had not owned a map since it was founded. Once, while attending the Senate, Catherine took out 5 rubles, sent to the Academy of Sciences for the purchase of a printed atlas, and donated it to the Senate. The supreme controller of the state's economy, the Senate was unable to draw up a precise budget inventory. After Catherine's accession, it gave her a register of receipts, according to which they came to sixteen million. Catherine ordered the receipts recounted, and the accounting commission tallied them at twenty-eight million—twelve million had been unknown to the Senate.

On the other hand, the Senate displayed great energy in squandering state property and revenue. It farmed out all the customs houses for two million, and when Catherine took them under state administration, the Petersburg customs house alone yielded more than three million in receipts. At the end of Elizabeth's reign, the Senate had arbitrarily turned over state factories to the private ownership of preeminent courtiers—the Shuvalovs, Vorontsovs, Chernyshevs, and others—and they were allocated some three million rubles to run them. The factory owners squandered the loan in the capital, the factory peasants were paid for their work either badly or not at all, and 49,000 of them revolted. Pacification detachments armed with cannon had to be dispatched, and the factories reverted to the treasury on account of their debts. All told, in the form of loans and by other means, the owners had grabbed some four million in cash and more than 7 million in land and mines, and they became indignant at the injustice of the treasury when it demanded the return of funds that had long since been wasted.

There was no trust in the government. Instead, everyone was in the habit of assuming that only orders detrimental to the common good could issue from it. Thus the state had lost its meaning in popular opinion and had even turned into a kind of conspiracy against the people, from whom, as Catherine remarked, the mistakes of judges and other officials were concealed. If we add to this the absence of fundamental laws—with the exception, perhaps, of the anarchistic statute on succession to the throne—Catherine's description gives a complete picture of Asiatic despotism, where the caprice of individuals takes the place of laws and institutions. Peter I had left Russia an "unfinished building" in the form of a great shell without a roof, windows, or doors, merely openings for them. After him, under the rule of his collaborators, then of sojourning foreigners, and later of home-grown Elizabethan statesmen, nothing at all had been done to complete the edifice. The stockpiled construction material, in the form of institutions, regulations, statutes, and so forth, had just been damaged.

Once she came to the throne, Catherine wanted to see the people, the country that had been so badly governed, to view its life up close, directly, not from the distant prospect of the palace and the tales of the court. With this objective, she undertook a series of trips in the first years of her reign: in 1763 she journeyed to Rostov and Yaroslavl; in 1764 she visited the Baltic gubernias, in 1765 she traveled along the Ladoga Canal (which she found beautiful but neglected); and finally, in the spring of 1767, she decided to visit "Asia," as she called it, that is, to travel down the Volga. Accompanied by a great entourage of some 2,000 people and the entire diplomatic corps, she boarded a barge at Tver and sailed downstream to Simbirsk, whence she returned by land to Moscow.

On this trip she collected a number of instructive observations. First, she saw what suitable material for governing she had in her subjects, how little needed to be done for the people in order to make them favorably disposed toward her: everywhere the empress was met with indescribable rapture. Catherine wrote en route that even the non-Russians (meaning the foreign ambassadors) more than once shed tears at the sight of the people's joy, and in Kostroma, Count Ivan Chernyshev, who was in charge of the expedition, wept throughout a banquet, touched by the "decorous and affectionate" behavior of the local gentry. In Kazan, people were ready to lay themselves instead of a carpet beneath the feet of the empress, "and in one place along the road," Catherine wrote, "the peasants brought candles to set before me, with which they were chased away." This was the reply of the simple folk of the Volga to the Parisian philosophes who glorified Catherine as the Minerva of Tsarskoe Selo. Her fleeting travel observations may have inspired Catherine with no few governmental considerations. She encountered cities "beautifully situated but abominably built." In their culture the people were inferior to the nature that surrounded them. "Here I am in Asia," Catherine wrote to Voltaire from Kazan. She found this city particularly striking in the diversity of its population. "This is a separate empire," she wrote, "so many different objects worthy of attention, and one could collect ideas here for ten years." Simbirsk was a most wretched town, and all the houses had been confiscated for tax arrears. The people along the Volga seemed to her prosperous and very well fed: everyone was eating bread, and no one complained. In the towns prices were high, but in the villages last year's unthreshed stocks were abundant; the peasants held back from selling their grain out of fear of a bad harvest.

While the observations she was amassing had not yet taken the shape of an integral plan of reform and foreign policy was not distracting her attention, Catherine hastened to darn the most serious rents in the government that she had noted in her picture. In view of peasant disturbances and rumors, a decree issued on the sixth day after her accession reassured landowners of the inviolable possession of their estates and peasants. Many tax farms and monopolies were abolished; to reduce the price of grain, its export abroad was temporarily prohibited; the state price of salt was reduced from fifty to thirty kopecks a *pud*, and to make up for the loss of salt revenue Catherine reduced her household maintenance by 300,000 rubles, to 1 million, which was obtained from the salt duty. Moreover, the empress declared to the

Senate that, since she herself belonged to the state, she considered everything of her own to be the state's property as well, and henceforth no distinction was to be made between her and the interests of the state. The senators arose and with tears in their eyes thanked her "for such judicious sentiments," Catherine adds.

A register of receipts and expenditures was established. Catherine persistently tried to limit the application of torture to criminals and the confiscation of their property, but she could not bring herself to abolish the two practices by law. A stern manifesto against bribery was issued. The population of Petersburg was treated to the edifying spectacle of the Senate's senior secretary pilloried in the square in front of the Senate with the inscription "Violator of decrees and bribe taker" on his chest. New salary standards for state servitors were introduced and pensions were established—but to cover the new expenditures the price of salt was raised. Even the flywheel of the bureaucratic machine, the undisciplined Senate, did not escape punishment: in 1763 it was given a severe reprimand "for internecine discord, enmity, hatred," and partisanship. When the opportunity arose, reference was also made to the impropriety of senators' holding tax farms on alcohol, in regard to which neither they nor the procurator-general himself had been squeamish. The difficult task of secularizing the populated ecclesiastical estates was completed, affording the treasury a net profit of 890,000 rubles in Great Russia alone after expenditures for ecclesiastical and charitable institutions (the decree of February 26, 1764). Finally, a Commission on the State Land Survey was established in 1765, a fundamental task that had not been carried out successfully under Elizabeth.

These measures of the first three years must have produced a favorable impression and even a practical effect, alleviating the tax burden to some degree, promoting general tranquility, injecting some life into the stagnant administrative swamp, giving a warning to officials, and, what was most important to Catherine, inspiring a certain trust in her government. She herself, as was her wont, was very much satisfied with the success of the measures she had taken. In one early note she wrote that trade was picking up, monopolies were abolished, insurgents were pacified, people were working and paying, justice was no longer being sold, the laws were respected and carried out, all the judicial institutions had returned to their duties, and so forth.

All these measures were mere details, however, almost trifles for the most part. In the manifesto of July 6, a general reform of the government had been promised, and state institutions had been announced that would operate undeviatingly within the confines of the law. Meanwhile, there remained one noticeable gap in the central administration: legislative authority, concentrated solely in the person of the sovereign, lacked any regular structure, there being no institution to facilitate its work. The procurator-general of the Senate had legislative initiative, but only of an accidental sort, when a matter came up within the confines of the Senate's supervisory and judicial competence that required a new law. Soon after her accession, Catherine commissioned Nikita Panin, who had drafted the July manifesto, to draw up a plan for the missing institution. Panin presented a report and a draft of a manifesto on an Imperial Council and a reorganization of the Senate, which was to be divided into departments. A new supreme administration was constructed out of these two institutions. Panin harshly criticized Elizabeth's government, in which "the power of persons rather than the authority of state institutions operated," and, using the domestic cabinet of the empress, "a private office having no state form," all affairs were irresponsibly manipulated by favorites, minions, and accidental and wild individuals, reminding Panin of "those barbaric times" when established government and written laws did not yet exist.

To the extent that one can understand Panin's long-drawn-out and diplomatically vague exposition, his Imperial Council, divided into four departments, each headed by a state secretary, was a purely consultative institution that in no way encroached on the plenitude of the supreme power. All matters requiring new laws would come before it, except those matters brought to the sovereign's discretion by the Senate, and the appropriate state secretaries would draft proposed laws, which were to be discussed by the imperial councillors and presented to the sovereign for confirmation. The Council would be a regular institution, established by a promulgated law, with a legal order of procedure; every new law would issue from it over the monarch's signature and would be countersigned by the appropriate state secretary. This was not, however, the old Supreme Privy Council, which, merging with the person of the monarch, had become a participant in legislative power. The Senate would remain the supreme institution, independent of the new Council. According to the draft of the manifesto, the Council was "the place in which we labor for the empire." It was a legislative workshop, carrying out the preliminary work of legislation in an appropriate form and procedure, through which "a good sovereign in his great labors may limit the commission of errors characteristic of human beings." The supreme authority was not limited, only restrained in practical terms by the organization of the legislative function.

Panin's proposal foreshadowed in a vague and clumsy fashion the future State Council of Michael Speransky, which proved to be completely safe politically. Catherine signed the manifesto on December 28, 1762, and appointed the members of the Council, but then she fell to thinking, consulted with various people, and buried the matter. Whether divining Catherine's secret thoughts or displaying the sincere zeal of a servile courtier, the master of ordnance, Alexander Vilbua, spoke with particular farsightedness when he declared that a Council established by law would in time rise to the significance of a co-ruler, would bring the subject too close to the sovereign, and might generate a desire to share the latter's power; the empress's reason needed no Council, and to alleviate the pressure of business coming before her, her private cabinet need only be divided into departments—to put it more simply, the state councillors should be replaced by personal secretaries. Only Panin's idea of dividing the Senate into departments was realized, but on the basis of a different plan (December 15, 1763). Reform of the central administration was limited to this measure. The legislative function, which remained unregulated, continued to employ accidental or makeshift methods. On particular issues the Senate was given legislative powers or commissions were created, while the Commission on the Rights of the Nobility of 1763 was charged, along with many other matters, with drawing up the new plan for dividing the Senate into departments. With the start of the first Turkish war, Catherine began to convene a council, principally on military matters, which soon became permanent but remained private.

Catherine wanted to conduct a purely personal policy, not masked in any way by a standing, purely consultative, but legally formalized and responsible institution. In the sphere of government closest to her, she would not allow even the shadow of a law capable of dimming the luster of her solicitous autocracy. According to her thinking, the purpose of law was to guide the subordinate organs of government. It had to act like the warmth of the sun in the earth's atmosphere: the higher it is, the weaker it is. Power, not just unlimited but undefined, devoid of any juridical form, is the fundamental fact of our political history as it had developed up to Catherine's time. She protected this *local fact* from any attempts to give the summit of the government a regular structure. But she wanted to cloak this indigenous fact in the *ideas of the age*. The way those ideas developed in her mind made such a logically difficult application of them possible. Even before her accession, as we saw, she concentrated her assiduous reading on historical and political literature and especially on the literature of the Enlightenment. Foreign adherents of this literature did not apprehend it in a uniform fashion. Some drew from it a stock of abstract principles and radical methods: when they talked about organizing a humane society, they loved to base it on principles that were drawn from pure reason and untested in historical reality, and when they turned to real, existing society, they found it deserving only of *total* demolition. Others made what might be called a gustatory rather than a nutritional use of this literature: they were enthralled by its abstract ideas and bold plans, not as a desirable way of life but simply as diverting and savory turns of daring but idle thought.

Catherine treated this literature more cautiously than the political radicals and more seriously than the frivolous liberals. From this rich source of new ideas, she tried, in her words, to extract only what would nurture the great spiritual qualities of the honest man, the great man, and the hero and prevent vulgarity from obscuring "the classical taste for honesty and valor." Traces of this study and of the reflections it plunged her into were preserved in the notes, excerpts, and passing remarks in French or Russian that she left behind. Even before her accession, she writes:

> All I want, all I desire, is the good of the country to which God has brought me. The country's glory is my own glory—that is my principle; I would be very happy if my ideas might further it. I want the country and its subjects to be prosperous—that is the principle from which I start. Power without popular trust means nothing to the person who wants to be loved and glorious. This is easy to achieve: take as the rule of your actions and your statutes the people's welfare and justice, which are inseparable from one another. Liberty, the soul of all things! Without you, everything is dead. I want people to obey the laws, but I do not want slaves; I want as a general objective to make people happy, but I do not want caprice, eccentricity, or brutality.

How these notes remind us of those intimate albums that school-girls kept in our grandfathers' times to inscribe their favorite poems and first girlish dreams. But Catherine's "principles," for all their placid freethinking, had a more practical, educational significance for her: they taught her to reflect on issues of political and social life, to clarify to herself the basic concepts of law and society. Whether following her own cast of mind or the spirit of the literature she read, however, she gave her principles a somewhat unusual meaning. To her, reason and its satellites—truth, justice, equality, liberty—were not militant principles, implacably contending for supremacy over humanity with tradition and its satellites—falsehood, injustice, privilege, bondage—but were just as much elements of social life as their opponents, merely a bit cleaner and more noble. Since the creation of the world, these noble principles had been abased; now their dominion had come. They could coexist with principles of the other order, but any action, whatever its objective, had to absorb these principles in order to succeed. "The crudest mistake," Catherine wrote to d'Alembert, "that the Jesuit order made, and that any institution can make, is to fail to base itself on principles that reason cannot refute, for truth is unconquerable." These principles are a good agitational device. "When truth and reason are on our side," we read in one of her notes, "we must bring them before the eyes of the people and say: such-and-such a reason led me to do such-and-such; reason must speak for necessity, and rest assured that it will win out in the eyes of the crowd." The ability to reconcile the principles of the two different orders when it comes to governing is political wisdom. It inspired Catherine with some ingenious ideas. "It is contrary to the Christian religion and justice," she writes, "to turn men, who are all born free, into slaves. In some countries of Europe, a church council emancipated all the peasants; such a revolution in Russia now would not be the way to gain the love of the landowners, who are filled with stubbornness and prejudice. But there is an easy method: to decree the emancipation of peasants when estates are sold; in a hundred years, all, or almost all, land changes owners—and then, the people are free." Or: our empire needs population, therefore it is hardly useful to convert to Christianity those non-Russians among whom polygamy prevails. "I want it established that people flatter me by speaking the truth: even a courtier will do that if he sees it as the path to favor." When principles are viewed from a utilitarian perspective, bargains can be struck with them. "I have found that in human life honesty helps you out of difficulties." Injustice is allowable if it achieves a benefit; only useless injustice is unforgivable.

We see that reading and reflection gave Catherine's thinking a dialectical flexibility, the capacity to bend to either side; it gave her a rich supply of maxims, of commonplaces, of examples, but it did not give her any convictions. She had aspirations, dreams, even ideals, but no convictions, because the recognition of truth did not fill her with the resolve to construct a moral order within and around her, without which the recognition of truth becomes simply a pattern of thought. Catherine had one of those mental constitutions that do not understand what a conviction is or why it is needed, at what point it becomes a consideration. Her ear suffered from a similar defect: she could not tolerate music, but she laughed heartily when she heard a comic opera in her Hermitage in which coughing was set to music. Hence the motley and eclectic character of her political views and sympathies. Under the influence of Montesquieu, she wrote that laws are the greatest good that people can give and receive, but, following the free, unfettered play of her thoughts, she felt that "leniency and the conciliatory spirit of the sovereign do more than millions of laws, while political liberty gives a soul to everything." She acknowledged within herself a "perfectly republican soul," but she considered the most appropriate mode of government for Russia to be autocracy or despotism, which she did not fundamentally distinguish (the learned writers of the day also had trouble differentiating these two forms of one and the same kind of government). She herself assiduously practiced this kind of government, although she agreed that the combination of a "republican soul" and despotic practice might seem odd.

Under Catherine, aristocracy came to Russia along with despotism. "Although I am free of prejudices and by nature of a philosophical mind, I feel a great inclination to honor ancient families. I suffer at seeing some of them reduced to poverty here; I would like to improve their position." And she deemed it possible to improve their position, by restoring entail and adorning the elders of a family with decorations, posts, pensions, and lands. This did not prevent her from regarding as foolhardy the aristocratic scheme of the Supreme Privy Council.[1] The traditions of German feudalism found room in her capacious mind alongside the habits of Russian government and the political ideas of the Age of Enlightenment, and she used all these methods according to her own inclinations and considerations. She boasted that,

---

[1]See chapter I, note 5.

like Alcibiades, she got along both in Sparta and in Athens. She wrote to Voltaire in 1765 that her heraldic device was the bee, which flies from blossom to blossom gathering honey for its hive, but the makeup of her political ideas was more reminiscent of an anthill than a beehive.

Catherine soon found broad application for her ideas. In her words from a later note, during the first years of her reign she saw from the petitions submitted to her, the work of the Senate and Colleges, the senatorial debates, and discussions with many other people that no uniform rules had been established, and the laws, issued at various times and reflecting different frames of mind, seemed contradictory to many people. Hence, everyone wanted and demanded that lawmaking be put in better order. From this she drew the conclusion that "the *mode of thought* in general and civil law itself" could be improved only if she established written and confirmed rules for the entire population of the empire and on all subjects of legislation. To that end she began to read and then to write the *Instruction to the Commission on the Code of Laws*. For two years she read and wrote. In a letter of March 28, 1765, to her Parisian friend Mme. Geoffrin, very well known at the time for her literary salon, Catherine wrote that for the past two months she had spent about three hours each morning working out the laws of her empire: this is a reference to the composition of the *Instruction*. It means that the work began in January 1765, and by the beginning of 1767 the *Instruction* was ready.

In the critical edition of the text of the *Instruction* that our Academy of Sciences produced in 1907,[2] the abundant material from which this document was composed has been carefully analyzed and its sources identified. The *Instruction* was a compilation drawn from several works of contemporary Enlightenment literature. The main ones were Montesquieu's celebrated book *The Spirit of the Laws* and the work of the Italian criminologist Beccaria *On Crimes and Punishments*, which came out in 1764 and rapidly gained wide renown in Europe. Catherine called Montesquieu's volume the prayer book of sovereigns with common sense. The *Instruction* consisted of twenty chapters, to which two more were subsequently added. The chapters were divided into articles, short statements like those in which statutes are written. In all, there are 655 articles in the printed *Instruction*, 294 of them borrowed

---

[2]N.D. Chechulin, ed., *Nakaz Imperatritsy Ekateriny II* (The Instruction of Empress Catherine II) (St. Petersburg: Imperial Academy of Sciences, 1907).

from Montesquieu. Catherine also made extensive use of Beccaria's treatise, which was directed against the vestiges of medieval criminal procedure, with its tortures and similar forms of judicial evidence, and took a new look at the responsibility for crimes and the expediency of punishments. Chapter 10, the most extensive in the *Instruction*, "Of the Forms of Criminal Courts," was taken almost in its entirety from that book (104 articles out of 108). A critical analysis of the *Instruction*'s text also found traces of borrowings from the French *Encyclopedia* and the works of the contemporary German writers Bielfeld and Justi. Researchers find that only about a quarter of the articles in the entire *Instruction* were not borrowed, and those for the most part are headings, questions, or explanatory interpolations gleaned from the same sources, though original articles of a very important nature are also encountered.

Catherine did not overrate her authorship of the *Instruction*—in fact, she underrated it. When she sent Frederick II the German translation of her work, she wrote, "You will see that like the crow in the fable I have decked myself out in peacock feathers[3]; what belongs to me in this work is merely the arrangement of the material and a line or a word here and there." The work proceeded in the following manner. From her sources Catherine wrote out passages, either verbatim or in her own paraphrase, that corresponded to her program, sometimes distorting the meaning of the source. The excerpts were crossed out or supplemented, assigned to chapters subdivided into articles, translated by her secretary Gregory Kozitsky, and amended again by the empress. Catherine decided not to do the translation herself, since at that time she did not yet feel completely at home in Russian. Given this procedure, defects in the work were inevitable. A sentence taken out of the context of the source would become unclear. In the Russian translation of complex discussions, the lack of fixed terminology sometimes makes it difficult to ascertain the meaning; in such passages the French translation of the *Instruction*, which was made at the same time, is more intelligible than the Russian original, though the latter was borrowed from the same French source. Individuals whom Catherine familiarized with parts of her work before its completion pointed out the unintelligibility of many of the *Instruction*'s passages. In places, even contradictions crept in: in one article, taken from Montesquieu, capital

---

[3]A reference to a fable by Ivan Krylov. See chapter 4, note 3.

punishment is allowed; in other articles, composed according to Beccaria, it is rejected.

The *Instruction* suffered a great deal from the censorship, or criticism, to which it was subjected before it was published. By Catherine's account, when her work was sufficiently advanced she began to show parts of it to various individuals, in accordance with their taste. Nikita Panin said of the *Instruction* that these were maxims capable of overturning walls. Whether influenced by the comments she heard or as a result of her own reflection, she crossed out, tore up, and burned a good half of what she had written—so she informed d'Alembert at the beginning of 1767, adding, "And God knows what will become of the rest of it." What became of it was this. When the deputies to the Commission came to Moscow, Catherine invited "several persons, highly diverse in their thinking," to a preliminary discussion of the *Instruction.* "Here debates arose over each article; I gave them the freedom to ink out and delete whatever they wanted; they crossed out more than half of what I had written, and what remained was the *Instruction on the Code of Laws* as printed."

If, as may be supposed, this was a second round of abridgment, then in the printed *Instruction* we are reading no more than a quarter of what was originally written. This, of course, must have greatly impaired the harmony of the work. Chapter 11, on the serf status, suffers particularly from incoherence. The reason is that in the printed edition some twenty articles were cut out of the original version, dealing with types of serf bondage, measures against abuses of power by masters, and methods of emancipating serfs. Those were things the gentry censor-deputies feared most. Despite the objections and abridgments, Catherine remained very satisfied with her work and regarded it as her political confession. She wrote—even before it appeared in print that she had said everything in it, she had emptied her sack, and for the rest of her life she would not say another word—that all who saw her work agreed unanimously that it was beyond perfection, but it seemed to her that it still needed a little cleaning up.

In its twenty chapters, the *Instruction* speaks of the autocratic power in Russia, of the subordinate organs of government, "of the repository of the laws" (the Senate), "of the status of all those living within the state" (on the equality and freedom of citizens), "of the laws in general," "of the laws in particular" (specifically on making punishments conform to crimes), "of punishments" (especially their moderation), "of the judicial process in general," "of the procedures of criminal courts" (criminal law and legal procedure), "of the serf status," "of increasing the population in the state," "of manufactures (handicrafts) and trade," "of education," "of the nobility," "of the middling sort of people" (the third estate), "of the towns," "of inheritances," and "of the composition (codification) and style of laws." The last chapter, the twentieth, sets forth "the various articles that require explanation" and speaks specifically of trials for high treason, of extraordinary tribunals, of toleration, and of the symptoms of the decline and ruin of a state. Two supplementary chapters discuss good order, or policing, and the state economy, that is, revenues and expenditures.

We see that despite the cuts, the *Instruction* quite broadly encompasses the realm of lawmaking and touches on all the basic parts of the state structure, the supreme power and its relationship to its subjects, the government, the rights and obligations of citizens, the social estates, and, most of all, legislation and the courts. Moreover, it makes a number of revelations to the Russians. It proclaims that the equality of citizens consists of everyone's being subject to identical laws, that there is such a thing as state freedom, or political liberty, and that it consists not only of the right to do whatever the laws allow but also of not having to do what one should not want to do and of the peace of mind that comes from being confident of one's security. Such freedom requires a government under which one citizen does not fear another and all fear only the laws. The Russian citizen had never seen anything like that in his own country. The *Instruction* taught that what must restrain people from crime is innate shame, not the lash of the government, and that if people are not ashamed of punishment and are restrained from vice only by brutal retributions, then a brutal government, which brutalizes people by inuring them to violence, is to blame. Frequent use of executions has never reformed people. Unhappy is the regime in which brutal laws have to be instituted. The *Instruction* sharply condemns torture, to which Russian courts so readily resorted, as an institution contrary to common sense and humane feeling; and it recognizes that prudence demanded placing limitations on the confiscation of a criminal's property, an unjust measure but one customary in Russian judicial practice.

The senseless brutality and arbitrariness with which cases of high treason were prosecuted is well known: a careless, ambiguous, or stupid word about the government would elicit a denunciation, the dreaded "word and deed,"[4] and lead to torture and execution. Words, the *Instruction* affirms, never turn into a crime unless they are combined with actions: "He who turns words into a crime deserving of death perverts and subverts everything." Especially instructive for Russian judicial and political practice was the *Instruction*'s opinion of extraordinary tribunals. "In autocratic governments," it says, "the most useless thing is the appointment sometimes of special judges to try one of their subjects." Religious toleration was permitted in Russia, but, out of political considerations, only within very narrow limits. The *Instruction* recognizes that not to allow different religions in so heterogeneous a state as Russia would be a defect very harmful to the tranquility and security of its citizens and, on the other hand, regards religious toleration as the sole method "of bringing all the stray sheep back to the true flock of the faithful." "Persecution," the *Instruction* continues, "irritates the human mind, but permission to believe according to one's own law softens even the most obdurate hearts." Finally, the *Instruction* more than once touches on the question of whether the state, that is, the government, is fulfilling its obligations to its citizens. It points to the horrifying rate of child mortality among the Russian peasants, which carries off upward of three-quarters of "this hope of the state." "What a flourishing condition this realm would be in," the *Instruction* bitterly exclaims, "if by judicious institutions we could avert or prevent this evil!" Alongside child mortality and imported infectious diseases, the *Instruction* places among the afflictions ravaging Russia the senseless exactions with which landowners burden their serfs, forcing them for long years to abandon their homes and families for wagework and "to wander over almost the whole of the state." Half ironically, half complaining of the government's lack of concern, the *Instruction* remarks that "it is highly necessary that the law prescribe to the landowners" a more considered method of taxing their serfs.

It is difficult to explain how these articles evaded the censorship of the gentry deputies and crept into the printed *Instruction*. The chapter on increasing the population of the state, following Montesquieu, paints a horrifying picture of a country desolated by chronic disease and bad government, where, born in despair and poverty, amid violence and weighed down by the false notions of the government, peo-

---

[4]The traditional phrase "the sovereign's word and deed" was used in accusations of sedition or treason.

ple see their ruin without observing its causes and lose heart and the energy to work, so that fields capable of feeding the entire nation scarcely provide sustenance for a single family. This picture vividly calls to mind the mass flights of the people abroad, which in the eighteenth century became a real calamity for the state. In its list of methods for preventing crime, the *Instruction* seems to enumerate in the words of Beccaria the shortcomings of the Russian government. "Do you want to prevent crimes? Have the laws favor particular ranks of citizens less than each individual citizen; have people fear the laws and no one but the laws. Do you want to prevent crimes? Have enlightenment disseminated among the people. Finally, the most reliable, though the most difficult way of making people better is to perfect education." Everyone knew that the Russian government did not concern itself with these methods. "A book of good laws" also would curb the inclination to do harm to one's neighbors. This book should be distributed so that it could be purchased at a small price, as a primer, and it should be prescribed that reading and writing be taught in the schools from such a book alternately with church books. There was still no such book in Russia, however; the *Instruction* itself had been written for the purpose of compiling one. Thus a document bearing the imperial signature informed Russian citizens that they were deprived of the fundamental benefits of civil society, that the laws by which they were governed did not conform to reason or justice, that the ruling class was harmful to the state, and that the government did not fulfill its essential obligations to the people.

This is the form Russian reality assumed in the light of the ideas proclaimed by the *Instruction*. How could those ideas be transmitted to a milieu with so little affinity for them? The *Instruction* found a method and designated a transmitter. In its introduction, it takes the general position that the laws must correspond to the natural situation of the people for whom they are composed. In subsequent articles it draws two conclusions from this thesis. First of all, Russia by its situation is a European power. The proof of this is the reforms of Peter the Great: bringing European manners and customs to a European people, they succeeded the more easily because previous manners in Russia did not at all accord with its climate and had been conveyed to us by alien peoples. Let us suppose that to be true, contrary to all probability. The unspoken conclusion that follows is that the Russian laws must have European foundations. Those foundations were provided by the

Instruction in the deductions it assembled from European political thought. The result was something like a syllogism with an unstated conclusion, which Catherine found it inconvenient to articulate. The *Instruction* does not conceal its sources. Montesquieu, Beccaria, and the other Western writers whom it used, however, had no legislative authority in the eyes of the Russian deputies to the Commission on the new Code of Laws. They took the precepts of the *Instruction* only as an expression of the thought and will of Russia's supreme power. It would have been more appropriate to address this syllogism to the Western European educated public—which might have had its doubts as to whether Russia had attained such political maturity that these lofty ideas could be placed at the foundation of its Code of Laws.

The other conclusion, drawn from the natural situation of Russia, was that because of its vast size it should be governed by an autocratic sovereign: "It is requisite that the speedy resolution of affairs sent from distant parts compensate for the delay caused by the remoteness of those places." If, speaking in the language of that period, the entire "reason" for autocracy lay in Chita's distance from Petersburg, then a syllogism might be constructed on this second conclusion, too, a much more unexpected one. Montesquieu's book, the principal source of the *Instruction*, is an ideal depiction of a constitutional monarchy. The first term of the syllogism is the same: the laws of a state must correspond to its natural situation. The second term is: Russia, by virtue of its natural—that is, geographical—expanse must have an autocratic form of government. The conclusion is: the principles of constitutional monarchy must lie at the basis of Russia's laws. This syllogism has the form of a paralogism, but such was Catherine's actual thinking. Free of political convictions, she exchanged them for the tactical devices of politics. Without letting a single thread of autocracy out of her hands, she would allow the indirect and even direct participation of society in the government and was now summoning representatives of the people to collaborate in the compilation of a new Code of Laws. Autocratic power, according to her thinking, was assuming a new aspect: it was becoming a kind of *personal and constitutional absolutism*. In a society that had lost all sense of law, even something as accidental as the felicitous personality of the monarch could pass for a legal guarantee.

Catherine As a Young Girl. Engraving by Rosina Lischevska, 1740.

Empress Elizabeth. Portrait by Vigilius Ericksen.

Grand Duchess Catherine. Portrait by Georg Groot.

Grand Duke Peter. Portrait by Georg Groot.

Catherine II in Her Coronation Attire. Portrait by Stefano Torelli.

Empress Catherine II. Portrait by Fyodor Rokotov.

Empress Catherine II. Portrait by Johann Baptist Lampi.

Empress Catherine II in Traveling Clothes. Portrait by Michael Shibanov.

～ VI ～

The Commission of 1767

In 1700 a commission composed of senior officials and a few clerks was charged with supplementing the Code of Laws of 1649 with those statutes enacted since its publication. Ever since, a series of commissions had worked unsuccessfully on this project. They had employed various methods: they tried making the old Code of Laws the basis of their work, supplementing it with the new decrees; they tried combining the old Code of Laws with the Swedish code, replacing the inappropriate points of the latter with articles of the former or with new enactments; to the makeshift codifiers, who were military and civil officials, they added appointed or elected experts, "good and knowledgeable people," sometimes consisting only of officers and gentry, more often drawn from other estates, the clergy and merchants, as well. Codification commissions of the latter type reflected a dim memory of the participation by Assemblies of the Land in the compilation of the most important codes of old Rus: the Code of Laws [*Sudebnik*] of 1550 and the Code of Laws [*Ulozhenie*] of 1649. The Commission of 1754, consisting of officials of the central government with the participation of "*Des-sciences-académie* Professor" Strube de Piermont, prepared two parts of a new code of laws. In 1761, when the commission proposed a second examination of its work jointly with the Senate, the latter ordered that each province send two deputies elected from the gentry and one from the merchants, and it was suggested to the Synod that deputies be elected from the clergy. On this occasion, too, the task remained unfinished: the deputies were dismissed in

1763, although the commission continued to exist until the summoning of new deputies in 1767.

It was left to Catherine to complete this longstanding project after eliminating what experience showed to be the reasons for the failure of previous efforts. The project now was organized on a different basis than before in many respects. It began directly with the manifesto of December 14, 1766, summoning deputies to a proposed Commission for the Compilation of the Draft of a New Code of Laws, as it was officially called. Representation was considerably broadened. The commission was composed of representatives of governmental institutions and of deputies from various categories or classes of the population. The Senate, the Synod, all the Colleges, and the main chancelleries of the central government sent one representative each. In order to understand the procedures for the election of deputies from the population, it must be remembered that the empire at that time was divided into twenty gubernias, which were subdivided into provinces, and the provinces into districts. There was to be one deputy from the home owners of each town, one deputy from the gentry landowners of each district, and one deputy per province from the single homesteaders, the soldier-farmers, the state peasants, and the settled elements of each non-Russian tribe, baptized or unbaptized—a total of four deputies per province where these four categories of the population were present. The number of Cossack deputies was left to their senior commanders to determine.

District and town elections were direct; those in the provinces were in three stages. The gentry landowners of a district, under the chairmanship of a marshal of the nobility elected for two years, and urban householders, under the chairmanship of a mayor also elected for two years, chose their deputies to the commission directly; only very large towns could first choose electors from different parts of the town. Single homesteaders and other free rural inhabitants in the aforementioned categories "who have a house and land in the *pogost* (rural parish)" elected *pogost* representatives, who chose district representatives, and from the latter the provincial deputy was elected.

Thus central governmental institutions, some social estates, non-Russian tribes, and places of residence were represented in the commission. According to the letter of the "Rules of Procedure" for the town elections, all householders, who could be individuals of any rank, were to participate in them. This suggests the idea that the town elections had an all-estate character, which contradicted the entire structure of contemporary Russian society. Let us remember, however, that Catherine at the time dreamt of creating in Russia "a middling sort of people," similar to the middle class in the West. The *Instruction* assigned to this class, which was still called *meshchane* [townsmen], those people who, being neither nobles nor tillers of the soil, were engaged in "the arts, sciences, seafaring, commerce, and trades," as well as all non-noble graduates of Russian schools and foundling homes, and, finally, the children of government clerks. The principal attributes of a townsman were possession of a "house and property" in a town and payment of municipal taxes. As yet, however, there was no such class in Russia, only some discrete elements of one. For the elections there was only one discernible mark of a townsman: home wnership. In Catherine's thinking, the town was an estate, but a fictitious one; in actuality, therefore, the town elections were neither single-estate nor all-estate but simply non-estate. From the documents that have been preserved, we see that clergy took part in the town elections along with government clerks. The Senate would not confirm deputies elected solely by merchants where there were home owners of other ranks. In the Ukrainian towns, even the gentry participated in the elections alongside the townsmen. In Petersburg, which by Peter's orders had been built up with gentry houses, home owners who were high-ranking noble officials completely swamped the merchants: a senior commandant was elected mayor, and the deputy from the capital was Count Alexis Orlov. Following Petersburg's example, the elections in the old capital assumed the same character, a Prince Viazemsky being elected mayor and a Prince Golitsyn the deputy.

Its broadened representation notwithstanding, however, the commission was far from including in its membership all strata of the empire's population. Without even mentioning the serfs, we see no deputies from the parish clergy (though they did participate in the town elections), the court peasants, or even the former ecclesiastical peasants (or "economic" peasants, as they were called, from the name of the College of Economy, which administered them), though they had joined the free rural inhabitants at the time of the secularization of 1764.

In all, 564 deputies were selected. The quantitative distribution of representatives corresponded neither to the size of the represented groups of the population nor to their significance in the state. The towns had the most deputies, because every town, big and small—the capital, Moscow, and the district town of Bui, which had a total of a few hundred inhabitants—sent one deputy. Town deputies made up 39 percent of the commission's membership, while townsmen did not constitute even 5 percent of the empire's total population. The proportion of representatives by classes was as follows:

Governmental institutions	Approx. 5%
Gentry	30
Towns	39
Rural inhabitants	·14
Cossacks, non-Russian tribes, other classes	12

Catherine had to overcome the ingrained indifference and distrust with which the population was accustomed to greeting appeals from the government for public assistance, knowing from experience that nothing would come of them but new taxes and incoherent orders. That was how it had regarded the Senate's decree of 1761 calling on "society"—the gentry and merchants—to assist the government with advice and participation in the compilation of a new code of laws, reminding "sons of the fatherland" of their duty and of the opportunity "to leave an unforgettable memory of yourselves to future generations." Those words of the Senate's decree sounded like an absurd joke to the ordinary individual, especially alongside the codification commission's threat to confiscate villages from the gentry representatives if they failed to appear. Now the government tried to signify its trust in its subjects in a more seemly fashion. The manifesto summoning the deputies was read in all the churches on three Sundays in succession, and it proclaimed that on the part of the throne mercy was regarded as the foundation of the laws, while gratitude and obedience were expected on the part of the subjects. The deputies were being summoned to "a great cause." Their election must be carried out "calmly, courteously, and quietly." The deputies were assigned a salary; their rank was raised to an unprecedented height and became the most privileged in Russia. They were placed under the empress's "own protection" for life, and "whatever the sin" they might fall into, they were exempted from the death penalty, torture, and corporal punishment. Their property was subject to confiscation only for debt, and their personal safety was protected by a double penalty. They were given special badges to wear, which noble deputies upon the completion of their mission were allowed to insert into their coat of arms "so that their descendants may know in what a great cause they participated." No Russian subject at that time enjoyed such preferences.

In Great Russia the elections on the whole proceeded smoothly. Incidents such as the struggle between the town of Gorokhovets and its commandant over the town's deputy or the refusal of a mad Novgorodian noble to participate in the elections on the grounds that the nobility had been freed from compulsory service were rare. On the other hand, in Ukraine the elections provoked noisy disturbances, stirring up long-accumulated hostilities between the Great Russian administration and the indigenous society, the gentry and the townsmen, and the rank-and-file Cossacks and their officers.

The most important innovation of the Commission of 1767 was the instructions that the electors were required to provide to their deputies setting forth their "social needs and burdens," exclusive of private matters resolvable by a court. The electors responded eagerly to this requirement, sensing in it, if not a right, then a permit opening a direct path to the throne for their mundane requests. In addition, the deputy's instruction conferred on the deputy himself the customary significance, which everyone understood, of a petition bearer for the needs of his community: the contemporary understanding of popular representation did not go beyond this. The deputies brought more than twice as many instructions as there were deputies themselves, almost 1,500. Particularly numerous, over 1,000, were those brought by the rural deputies. The explanation for this abundance lies in the procedures for drawing up the instructions to those deputies. In the direct elections, those of the towns and the gentry, the electors, after choosing their deputy, formed from their ranks a five-member commission. For three days this commission heard statements by the electors concerning their needs, then in another three days it put these statements together in an instruction, which it read to the electors and with their signatures handed it over to the deputy. In the three-stage elections for provincial deputies from the rural categories, the *pogost* or parish electors drew up a "most humble petition" concerning their needs, which their representative transmitted to the district representative, who transmitted it to his provincial deputy. Hence, the provincial deputy of the single homesteaders or state peasants took with him to the commission as many petitions, or instructions, as there were parishes containing inhabitants of his category in the province he represented. The peasant deputy of

Arkhangelsk Province brought 195 parish instructions. More often, however, a composite district or even provincial instruction was compiled from the parish petitions. The first instruction heard by the Commission of 1767 was from the state peasants of Kargopol District of Belozersk Province, Novgorod Gubernia.

Social discord also fostered the propagation of instructions, when the electors could not come to an agreement about their needs and it became impossible to compile an instruction. This occurred especially often in the towns, which Catherine imagined to be cohesive societies with a harmonious understanding of their needs and interests. The urban classes, when they disagreed in their opinions, resolved their discord by various means or gave their deputy several instructions that conflicted with or were even antagonistic to one another; or they compiled a common instruction out of articles dictated by representatives of the different classes of the urban population, unabashed at the intrinsic nonsense of such an instruction; or, even more simply, they stitched together various instructions inscribed "from the white clergy," "from the merchants," "from the proprietors of factories," and so on. (All these devices have been elucidated in detail by Alexander Kizevetter in his article on the urban instructions.[1]) Astrakhan, despite the regulations governing the elections, even chose five deputies and provided each with a separate instruction. Finally, in the deputies' instructions of 1767, both urban and gentry, we encounter borrowings from each other, as was the case with the "testimonies" of the elected representatives at the Assemblies of the Land in the seventeenth century.

A deputy was responsible to his electors for the timely presentation of their petitions to the proper quarter. Over and above the instruction, however, he was granted the right to petition in regard to whatever he saw fit, except that he could not contradict his own instruction and in case of disagreement with it was supposed to resign his mandate.

Previous codification commissions made up of high officials had not mingled with the estate deputies whom they summoned to assist them in their work: strictly speaking, they were the ones who drew up the proposals for the new code of laws, using the deputies as an auxil-

---

[1]A.A. Kizevetter, "Proiskhozhdenie gorodskikh deputatskikh nakazov v ekaterininskuiu komissiiu 1767g." (The Origin of the Instructions to the Town Deputies to Catherine's Commission of 1767), *Russkoe bogatstvo* (Russian Wealth) (St. Petersburg), 1898, no. 11: 32–57.

iary instrument. Now the representatives of governmental institutions formed part of the Commission on the same footing as the estate deputies and were not its directors or even equal participants in it: in view of their official duties, they were allowed to sit in the commission only two days a week instead of five. The manifesto of December 14 had assigned the commission a twofold task: the deputies were being convened not just to air the needs and deficiencies of each locality; they were to be admitted to the commission to prepare the draft of a new code of laws. In accordance with that task, the commission was given a very complex organization. From the Great Commission, as the full assembly was called, three small ones, of five deputies each, were elected. The *Directorial Commission*, managerial in nature, proposed to the full assembly the formation as needed of codification subcommissions, with no more than five members each, to work out separate parts of the code of laws. It then supervised their work, checked the proposals they drew up against the *Great Instruction* (as the empress's *Instruction* was called, to distinguish it from the deputies' instructions), corrected them, and brought them before the full assembly, always explaining its emendations. The *Expedition Commission*, editorial in function, worded or rectified the proposals of the subcommissions and the enactments of the Great Commission itself "according to the rules of language and style," removing ambiguous, obscure, and incomprehensible words and rhetoric. Without it, all the other commissions and the Great Commission itself would have been "out of action" in view of the illiteracy and inability to express abstract ideas of any sort that prevailed even in the ruling circles. The third, or *Preparatory Commission*, sorted out the deputies' instructions, made extracts from them "by topics," and brought them before the full assembly. These three small commissions constituted a kind of administrative bureau of the Great Commission.

The chairman of the full assembly, the marshal, or deputies' marshal, as he was called, was appointed by the empress from a list of candidates proposed by the commission and the procurator-general. The marshal acted hand in hand with the procurator-general, the representative at the commission of the supreme power, arranged the full assembly's order of business in concert with him, and sat with him on all the subcommissions. The main task of the procurator-general was to allow nothing contrary to the sense of the *Instruction* into the enactments of the commission. Catherine imparted especially great importance to the journal of the commission's sessions: it had to be kept in such a way that future ages would be able to find, in the execution of the commission's "great cause," instructions on how to organize themselves more soundly. Even our present building, we read in the Rules of Order of the commission, "would have been less of a burden for us" if we had had such minutes from past times. For the daily minutes in the full assembly and in all the subcommissions, capable individuals were to be appointed from the nobility, with one to be "director of the daily minutes" and subordinated to the empress herself. He, the marshal, and the procurator-general formed a kind of presidium of the commission and sat at a separate table in the hall of the full assembly, the director in the middle and the marshal and procurator-general at each end.

The commission's order of business corresponded to its complex organization. A legislative item, initiated in the full assembly, passed with the assembly's preliminary judgments to the Directorial Commission, which directed it to the proper codification subcommission. The latter, having composed a draft, communicated it to the central College or chancellery within whose purview it fell, and with the latter's opinion and its own conclusion sent it back to the Directorial Commission. The Directorial Commission, after checking the draft against the *Instruction*, either sent it back for correction or transmitted it to the Expedition Commission for grammatical and literary improvement, and only then, through the same Directorial Commission, did the draft come before the full assembly for final discussion. We see that the general idea of the Muscovite Assembly of the Land may have contributed to the structure of the Commission of 1767, but in the details of its organization and its order of business it followed the parliamentary usages of the constitutional countries of Western Europe.

Along with pleasant observations, Catherine had brought back from her Volga journey more than six hundred petitions, the greater part of which were filled with complaints by the serfs about the severity of their masters' exactions. The petitions were returned with the instruction that no others were henceforth to be submitted. But the peasants were not to be stopped. Rumors circulated that the masters' peasants were to be taken over by the state, as the ecclesiastical peasants had been not long before. Whole villages of serfs began to submit requests to the empress for outright emancipation from the landowners, and to the exhortations of the authorities they stubbornly replied that they did not want to remain in obedience to their masters. That seemed an alarming sign, and the Senate was charged with devising appropriate methods to counter it. The Senate devised just two: by decree it forbade peasants to complain against their masters, and it ordered those who petitioned for freedom to be flogged publicly. There were instances also of peasants taking bloody reprisals against landowners. The factory peasants, who had just been pacified, rose again. At the same time, in the south, among the single homesteaders, a sect rapidly spread that rejected the rituals of the state church. The sectarians were sent into the army, and the widows and unmarried women were distributed as workers to the single homesteaders and peasants. The atmosphere in the countryside became oppressive and fear ridden.

At this time, on July 30, 1767, Catherine opened the Commission for a New Code of Laws with a solemn reception in the Kremlin, to which she came from the Golovin Palace in a ceremonial procession with staff-bearing marshals of the court, footmen, negroes, ladies-in-waiting, and other majestic ornaments that an age of formalized sentiment and symbolic thought had devised. The commission met in the Kremlin's Palace of Facets. At its first sessions, it organized itself, elected a marshal—Alexander Bibikov, the deputy of the Kostroma nobility—listened to the *Instruction* and other regulations pertaining to it, and elected members to the three small commissions. The *Instruction*, the daily minutes remarked, was listened to rapturously, even avidly. The deputies were particularly struck by the articles stating that persecution irritates men's minds, that it is better for the sovereign to encourage and the laws to threaten, that contrary to the flatterers who tell sovereigns every day that the people are created for them, "We think, and regard it as our glory to say, that We are created for our people." Many wept. The ecstasy reached its peak at the concluding words of the same article: "God forbid that at the conclusion of this legislation there be any nation on earth more just, and, consequently, more flourishing—a misfortune that I do not wish to live to see." The flood of enthusiasm called forth an excess of zeal: the Commission asked the empress to accept the title of "the Great, All-Wise, Mother of the Fatherland." In a beautiful personal reply to the deputies, Catherine neither accepted nor declined the proffered title, and, in a little note to the marshal, she even seemed to express her annoyance at the deputies: "I ordered them to make laws for the Russian Empire, and they make apologies for my qualities." Despite this, the Senate, associating itself with the commission in this matter, took it upon itself to find a suitable occasion to fulfill its wish.

The codification work of the Great Commission began only with the eighth session, with the reading and discussion of the instructions from the state peasants and soldier-farmers. The first to be read out was the instruction from the state peasants of Kargopol District; it elicited twenty-six speeches and written opinions. In fourteen sessions, a total of twelve rural instructions were read and discussed; after that, not a single deputy's instruction was read out in the full assembly. After abandoning the deputies' instructions, the commission turned to the reading and discussion of the laws concerning the rights of the nobility, which provoked heated debate. After devoting eleven sessions to this subject and forwarding the laws that had been read out and the opinions that had been heard to the subcommission "on the review of the kinds of inhabitants of the state" (that is, the estates), the Great Commission turned to the reading and discussion of the laws concerning the merchants, which occupied forty-six sessions. Alternately with discussions of the merchants and of other questions that arose by chance, the privileges of Livonia and Estonia were read and discussed at ten sessions.

In December 1767, the commission's sessions in Moscow were terminated, and it was transferred to Petersburg, where it resumed its work on February 18, 1768, in the Winter Palace, with the reading and discussion of the laws concerning justice. Over the course of five months, it devoted approximately seventy sessions to this subject, at which 200 deputies' opinions were heard. Meanwhile, there came before the full assembly the draft of the "rights of the nobles," that is, of the gentry, which had been prepared by the subcommission "on the kinds of inhabitants of the state." This subject, which had already been discussed by the deputies, again occupied their attention for a full three months. It was decided to return the draft to the subcommission to review it and reconcile it with the numerous deputies' opinions. After that, the deputies occupied themselves with reading and discussing the laws on service estates and hereditary estates. This was where the decree terminating the work of the Great Commission found it in December 1768. Rumors about the commission had created a ferment among the people, eliciting talk of changes in the laws, and at this point, by chance, the war with Turkey occurred, requiring those deputies who were in military service to return to the army. The decree ordered the general assembly to disperse until it was convoked again, leaving only the subcommissions, which continued to work for many years. There was no second convocation of the full assembly. In the year and a half of its activity, the Great Commission had had 203 sessions.

From this survey we see that no plan of work had been drawn up, topics were assigned accidentally, and questions succeeded one another without being resolved. For some reason the commission began with the deputies' instructions, which were read in their entirety, although there was already a subcommission to give them a preliminary review. The statements in the instructions were subjected to minute scrutiny and elicited distrust and a demand for verification at the local level. The Kargopol peasants asked in their instruction to be allowed, contrary to a decree, to trap birds and game year round. Objections were raised to this request. The Arkhangelogorod peasant deputy Chuprov glossed over the argument with the remark that, "if trapping is allowed at any time, the animals and birds won't be reduced, and if it is forbidden, they won't be added to—decrease and increase depend on God's power." Geniality was not the prevailing tone of the debates, however. The same peasants asked for the construction of state granaries from which poor peasants would take grain in the spring, returning the loan at the new harvest. The Novgorod noble deputy responded that such storehouses were completely unnecessary and that in the hope of state grain the peasants would abandon farming, while the Vereia deputy of the nobility, Stepanov, called the Kargopol peasants lazy and stubborn. This harshness elicited a delicate objection from the Kopore noble deputy, Count Gregory Orlov, that the Vereia deputy probably had not spoken those words and the scribe had written them down incorrectly. Stepanov was surpassed by another noble deputy, Glazov, who advanced such an unseemly opinion, in which he so indecently reviled all the state peasants and their deputies, that the marshal stopped the reading of his memorandum. The question of excluding him from the commission arose, but he was treated leniently and was only fined five rubles and required to apologize to those he had insulted before the whole assembly.

Gradually, as the range of the discussion broadened, the commission rose from local details to general questions of state organization. Here, especially in its discussion of the laws concerning the nobility and the merchants, the debates began to tie conflicting and contradictory interests into a tangled knot. Until Peter I, the Muscovite government had pursued the intensive legislative and administrative development of estate obligations, for the fulfillment of which the estates were granted certain privileges or advantages. Now, to counterbalance the policy of imposing burdens, the deputies' instructions and speeches in the commission repeatedly insisted that those advantages be recognized as the rights of their estate, independently of their obligations. Furthermore, each of the higher estates wanted its rights to be a monopoly at the expense of the interests of the other estates. The nobles awarded themselves the sole right to own land populated by serfs, and the merchants awarded themselves the sole right to trade and industry, leaving to the free rural population only farming, without even the right to sell its agricultural products freely. The economic policies of Peter I had introduced a new interpretation into estate concepts that were a reflection, as in a pool of water, of the principles of the Code of Laws of 1649. We know how Peter tried to give his dignitaries a taste for manufacturing, while encouraging the owners of factories and mills by granting them the nobility's right to acquire land populated by serfs. Now the nobles, while defending their monopoly on the ownership of land and serfs, refused to give up the right to have factories and mills as well, while the merchants laid claim to the right to own peasant souls.

The topics of the debates in the commission reflect the structure of the society, and the arguments clearly indicate the public mood and the level of political consciousness. The commission had been instructed to allow each deputy to express his opinion "with the boldness needed to benefit this cause." And the deputies made extensive use of this right, fearing neither the government nor even stupidity. The nobility came forward in the commission as "the first estate of the realm." The champion of its rights was the most outstanding orator in the assembly, Prince Michael Shcherbatov, somewhat later a Russian historian and critic, now the deputy of the Yaroslavl nobility, well read and intelligent but more passionate than reasonable. We have already seen that, as the nobility's rights grew after Peter I, it tried to purge itself by shaking off extraneous elements of the lower classes that had adhered to it. Peter I's decrees on the elevation to hereditary nobility of nonnobles who were promoted to officer's rank stuck in the craw of the old nobility. Prince Shcherbatov took up arms against those decrees and the promoted nobility. In doing so he developed a historical and political theory of the noble estate according to which its present-day members, to whom a monopoly on honor and nobility, as well as serf ownership, belonged by right of heredity, turned out to be natural-born nobles, from time immemorial, behind whom stood ranks of ancestors distinguished by their glorious deeds. Thereby, of course, he set against himself the numerous service nobles, who accused the old nobility of class arrogance and exclusiveness, of scorning personal service and merit. One of their deputies declared that the nobility, as was evident from the laws regarding it read out in the commission, had originated from the most undistinguished families through merit in service. Among the twenty-three deputies who concurred in this opinion, there was not a single nobleman, but it shook Prince Shcherbatov's psychological equilibrium. In an extremely excited speech, his voice shaking, he traced all nobles either from Rurik and foreign crowned heads or from highly distinguished foreigners who came to serve the Russian grand princes. Having made such a bold challenge to history, he even called as his witnesses the holy places of the Kremlin, which had supposedly been saved from the yoke of the non-Orthodox by noblemen of ancient families. Another defender of the service nobility asked whether the Russian noble gentlemen could say of their ancestors that they had all been born of nobles and thus brought Prince Shcherbatov to the question: Of whom was the first noble born? None of the natural-born noblemen responded, and the question of the first noble was not resolved as aptly as Mrs. Prostakova's problem of the first tailor.[2] But even Prince Shcherbatov was surpassed by the deputy of the Mikhailovsk nobility, Naryshkin, who took the subject to its ultimate conclusion by declaring bluntly that "noble rank is considered among us to be something holy, distinguishing one man from the rest: it gives him and his descendants the right to own another who is their like." After that, it remained only to speak of the nobility's canonization.

With no less difficulty the nobility, weakened by its own inconsistency, also defended itself against the merchants. Prince Shcherbatov and other noble deputies stood for a strict demarcation of estates, so

---

[2]Mrs. Prostakova, a crude and uneducated landowner, is a character in Denis Fonvizin's satirical play of 1781, *The Minor*. As the play opens, she is berating a servant for sewing a badly fitting coat; to the servant's objection that he was never taught to be a tailor, she replies that learning is unnecessary, for, after all, from whom did the first tailor learn to sew? The servant's response is that perhaps the first tailor sewed even worse than he does.

that each class, as one noble instruction put it, "has its own privileges, and one does not trespass on the prerogatives of another." Not content with its landowning monopoly, however, the nobility wanted to enjoy the right of manufacturing as well. Here, too, Prince Shcherbatov proceeded from the highest principles and in a very original fashion deduced this claim from "the very essence of mills and factories." A state is sound when it rests on distinguished and well-to-do families as its unshakable pillars. The greatness of the Spanish and French states was based on distinguished families. The implied conclusion was that distinguished families have to become rich in some way. Ownership of land is the right of nobles alone; ores originate in the land, consequently mineral works should constitute one of the nobility's rights. Deputies of the merchants objected with the sarcastic reproach that factories and other commercial enterprises were unbecoming to the noble Russian gentry, that its business was to try to improve the agriculture of its peasants. One town deputy pointed out a sharp difference between a merchant and a landowner when it came to manufacturing: the merchant who builds a factory provides wages to an entire rural area, assisting it in the scrupulous payment of taxes and the masters' dues, while the landowner-manufacturer only burdens his serfs with new unpaid labor and, moreover, conducts the business badly, since he does not know its secrets.

But the town, too, encroached on the "prerogatives" of others. The merchants' deputies persistently sought the right to own serf stewards and workers in view of the unreliability of hired ones: the latter took money in advance and ran away without working it off. Especially negligent were hired hands who had been the servants of landowners: they were lazy and thieving—a sign of the education they had received from their masters. Serfdom was a bone that state power threw to all classes of Russian society. With the manifesto of February 18, 1762, serfdom in the hands of the nobility lost its political justification; while remaining legal, it ceased to be just. As is evident from the instructions, the idea had already disappeared from the consciousness of the nobles that their ownership of land inhabited by serf souls was a conditional right, a right *and* an obligation, that they were only half property owners and half responsible police (and judicial) agents of the state. One instruction asked for confirmation in the proposed new code of laws that "the authority of the landowners over their servants and peasants, legalized since olden days, is irrevocable; as it has been

hitherto, so shall it be henceforth." Such a viewpoint actually undermined the nobility's serf monopoly, however: if the right to own populated land was mere private property, there was no reason to withhold
it from non-nobles. Other classes of society did not contest the
nobility's possession of this right but wanted to share it. The loftiest
considerations of state had to be contrived in order to justify its belonging exclusively to the gentry, meaning that a speech by Prince
Shcherbatov was needed—that was his role in the commission. He set
forth a new political syllogism. Nobles are obligated by their rank to
serve sovereign and fatherland with particular zeal. This service consists of governing other subjects of their sovereign, for which their
education must prepare them. For such preparation nobles are also
given the right to own villages and *slaves*, on whom they learn from
infancy how to govern parts of the empire. The conclusion follows of
itself. Slaveholding must be a privilege only of the ruling estate. Thus,
serfdom was a school for Russian statesmen and the slave owner's
village a model for the government of the Russian Empire. On this
occasion, too, the quick-tempered prince was unable to hold his
tongue.

No less remarkable, however, was the opinion of the Kerensk nobility, which in its instruction justified the unlimited power of the landowner over his serfs on the grounds that the Russian people "do not
compare in character with the peoples of Europe." Furthermore, merchants could acquire serfs, should they be permitted to do so, only
without land, on a retail basis. "We should be ashamed," Prince
Shcherbatov continued, "at the very thought of reaching such a degree
of severity that those equal to us by nature are equated with cattle and
sold individually." But the prince did not count on the gentry's shame,
knowing how readily nobles sold their serfs individually, and he expressed his firm confidence that the commission would prohibit by law
the sale of people individually without land—a shameful business, the
prince acknowledged, at the very thought of which his blood boiled.
Thus a speech directed against the claims of the merchants involuntar-
ily turned into one against the orator's own noble brethren. Meanwhile,
almost half a century earlier, Peter I had expressed to the Senate his
desire, or demand, to put a stop to the individual sale of serfs.

Prince Shcherbatov also demonstrated by means of a statistical calculation that the acquisition of serfs by merchants would be detrimental to the national economy. Of the 7,500,000 peasant souls, there were

no more than 3,300,000 actual workers tilling the soil for the 17,000,000 inhabitants of Russia as a whole. Consequently, each plowman had to prepare grain for more than five people. If each of the 20,000 merchants bought two families, the number of plowmen would be reduced by an additional 40,000. But the same statistics that Prince Shcherbatov drew on to defend the gentry's monopoly on peasant ownership were used by the merchants to defend their monopoly on trade against the peasants. One of their deputies calculated that as a result of the peasants' commercial activities there were not even 2 million tillers of the soil left, the result being an abundance of vacant land and high prices. The gentry was not satisfied with the land it already owned and set its sights on the former ecclesiastical lands and their peasants; in the nobility's instructions we encounter an item "concerning the sale to the gentry of 'economic' villages."

Given the totally impervious slave-owning "mentality" of the bulk of the gentry, it was useless to raise the question of the abolition of serfdom directly. The deputy of the Kozlov nobility, Korobin, tried to approach this untouchable question obliquely. When the commission was discussing peasant flight, he pointed to the landowners' scandalous arbitrariness in disposing of the peasants' labor and property as its main cause, and he proposed that, without infringing on the landowner's power over the person of the serf, his right to what the serf acquired by his own labor be limited. Korobin was supporting the empress's *Instruction*, Article 261 of which stated that "the laws may do something beneficial for the slaves' private property." The commission found it impossible to divide the landowner's powers in this way, however, and Korobin attracted only three votes, while eighteen opposed him.

Nevertheless, Korobin's proposal was the correct approach to the issue. Power over the person of the serf belonged to the landowner as a police agent of the government. Korobin separated that power from the rights of the private owner of serf souls. The refusal of the law to defend the serf's property made him into an object. Legal defense of the property of the serf would have led to legal protection of his labor and of his person as a taxpayer. The Edict of February 19, 1861,[3] in fact opens by dividing the landowner's judicial and police powers from his ownership rights. The entire falsity of the government's and the

---

[3]Alexander II's decree emancipating the serfs.

landowners' view of the question of serfdom, which muddled and delayed its resolution for several generations, lay in the confusion of these two different elements. This confusion obliterated any distinction between a right and an abuse. It explains the appearance of an article in the instruction to the deputy from one of the *governmental* offices "on making a law on how to proceed in those instances when, as a result of blows by landowners, death occurs to their servants." In old Rus the law did not punish a master whose blows caused the death of his slave, who was considered an object. In the eighteenth century, however, the serf was not an object, not a *slave*, as Prince Shcherbatov and other noble deputies thoughtlessly called him, but a *revision soul*, a state person, though one not possessing full rights, and causing him mortal blows made one liable to the charge of ordinary murder. If even a governmental office felt the need for a special law regarding such cases, this meant only that the state authorities did not understand their own laws and did not know how to apply them.

Catherine was incensed at the deputies' view of the serfs as slaves. In one of her outbursts of indignation, she dashed off the comment: "If the serf cannot be considered a person, it follows that he is not a human being; let him be considered a brute, then, for which the whole world will ascribe to us considerable glory and love for mankind. Everything done in regard to the slave follows from this God-pleasing principle and is done entirely for cattle and by cattle." But the commission viewed serfdom not as a question of rights but as booty, and, as though it were a trapped bear, all classes of society hastened to grab their share—merchants, government officials, Cossacks, and even state peasants. The clergy, too, showed up at the division and seized the edge of the bear's ear: it inserted a petition in one of the town deputies' instructions that clerics and church servants be allowed to buy peasants and house serfs on an equal footing with merchants and non-nobles.

Neither the commission's organization nor its procedure was appropriate to the task it had been assigned, and the mood of the deputies as it came to light directly impeded its successful fulfillment. Representatives of the most diverse social circumstances, beliefs, ideas, and levels of development appeared before the government. Alongside Petersburg generals and senators sat elected representatives of the Cheremiss of Kazan and the Teptiars of Orenburg. Summoned to work on one and the same project, and a very complex one, were a member of the Holy Synod, Dimitry Sechenov, the highly educated metropolitan of

Novgorod and Velikie Luki; the deputy of the Meshcheriak service-men of Iset Province in the Urals, Abdullah-Murza Tavyshev; and even a representative of the non-Christian Kazan Chuvash, Aniuk Ishelin. The deputies of the Samoyeds declared in the commission that they were simple people and did not need a code of laws, only that their Russian neighbors and governors be forbidden to oppress them—they needed nothing more. Even two wild animals from Siberia, who had patents of princehood from Tsar Boris Godunov, were sent to the commission: they were the princes Obdorsky and Kunovatsky of the nomads at the mouth of the Ob River. It would be difficult to put together an all-Russian ethnographic exhibition more complete than the Commission of 1767.

These bearers of outlooks so remote from one another merely formed the opposite ends of the long chain of intellectual and moral variations that made up Russian society. The dissonance of needs and opinions that resounded in the deputies' speeches and the clash of interests in the instructions of the different estates were natural. But how was the lawgiver to bring all these voices into harmony, to detect dominant motifs, to extract from these conflicting interests a legislative principle that would reconcile them—as Catherine put it, to sew a garment to fit all these peoples, of whom in Kazan alone she had counted approximately twenty? Moreover, the deputies' instructions and speeches, discordant as they were, were only one of the sources from which the principles of the new code of laws had to be derived.

The Russian codifiers had before them two additional sources: on the one hand, the *Instruction*, which revealed to them the profound political ideas of Western thinkers, and, on the other, the unsorted heap of Russian laws from various times, which lacked any common idea and were often contradictory. Thus the deputies stood amid three completely unrelated sets of ideas and interests. Either the laws did not accord with the articles of the *Instruction* or the needs of the population conflicted with the laws, while in other instances all three said something different. One incident showed the kind of misunderstanding this discord could provoke. As we have seen, among the groups the *Instruction* assigned to the "middling sort" of people, or the urban estate, were those artists and scholars who did not come from the nobility. The subcommission charged with reviewing "the inhabitants of the state" added the clergy to the "middling sort." The Synod objected, maintaining that the clergy was a separate estate and should be equal in rights to the nobility. The subcommission explained that it counted the clergy, as teachers of the people, in the category of scholars. But then the scholars of the Academy of Sciences protested, offended that they were being placed alongside the merchants in the category of people subject to taxes and army recruitment.

Finally, on previous occasions, in 1648 and 1761, elected representatives had been summoned to hear and examine an already prepared draft of a Code of Laws, or parts of it, that had been drawn up by a special governmental commission. Now the deputies formed the commission itself and took a direct part in compiling the draft, which required a great deal of specialized knowledge and an extensive preliminary study of Russian legislation, and there were too few such experts in the commission. Having distributed the parts of the Code of Laws to subcommissions composed of those same deputies, the full assembly, while awaiting their drafts, discussed general questions and read out laws and deputies' instructions in their entirety. This procedure greatly slowed down the pace of business: in a year and a half only one chapter of the Code of Laws was prepared—on the rights of the nobility.

All these inconveniences of the codification process raise the question: Was drawing up a draft of a new Code of Laws the real purpose of the commission? From the beginning of her reign, Catherine had heard talk around her of the need to put Russia's laws in order. Even before the commission, however, she herself had accepted the idea that those laws were completely worthless, and in 1767 she had written from Kazan that there she saw how little they corresponded to the circumstances of the empire: they exasperated a countless number of folk and only destroyed their well-being. When drawing up the manifesto on the convocation of the deputies, she had vacillated as to what path to choose in the manifesto: whether to continue the work that had been begun before her of putting Russia's laws in order by reconciling them with the *Instruction*, or to declare all such efforts fruitless and begin the project "from the other end"—which end, however, she did not specify in the surviving draft. In the manifesto of December 14, 1766, she chose the first path, but if by the second path she had meant a completely new code, the course of affairs in the commission showed her a third path, which was the one she took.

Alongside local needs and class claims in the deputies' instructions, both town and gentry, are statements regarding the absence of physicians, pharmacies, hospitals, almshouses, orphanages, state granaries, banks, post stations, schools—the simplest elements of a well-organized civil society. This was no longer an answer to the government's inquiry of the inhabitants concerning their needs but the inhabitants' question to the government concerning its lack of fulfillment of its obligations. Peter I had begun to introduce those elements, but the pathetic reigns that came after his death failed to continue what he had started and even neglected and undermined it. To judge by the deputies' statements, Russia resembled a ruined or not yet habitable house, containing only bare walls and dark corners, taxpayers and governmental offices. Especially bitter were complaints about the administration of justice: this was just about the sorest point of the instructions, regardless of estate. Nobles complained of the multitude of jurisdictions and were bitterly opposed to bribes. Naively presuming that a government official might be restrained from something by the voice of conscience, both trusting and distrusting that conscience, they proposed binding all those who served in governmental offices by a special oath "not to touch bribes" and subjecting those who violated the oath to a mandatory death penalty, however petty the bribe. They wanted to have nothing to do with the governor's office or other chancelleries aside from their own elected authorities. The noble deputy Lermontov even proposed abolishing the College of Justice as a breeding ground of judicial red tape and slander, with cases to be transmitted from local courts directly to the Senate. Townsmen asked for a reduction in the number of courts and for the fining of judges, while single homesteaders and state peasants asked "that no matters pertaining to them except tax assessment be conducted in governmental offices."

The estates shunned the crown courts and administrative institutions as though they were refuges of the Evil Spirit. Instead of the expensive formal courts, with their protracted written procedure, gentry, townsmen, and peasants alike requested a nearby, swift, and inexpensive oral court for petty cases (of the first instance), with judges elected from their own ranks to whom the police would also be subordinated, or special elected officials to whom police matters would be entrusted. Nobles proposed the establishment of justices of the peace after the example of England and Holland. In connection with elected courts, a tendency emerged to close ranks in estate associations, to organize on a corporate basis. The town instructions expressed the desire that the post of mayor, temporarily created for the election of deputies to the commission, become permanent and that mayors be chosen "by all citizens in general." The single homesteaders and peasants petitioned for the election of judges "by the whole society of the whole district" and from the latter's ranks—but not from the gentry, who act "according to their own customs," demanding carts, foodstuffs, and other things and giving beatings when peasants object.

This corporate sentiment expressed itself with particular force in the nobles' instructions, combining with their claim to occupy the dominant position in provincial society and administration. Nobles petitioned for periodic district congresses, which would have the right to supervise the course of affairs in the district and, in the event of a violation of the law or oppression on the part of judges and officials, to inform the Senate. At the congresses, judicial and police authorities would be chosen, to whom not only the nobles and their serfs but also the "economic" and court peasants would be subject. Some instructions even wanted to replace the crown administration of the district with one elected by the nobility and asked that this estate be given the right to elect commandants and vice-commandants.

Standing out sharply from the general level was the unique instruction of the Dmitrov nobility. Beautifully written, it was completely devoid of pretensions. It recognized as the chief local deficiency of the gentry the constant quarreling and violence between the peasants of different owners, with which neither individual owners nor the protracted and "almost endless" crown courts, with their instances and written procedure, were able to cope. To provide a swift, nearby, and inexpensive court for these usually petty cases, the instruction proposed dividing a district into four circuits, each headed by a land judge elected from the nobility. These judges, acting under the guidance of the marshal, "with the greatest dispatch" would resolve suits between serfs orally, punishing the guilty peasants and "pacifying the landowners amicably." Every year the nobility would come together, elect a marshal (every two years) and new land judges, and receive a report from the previous ones. At the conclusion of the elections, the congress would turn into an agricultural conference: the nobles would exchange ideas on farming, inform each other of measures for putting their villages in order and of their agronomy experiments, devise new experiments, and assign them to each other. In addition, the marshal and the land judges would be required to persuade the gentry to teach their children useful sciences and languages, striving especially for a good knowledge of their native tongue. Also, they were "to urge strongly" that landowners hire a skilled teacher for each one hundred peasant homesteads to instruct peasant children in reading and writing and the first principles of arithmetic, explaining to each landowner how much more useful a literate peasant would be to him. "It is not just for plowing that the state needs the peasant, while literacy will not prevent him from tilling the soil, the more so as those years in which children may be taught reading and writing go almost entirely to waste." The marshal would also remind the landowners how an excessive number of house servants ruined them and persuade them all in every way possible "to prescribe a law to themselves" "that no one let the least bit of land lie idle," with the land judges to look after this matter.

Educated men, imbued with a sense of duty to their fatherland, called on their landowning brethren to work locally for agriculture and peasant enlightenment, protected from the state authorities by modest self-government. The same inclination toward local activity, though in the crude forms of class egotism and domination, along with usurpation of the rights of others, runs as a very perceptible thread through other noble instructions as well. The demarcation of estates on which Prince Shcherbatov insisted and the precise apportionment of rights among estates that had closed ranks in local associations were the predominant interests of the classes represented in the commission on the new Code of Laws. But they did not content themselves with the codification of their rights: articles of the law were playthings in the hands of government clerks. The instructions wanted the articles on the rights of the estates to be developed into elective estate institutions, which would not be circumvented so easily. This desire, so insistently expressed, helped Catherine end her vacillations regarding the nature of the new Code of Laws she had planned. Seeing that neither a codification of the old laws nor a new code in the spirit of the *Instruction* would issue from the work of the commission, she turned her thoughts to provincial reform.

For us, the main significance of the Commission of 1767 lies in the concern for estate rights that predominated in the deputies' speeches and instructions. Catherine assessed this significance in her own way. She praised the commission, comparing it to the French representative assemblies under Calonne and Necker, and wrote: "My assembly of deputies proved successful because I said to them: you know what my principles are; now voice your complaints. Where does the boot pinch your foot? We will try to fix it." Many years later, not long before her death, Catherine recalled that the Commission had given her "light and information on the whole empire, whom we were dealing with and whom we had to tend." She did not explain how she understood the society with which she was dealing, but society well understood the moment Catherine afforded it with her commission. Hitherto, lawmaking had concentrated most zealously on one element of state organization—state taxes. Society had been partitioned according to the kinds of obligations assigned to its classes. It knew no rights in the political sense; it was given only advantages (or privileges, preferences) as auxiliary means for fulfilling estate obligations. After the death of Peter I, however, one estate began to receive preferences that were not only unconnected with new burdens but were even accompanied by an easing of the old ones. This was taken as an injustice by the estates that were left out, and it imbued them with corresponding feelings toward the government and the gentry—feelings sharply expressed in ever-increasing peasant disturbances.

Even before her accession, Catherine had devised a method for averting legislative mistakes—spreading a rumor in the marketplace about an intended law and eavesdropping on what was said about it. Now, with the same objective, a representative assembly was convened in which "the voice of the people" could be heard. What was heard there, however, was a dissonance no better than that of the marketplace. One deputy advanced a new ecclesiastical dogma of the holiness of the nobility, while another was charged in his instruction with petitioning that military servicemen—usually those same nobles—refrain from insulting and beating merchants and pay for the goods they took from them. The deputies' speeches sounded such discordant notes that well-meaning deputies considered it their duty in the name of the *Instruction* to appeal to the assembly for peace, mutual love, and like-minded agreement. To the demand that nobles be freed from corporal punishment, torture, and the death penalty, deputies from the towns sharply objected that neither Holy Writ nor natural law tolerated partiality; that a thief is always a thief, be he baseborn (a commoner) or noble, and, besides, nobility is maintained only through noble actions; and that in Russia the government is monarchical, not aristocratic, and both the baseborn and the noble are equally subjects of the all-merciful sovereign. In short, a legal turning point in political consciousness had taken place with the permission of the government.

It had asked its subjects what they lacked, and the subjects had replied: estate rights and estate self-government. It is difficult to say what would have come out of the promised second convocation of the commission, but even without it legislation willy-nilly had to be recast from a system of obligations into a system of rights.

The demand for rights is the most characteristic symptom of Russian society's mood at this time, and the commission brought it to light. In doing so, it showed Catherine not only where to direct her reform efforts but also what should be done in that quarter. More than a hundred years earlier, elected representatives of the estates had been summoned to hear the Code of Laws of 1649, to supplement it, and to ratify it with their signatures. That code had consolidated the partition of society according to its obligations to the state, and Muscovite legislation had tended to those obligations with the greatest care. Each class was bound to state service by a specific requirement, which was joined to a particular economic benefit—landholding, urban trade, or farming—to help it scrupulously fulfill that requirement. Meeting again in 1767, deputies of the estates saw that their social structure and moral make-up had not budged from the foundations laid down by the Code of Laws of 1649, that their interests and ideas were rooted in the same division of estates that had been confirmed by the code. But now the deputies came with other thoughts, because they had been called together for other purposes. On the previous occasion, a draft of the Code of Laws had been read to the elected representatives in order to find out whether or not the "land" could bear the system of requirements that was being proposed for it. Grudgingly, the elected representatives had replied in the affirmative, merely petitioning for certain advantages to alleviate the burden. At times, especially under Peter I, the burden became unbearable and the service and taxed people fell on hard times. Assemblies of the Land were not convened, however, and popular discontent expressed itself either in uprisings and petty local disorders, which were brutally suppressed, or in peaceful complaints, which at best received no attention. Meanwhile, Peter's reforms confused the allocation of state obligations and economic benefits to the estates; they gave factory-owning merchants noble privileges, drew nobles into industrial enterprises, and made military service an obligation of all the estates. This practice of generalizing specific estate requirements and preferences, accompanied at the same time by a consistent legislative program that emancipated the estates, would have led to their equalization by virtue of common rights and obligations. But the accidental governments after Peter's death began to invest one estate with preferences unconnected with new burdens and even accompanied by an alleviation of the old ones. Such a one-sided emancipation severed that estate's obligations from the economic benefit associated with them and turned that benefit into a pure, totally unjustified privilege.

In the lower ranks of society, this violation of the balance between right and obligation was felt to be a political injustice, and at the beginning of Catherine's reign, rumors spread among the people that the gentry had forgotten divine law and the laws of the state and had banished justice from the Russian land. But within the gentry itself and the classes that stood closer to it on the social ladder (which Catherine combined under the rubric of "the middling sort of people"), this juridical contradiction was understood as a class right. Each of these estates, while defending its old privileges and seeking to obtain those of others, tried to evade the obligations associated with them, that is, they tried to shift them onto other classes. Hence, rivalry over estate rights is the strongest current that runs through the deputies' instructions and debates in the commission. Behind this rivalry, however, are glimmers of a certain advance in social consciousness, of some progress of civic sentiment: class egotism shyly tries to camouflage itself with specious motives or meets with a rebuff from individuals or certain social groups.

Catherine later wrote of her *Instruction* that it introduced far more unity into principles and arguments than had been the case previously, and "many people began to judge colors by their color, and not as blind people judge them; at the very least, they began to know the will of the lawgiver and to act in accordance with it." The *Instruction* was distributed to the deputies and was read in the full assembly and the subcommissions at the beginning of each month; it was cited in the debates, and the procurator-general and the marshal were not supposed to allow anything into the enactments of the commission contrary to the sense of the *Instruction*. Catherine even thought of prescribing that it be read in all the judicial institutions of the empire on the anniversary of its publication. But the Senate, with the knowledge of the empress, of course, gave it a special classification and circulated it only to the higher central institutions, withholding it from provincial governmental offices. Even in the central institutions it was made available only to qualified members; neither rank-and-file clerks nor outsiders were allowed to copy it or even to read it. The *Instruction* always reposed on the judicial bench, but only on Saturdays, when routine business was not being conducted, would those members read it, in an intimate circle, the way a prohibited book is read to selected guests secluded in a study. The *Instruction* was not intended for the public. It served as a guide only for the ruling circles, and only through their manners and actions were the subordinate and the governed allowed to experience for themselves the qualities of the maxims that the supreme power deemed it necessary to propagate for the good of its subjects. The *Instruction* was supposed to illuminate the stage and the auditorium like a lamp that itself remains invisible. The Senate devised this theatrical illusion to prevent misinterpretations by the people, but the very secretiveness of the *Instruction* could only foster the spread of rumors about new laws of some kind. The deputies and officials who read or heard the *Instruction* drew from it some new ideas, blossoms of thought, but their impact on the government and on society's way of thinking is hard to detect. Only Catherine herself in subsequent decrees, especially on matters concerning torture, reminded the appropriate authorities that the articles of the *Instruction* were binding acts and—to her honor, it should be added—sternly insisted "that no one under interrogation is to be subjected to bodily torture in any form."

Despite its weak practical impact, the *Instruction* remains a characteristic phenomenon of the reign, in the spirit of Catherine's entire domestic policy. She wrote to Frederick II in explanation of her work that she had to accommodate herself to the present, without, however, blocking the path to a more propitious future. With her *Instruction* Catherine put into circulation in Russia, albeit to a very restricted degree, many ideas that were not only new to Russia but had not even been fully assimilated into the political life of the West. She made no haste to embody them in facts, to build a Russian political order in accordance with them, reasoning that they might be only ideas, but sooner or later they would produce their own facts, the way causes produce effects.

By 1775 Catherine had concluded three difficult wars: with Poland; with Turkey; and with her own resurrected husband, the "Marquis de Pugachev," as she called him. With leisure, her disease, "legislomania," as she termed it, also returned. The idea of a new Code of Laws was not entirely abandoned—the subcommissions continued their work—but Catherine had no thought of convening the full assembly. Another legislative enterprise enticed her. A variety of motives drew her attention to this quarter. In an instruction to the governors in 1764, she had recognized that the gubernias were the parts of the state "that most of all require improvement," and she promised in time to take up this task. The local administration had just displayed its shortcomings, having been unable either to prevent the Pugachev conflagration or to extinguish it promptly. Moreover, all the estates represented at the Commission of 1767 had insistently and unanimously expressed the desire to conduct their own affairs through their elected representatives.

~ VII ~

Reform of Provincial Government

The commission failed to draft a new Code of Laws, but the deputies' instructions and debates revealed the needs and desires of the various classes of the population. Catherine herself valued the commission from this point of view, writing that it gave her "light and information" on whom she was dealing with and whom she had to tend. The new provincial institutions she introduced were the first practical application of her solicitude.

We need to recall the changes Peter I made in the structure of the central and local government. The old administration of the Muscovite state had had a dual character: it contained both estate and bureaucratic elements. Peter did not eliminate that dual character; he merely divided its formerly intermingled elements between two different spheres of government. The central administration was given a purely bureaucratic character and staff, while the estate element was maintained in the local administration through the participation of two classes of society. Peter's successors substantively altered the provincial administrative structure he had created. They found his governmental mechanism too complex, and they began to close numerous offices and chancelleries that they deemed superfluous and to merge departments that they considered overly subdivided. Peter had expended a great deal of effort to separate the courts from the administration in provincial government, and in the main gubernia towns he had instituted high courts[1] that operated independently of the governors. Under Catherine I, these high courts were abolished, and justice was entrusted to the administrative organs of the central government—the governors and commandants.

Similarly, Peter had concerned himself with the development of municipal self-government, having first created town ratushas[2] and then town magistracies, which also operated independently of the governors, under the supervision of a chief magistracy in Petersburg. In 1727, during the reign of Catherine I, the town magistracies were subordinated to the governors, and in the same year, during Peter II's reign, the chief magistracy was abolished altogether, while the town magistracies were given a simpler composition: they were turned into the old ratushas but with just a civil jurisdiction. Thus, the estate element in provincial administration was weakened after Peter's death, and participation by the classes of local society was restricted. Provincial administration remained in this form until Catherine II.

Transformation of the central administration began to take a very different course. The old, customary directors of that administration, the boyars, had been destroyed. Their place was taken by a new official elite consisting of promoted administrators. Partly in accordance with habits and traditions inherited from the old boyars and partly under the influence of familiarity with the political systems of Western Europe, this officialdom adopted some of the political mannerisms of an aristocracy and sought to transform itself from a mere governmental instrument into a governmental class, an autonomous political force. It may therefore be termed an official aristocracy. Under the influence of its tastes and aspirations, changes were introduced in the central administration after Peter's death. In order to give a privileged place to the representatives of this elite, who did not want to be lost in the crowd of senators, a series of new, higher institutions with legislative authority arose over the Senate, which was the supreme supervisor and monitor of the administration and the courts. There was the Supreme Privy Council under Catherine I and Peter II, the Cabinet of Ministers under Anna, the Conference under Elizabeth, and the nine-member Council under Peter III.

---

[1]*Gofgerikhty* (from the German *Hofgerichte*), or, in Russian, *nadvornye sudy*, established by Peter in 1719. These were courts under the jurisdiction of the central College of Justice rather than the provincial governors.

[2]*Ratusha*, from the German *Rathaus*.

The aspirations of the official aristocracy manifested themselves in a distinctive fashion in another area, too. The most bureaucratic element in the collegial institutions of the government was the procuracy, headed by the procurator-general of the Senate. The procuracy was the "eye of the sovereign," the guardian of the laws. Naturally, it inhibited the official aristocracy. As a result, soon after Peter's death something unexpected occurred: suddenly, in 1730, the procurator-general, the procurator of the Senate, and the ordinary procurators in the Colleges disappeared, and no one knew where they had gone, although the men who had occupied those posts were still alive. The former procurator-general Yaguzhinsky, for example, was still living at the time. In her manifesto of October 2, 1730, which restored the procuracy, Empress Anna admitted that "we do not know by what decree this office was set aside after the death of our uncle, or by whom it was abolished." Restored under Anna, the procuracy was abolished a second time during the regency of Anna Leopoldovna, and it is interesting that the culprit was none other than one of the distinguished representatives of the official aristocracy, Count Ostermann, who bore the rank of admiral of the fleet and was in charge of Russia's foreign affairs. Thus the official element began to grow stronger in the central administration at the same time that the participation of the "land," that is, the estate element, was on the decline in provincial administration.

As a result of all these changes, one class was given preference over the law at the center of the state, while individuals were given preference over the classes of society in the provinces. Freed from the pressure of the old elite at the center and from the supervision of society in the provinces, the new official aristocracy introduced into the government an unrestrained personal despotism that undermined the administrative order Peter had built.

Catherine was well aware of the defects in the administration. In a secret instruction to the procurator-general, Prince Viazemsky, she wrote that "all the governmental offices and the Senate itself have come loose from their foundations," in part because of her predecessors' negligence, in part "because of the weaknesses of the accidental persons in them." Catherine clearly recognized the task before her: she had to give the governmental offices firm foundations and set out precise laws and limits for their operation. These two promises had been solemnly made in the July manifesto of 1762.

A man close to Catherine hastened to present her with a plan for an institution based precisely on those principles. Count Nikita Panin, soon after the coup d'état, submitted a proposal to the empress for a permanent State Council. Count Nikita was not entirely alien to the aristocratic ideas of 1730. His long sojourn as ambassador in Stockholm had not been in vain, and the Swedish State Council, with its aristocratic membership, was his model of a supreme governmental institution. Panin's basic idea was that "the authority of the sovereign will operate with benefit only when it is intelligently divided among a small number of persons specially chosen for that purpose." The simple meaning of this abstruse expression is explained in his account of the source from which the principal shortcomings of the existing order arose. That source, in Panin's opinion, was the fact that the administration functioned on the basis of "the force of persons" rather than "the authority of state institutions," and also the fact that the government lacked certain basic foundations that would impart greater stability to its structural forms. To put it more simply, Panin meant to say that in Russia there were no fundamental laws that might restrain personal arbitrariness. Catherine was on the point of accepting Panin's proposal and had even signed the manifesto for the new permanent council— she had even appointed its members—but someone explained the meaning of Panin's idea to her, and the signed manifesto remained unpublished.

From time to time, Catherine convened a conference of intimates on important questions, but this conference was not an institution that was binding on her, as Panin's permanent council would have been, for it was not recognized by an actual law. Thus the central government under Catherine remained as undefined and disorganized as it had been before.

Provincial administration was suitable soil in which Catherine might sow the political ideas she had borrowed from her favorite works. Special considerations, moreover, impelled her to turn her primary attention to reorganizing the provincial administration. In the first place, in 1773–74, soon after the termination of the work of the Commission for the Compilation of the Draft of a New Code of Laws, the terrible Pugachev uprising broke out, which the local administration was unable either to prevent or to suppress promptly. In the second place, the noble deputies to the codification commission of 1767 had insisted with particular vigor precisely on the reorganization of the provincial administration. These were the incentives for the "Statute

for the Administration of the Gubernias," which was published on
November 7, 1775.

I will give a brief outline of this legislative document. The manifesto of November 7, 1775, which accompanied the publication of the
"Statute," pointed out the following defects in the existing provincial
administration: first, the administrative regions represented by the
gubernias were too vast; second, they were provided with an insufficient number of institutions, which were meagerly staffed; third, within
the administration different departments were lumped together—one
and the same office was in charge of administration proper as well as
financial matters and the courts, both criminal and civil. The new
gubernia institutions were designed to eliminate these defects. First of
all, Catherine carried out a new division of the provincial units: instead
of the twenty vast gubernias into which Russia was then divided, the
whole empire was redivided into fifty gubernias. The boundaries of the
old gubernias and regions had been based partly on geographical factors and partly on historical characteristics or circumstances.
Catherine's provincial units were based exclusively on population size.
The gubernias were regions of 300,000–400,000 inhabitants and were
subdivided into districts of 20,000–30,000 inhabitants.

Each gubernia was given a uniform organization, both administrative and judicial. The principal institution in the administrative system
was the *gubernia board*, headed by a *governor* or *governor-general*.
This was an executive, a police, and a managerial institution: it published and put into effect in the gubernia the decrees and instructions
of the supreme government, supervised the regular flow of business in
other institutions, compelled them to carry out their duties, kept governmental offices in good repair, and maintained peace and tranquility
in the gubernia. The district organ of the gubernia administration was
the *lower land court*, under the presidency of a land superintendent, or
captain; this was also an executive and police institution. The land
captain implemented the edicts of the gubernia departments; supervised commerce in the district; took measures to prevent epidemics,
concerned himself with "the preservation and health of humanity";
watched over the repair of roads and bridges as well as over the moral-
ity and political reliability of the inhabitants of the district; assisted the
courts (meaning that he carried out preliminary investigations); and in
general acted, as the law put it, "zealously and with careful gentleness,
benevolence, and philanthropy in regard to the people." The authority

of the land captain extended to the entire district, with the exception of the district town; here, a police chief,[3] or commandant, corresponded to him. Financial administration was concentrated in the *Fiscal Chamber*, which was in charge of revenue collections, contracts, and construction. The gubernia and district *treasuries*, which held revenue receipts, were subordinated to the Fiscal Chamber.

The courts were given an extremely complex structure. Two chambers formed the highest judicial instances at the gubernia level: the *Criminal-Affairs Chamber* and the *Civil-Affairs Chamber*. These were judicial institutions for all the estates. Cases were assigned within them strictly on the basis of their substance. Below these judicial institutions in the gubernia were class courts in which cases were mixed by substance but divided by estate: a *superior land court* for nobles, a *gubernia magistracy* for merchants and town dwellers, and a *superior tribunal* for free rural inhabitants. The two higher judicial instances were located in the gubernia seat. Lower instances were dispersed in the district towns: a *district court* for nobles, a *town magistracy* for merchants and town dwellers, and a *lower tribunal* for free rural inhabitants. In addition, police administration of the district was centered in the *lower land court* under the presidency of the land captain. Estate courts on the district level were subordinated to estate courts on the gubernia level, and the latter to non-estate chambers with an appellate and review function, that is, cases were transferred from a lower instance to the highest on appeal by the litigants, for verification of decisions made by the lower instance, or for pronouncement of a final decision.

Additional judicial institutions with specialized functions were formed in the gubernia seats. Some criminal and civil cases of a special nature were concentrated in the *gubernia conscience court*. The conscience court dealt with those criminal cases in which the source of the crime was not the conscious will of the criminal but either an accident or a physical or moral deficiency—minority, weakness of mind, fanaticism, superstition, and so forth. The conscience court dealt with those civil cases that the litigants themselves brought before it. In such cases, the conscience court operated like our "peace court":[4] it was supposed to seek first of all to reconcile the parties. For the administration of educational institutions, almshouses, orphanages, and other charitable

---

[3]The *gorodnichii*, an appointed urban official.

[4]The judicial reform of 1864 created elected justices of the peace on the local level.

institutions, an *office of social welfare* was created. In their composition, both the conscience court and the office of social welfare were all-estate institutions. Their assessors were elected from the three main classes of local society. In addition, guardianship offices were created in the district-level estate courts: in the nobles' district court a *nobles' guardianship*, under the presidency of the district marshal of the nobility, to administer the affairs of noble widows and orphans; and in the town magistracy an *orphans' court*, under the presidency of the district town's mayor, for the guardianship of widows and orphans of merchants and town dwellers.

The unusual complexity of the gubernia governmental mechanism Catherine created is readily apparent. We see, first of all, the particularly strong influence exerted on these institutions by the ideas that were being disseminated at the time in the political literature of the West, most of all the idea of the separation of powers. Without a strict separation of powers—legislative, executive (or administrative), and judicial—the progressive writer of the time could not conceive of a proper organization of the state. Catherine paid very generous tribute to this idea in her gubernia institutions.

The complex structure of the estate courts came from another source. To be sure, the *Instruction* repeated Beccaria's idea that it was useful for the proper administration of justice to establish a court of peers so as to limit the pressure exerted on the court by the upper classes, the nobility and clergy. But in spite of the idea expressed in the *Instruction* of the equality of all before the law, the estate courts that were created smacked of something feudal, the medieval division of estates. This source can readily be discerned if we review the instructions of the noble deputies to the Commission of 1767. Many instructions expressed the decided wish of this estate to organize itself into district corporations and to take an active part in local administration and justice. For the election of deputies to the commission, the nobility had assembled by district and elected district marshals. Now, in the commission, the nobles expressed the desire to retain the right to elect district marshals, to assemble at certain intervals, and to monitor the operation of the local administration. Some instructions even demanded that the district administrators, the commandants, be chosen by the local gentry. Procedures for the nobility's participation in the administration were defined with particular precision in the instruction of the Borovsk nobles: it demanded that the district nobility assemble for a congress every two years and elect a candidate from the whole district who would function with the assistance of an elected commissar from each precinct, or subdistrict. The district *Landrat* would administer justice to members of all estates; the precinct or subdistrict commissar would assist him in the conduct of preliminary investigations.

The gubernia institutions of 1775 distinctly reflected the desires expressed in the nobles' instructions. Obviously, the idea of a district *Landrat* was embodied in the person of the district land captain; only the idea of a subdistrict commissar, or precinct constable, was postponed, to be realized subsequently in the reign of Emperor Nicholas I.

Thus, the desires expressed by the gentry formed the source of the contradiction discernible in the structure of the gubernia institutions. The legislator, guided by progressive West European writers, clashed with the nobles, who were guided by practical East European interests. If we examine the personnel of the administrative and judicial institutions Catherine created, it is readily apparent that this contradiction was inspired by the interests of one estate. The idea that everyone should be judged by his peers, as expressed in the *Instruction*, was not consistently followed in the gubernia institutions. As we saw, those institutions consisted of three layers. The topmost layer was composed of non-estate institutions: the gubernia board, the fiscal chamber, and the criminal- and civil-affairs chambers. All the personnel of those institutions were appointed by the crown, without any participation by local society.

The second layer consisted of estate courts on the gubernia level (the superior land court, the gubernia magistracy, and the superior tribunal), as well as all-estate institutions (the conscience court and the office of social welfare). The personnel of the institutions in this second layer were of a mixed character: the president was appointed by the crown, but the other members, called councillors and assessors, were in each institution elected by a certain estate and in the conscience court and the office of social welfare by all three estates. In the third and lowest layer, consisting of district courts and the lower (police) land court, the institutions were collegial but their personnel was drawn entirely from the "land": both the president and the assessors were elected by the estates. Only the president, or judge, of the lower tribunal, which dealt with cases of free farmers, was an official appointed by a higher local authority. To all appearances, participation in local administration and the courts at the lowest and middle levels was divided fairly evenly among all the classes of society. It is quite evident, however, that a certain predominance was given to one estate—the nobility. The lower land court was a police institution for the entire district (although its assessors in cases involving free farmers included the assessors of the lower tribunal), but the president of the lower land court, the land captain, was elected only by the nobility. Moreover, not all districts had lower tribunals: their opening was left to the discretion of the governors, and they were instituted only in those regions where there was a sufficient number of people—between 10,000 and 30,000 souls—belonging to the categories over which they had jurisdiction.

Thus police order in the district, the maintenance of safety and tranquility and a court without distinction by estate were concentrated in noble institutions. There was another form, too, in which the predominance of one class was expressed—in the gubernia administration. The highest gubernia institutions did not have a class character, but the government usually recruited the personnel of those institutions from the same class whose representatives were elected to the nobility's estate institutions: the governor and the president and assessors of the highest gubernia administrative and judicial institutions, as well as of the chambers, by origin usually belonged to the gentry. Thus the predominant position of the nobility in local administration was expressed in two forms: (1) in the election of the personnel of the nobility's estate institutions, and (2) in the noble origin of the personnel of non-estate institutions. As a result of this predominance, the nobility became the leading class in the local as well as the central administration. The noble held sway in the local administration as the elected representative of his estate; he held sway there also as a crown official appointed by the supreme authority.

After some time the structure of the provincial administration was crowned by two estate charters, to the nobility and to the towns. Both of these charters were signed on the same day, April 21, 1785. The following are their main features. The Charter to the Nobility completed the corporate structure of the noble estate: over the district noble assemblies and their marshals, which had convened for the first time to elect deputies to the Commission of 1767, gubernia noble assemblies headed by gubernia marshals now arose. The gubernia institutions of 1775 were introduced over the course of some twenty years, and once they were established the nobles of all the districts traveled to the gubernia seat and elected gubernia representatives of the nobility. The nobility's right to elect gubernia marshals was recognized in the charter of 1785. This charter at last defined the rights of the nobility: a noble enjoyed full ownership rights to his immovable property and his peasants, transmitted his rank to his wife and children, and could not be deprived of that rank except by trial for certain crimes; a noble's conviction of a crime required confirmation by the supreme power. A noble was freed from personal taxes, from army recruitment, and from corporal punishment. Noble assemblies had the right to petition the supreme government in regard to the needs of their estate.

The urban categories of the population also received a definitive organization. Until this time, judicial affairs and the maintenance of order in the towns were centered in the gubernia and town magistracies. Under the Charter to the Towns of the Russian Empire of 1785, alongside the magistracy as a judicial institution, there now arose municipal police and economic institutions. The town population was divided into six categories: distinguished citizens; actual residents (meaning those who owned houses and land in the town and did not engage in trade and industry); guild merchants; artisans; "guests" (or merchants from foreign countries and other towns); and, finally, tradespeople, who earned their living by unskilled labor or a handicraft and did not own real estate in the town. These categories were differentiated either on the basis of their origin or according to the size of their capital. Thus, merchants were divided into three guilds: the lowest amount of capital for merchants of the third guild was 1,000 rubles. Traders who did not have that much capital were counted as ordinary townsmen and were assigned to the artisan guilds. Two councils directed the urban economy and administration: a *general council* and a *six-member council*. The general council, under the presidency of a mayor, consisted of members from all the categories and had a managerial function, meeting at certain intervals or as need arose. The six-member council, consisting of one councillor from each of the six categories, also under the presidency of the mayor, was an executive institution and operated continuously, meeting on a weekly basis.

The two systems of self-government, the noble and the urban, did not develop with the same degree of success. The gubernia institutions brought an unaccustomed vitality into the life of the provincial gentry. Every three years, nobles came together in the gubernia seat and held elections for various positions amid the feasts and entertainments to which their brothers, the gubernia marshal and the governor, treated them. By contrast, urban administration operated very sluggishly under the heavy hand of the governor or governor-general. The liveliness that distinguished the nobility's estate institutions even prompted foreigners to exaggerate their danger: two Frenchmen traveling in Russia at the beginning of the 1790s, after hearing the nobility's speeches, predicted in their memoirs that "sooner or later these assemblies will surely lead to a great revolution."

It now remains for us to explain the reasons for the particular success of noble self-government alongside the weak operation of urban self-government. To do so, let us turn back for a moment to the history of the gentry.

The provincial and estate institutions were worked out under the distinct influence of (1) the political ideas Catherine borrowed from the literature of Western Europe, and (2) indigenous needs and influences. The influence of those political ideas on the organization of local administration in Russia, however, was almost exclusively formal: they found reflection in the technical details of the institutions, their forms, procedures, and mutual relations; and they manifested themselves in the strict division of departments and the delineation of the bounds of activity of the separate institutions; but the new principles were introduced inconsistently and did not exert an appreciable influence on the spirit of the new institutions. To be sure, two institutions were created, at the basis of which lay tasks unknown to the administration of old Rus. These were the office of social welfare, which oversaw educational and philanthropic institutions, and the conscience court, which decided cases on the basis of "conscience" rather than formal evidence. In the earlier governmental system, there had been no special department for popular education or public philanthropy, either in the central or in the local institutions; now there were gubernia offices of social welfare. Nor had conscience courts existed, either in the previous judicial system in Russia or in any of the other countries of Europe at the time. Curiously, however, these were precisely the two institutions that had the least appreciable effect and exerted the least impact on the course of affairs. The office of social welfare appeared at a time when there were practically no popular schools, nor were the towns given the resources to initiate them. The conscience court was established under conditions that paralyzed its activity. Thus in civil cases the conscience court, like a peace court, decided cases brought before it by agreement of the contesting parties.

If the innocent party was disposed to bring a case before the conscience court, the guilty party would oppose it, and then, not only could the conscience court not consider the case, it could not compel the resisting party to appear in court.

The institution of a conscience court was loudly hailed both in Russia and, especially, abroad. The French writer Mercier de la Rivière, with whom Catherine was acquainted, greeted this institution with the following ecstatic words: "The dawn of the prosperity of mankind has broken in the North. Sovereigns of the world, lawgivers of nations, hasten to the northern Semiramis, and kneeling before her be instructed: she is the first to establish a conscience court!" The judge of the conscience court of Ufa, however, admitted that in the twelve years of his judgeship not even twelve cases had come before his court, because his valet, at the request of the guilty parties, usually drove away all the petitioners who turned to it. According to the testimony of contemporaries, the same was true of the other conscience courts: in Catherine's entire reign, not even ten cases can be counted in all the conscience courts that were decided in a proper manner.

On the other hand, Catherine's gubernia institutions intensified the contradictions Peter's reforms had created in the administration. It is well known that an administration functions properly only when it rests on identical principles both at the center and at the local level. Under Catherine, the estate element Peter had introduced into the provincial administration was strengthened: the gubernia institutions allowed greater scope for the participation of the gentry and the urban population in local administration. But the central administration, which preserved its old bureaucratic character under Catherine, lacked even the ties with society that had existed in the seventeenth century. Thus the contradiction between the principles on which the administration rested at the center and in the provinces grew still more acute under Catherine.

At the same time, the predominance of the nobility further upset the balance of rights and obligations of the different classes of society. Previously, the gentry had had an importance in local administration commensurate with its state obligations. Now it was given an even greater importance in local administration after being freed of its most serious state duties. Second, the gubernia institutions were based on a principle that had been put forth in the *Instruction*, the principle that individuals of each status should be judged and administered by people of the same status. In its practical development, however, this principle was converted into the decided predominance of one estate, the nobility, in local administration.

Finally, an important defect of the administrative and judicial system Catherine created was its extreme complexity. Thus, as a result of the strict division of departments and the complex court structure, the number of officials, both elected and appointed, multiplied inordinately; where ten or fifteen officials had conducted business previously, there were now fully a hundred. This increased the high cost of the administration.

Much more important is the role of the gubernia and estate institutions in the history of our *society*. They expressed a characteristic tendency of the era we are studying: they carried out the state's emancipation of the two highest classes of society. We saw that the Charter to the Nobility formulated the rights of the nobles that had been created by earlier legislation; in the same way, the Charter to the Towns formulated the rights of the urban population. The latter were not distributed among all the urban classes in equal measure, but taken as a whole they emancipated the urban population by removing the special state obligations that had been imposed on it in old Rus. The urban groups received estate self-government and estate courts. Furthermore, guild citizens, that is, the uppermost stratum of the urban population, were freed from the soul tax, which was replaced by a 1 percent levy on the capital a merchant declared on his honor. Guild citizens were also freed from personal army recruitment: the citizen-merchant could redeem his personal service with a monetary payment. In addition, all guild citizens and townsmen were freed from fiscal "services" or "orders" for the collection of various kinds of excises, which in old Rus constituted the heaviest obligation of the urban population. Finally, merchants of the first two guilds were freed from corporal punishment, and the highest stratum of merchants, bearing the designation "distinguished citizens," could attain nobility under certain conditions.

Thus, the gubernia institutions and the estate charters were the first acts in the history of our society in which the rights of the two estates were formulated precisely and in detail and by which their special state obligations were removed.

This development is connected with another aspect of the gubernia institutions that is of even greater importance in the history of our society. As we have seen, the allocation of state obligations to the different estates in the seventeenth century destroyed their mutual ties and eliminated their joint activity. As a result of their estrangement, the Assemblies of the Land declined in the course of the seventeenth century. From then on, each estate bore its service and acted alone, lacking ties with any other estate. In the gubernia institutions, Catherine for the first time made an attempt to bring the estates together again to act in concert. In the office of social welfare and in the conscience courts and lower land courts, assessors elected by the three free estates—the nobility, the urban population, and the class of free rural inhabitants— worked under the direction of representatives of the crown. To be sure, those two institutions, as we have seen, occupied a secondary place in the structure of the local administration, but they are important as the first glimmer of the idea of restoring the joint activity of the estates, and this constitutes one of the best features of Catherine's gubernia institutions.

The gubernia institutions were of the greatest importance, however, in the history of the gentry: they consolidated its decided predominance in the local administration. As we have seen, that predominance was expressed in two forms: in the elected personnel of the nobility's estate institutions, and in the noble origin of the personnel of the all-estate crown institutions.

From now on, the nobility dominated the local administration, which completely depended on it. Urban self-government, under the supervision of a noble governor, developed slowly and worked sluggishly; noble self-government, on the other hand, proceeded briskly. The reason for the more successful development of noble self-government was the nobility's historical preparation for independent activity. In this respect, the gubernia institutions of 1775 and the Charter to the Nobility that completed them were merely the full realization of a long-standing desire on the part of this estate. We know that in old Rus the gentry (the men of service) formed tightly knit estate corporations by district. The basis for these district associations was service and the holding of service lands. The members of the gentry of a district defended the district town and formed its garrison. They went on campaigns in territorial, district regiments; elected officials from their ranks to deal with matters of service and land; and, finally, were bound to each other by a pledge of collective responsibility.

The creation of a regular army under Peter, if it did not destroy these district corporations, seriously undermined them. Regular regiments, which had no territorial basis, replaced the district militias. Thus, instead of district corporations, regimental corporations made their appearance. Officers of regiments and divisions formed companies, or corporations, and under Peter's laws all the officers of a regiment elected and pledged responsibility for the regiment's senior officers, and all the officers and generals of a division elected and pledged responsibility for staff officers. In setting up these regimental gentry corporations, however, Peter tried also to maintain the gentry's old local, provincial associations. At the end of his reign, the gentry was assuming a considerable importance in the national economy. The government began to regard this estate as its staff and police agents in the countryside. Therefore, even Peter tried to maintain the connection, based on land ownership, between gentry and police by granting the gentry participation in local administration. That participation was expressed, as we know, in the election of *Landrat*s, or councillors to the governor, by the gentry of a gubernia and in the election of district land commissars.

After Peter's death, as the gentry's service obligations grew weaker, its ties with the provinces grew stronger, and thus its corporate solidarity intensified. From the time of the December law of 1730, which recognized conditional estates along with patrimonial estates as the full hereditary property of the gentry, the latter became more settled and its landholding position in the provinces grew more stable. The law of February 18, 1762, removed the obligation of service from the gentry and encouraged its influx into the provinces from the centers. Henceforward it retained only its landholding position, and that position bound it to the provinces.

In accord with these changes, the gentry's political tastes also changed. Compulsory service had tied it to the capital, to the central government. That is why all of its interests until 1762 were focused on the center. In the first half of the eighteenth century, the gentry made governments. Even when it asked Anna to restore autocracy, it petitioned for the right to elect members of the Senate and Colleges and the governors, that is, to exert a direct influence on the composition of the central and provincial government. With the abolition of the gentry's compulsory service, the focal point of its interests shifted from the capital to the provinces. In the Commission of 1767, the gentry expressed broad claims to participation in local administration, but not a single noble deputy uttered a word about its participation in the central administration. The gubernia institutions of 1775 reinforced the long-held desire of this estate to become the governing class in the provinces, where almost half the population—the serfs—was already in its hands. Hence the gubernia institutions, despite the part that the ideas of the French writers played in them, reinforced a longstanding social and political fact of our history. So, even in the structure of local administration, the peculiarity that distinguished all of Catherine's political activity manifested itself: ideas unfamiliar to Russian society entered into each of her projects, but under cover of those ideas, old facts of our history were developed and reinforced.

To remember better the significance of the gubernia institutions in the history of the nobility, we can mark this phase of its development, in which it acquired local governmental importance, in the following way. In the Muscovite state, the gentry did not rule but was only an instrument of government—it *served* on a compulsory basis, and it served both at the center and in the provinces. In the first half of the eighteenth century, while making governments, it continued to render compulsory service at the center but had barely begun to rule in the provinces. In the second half of the century, having made a government for the last time in 1762, it ceased to serve on a compulsory basis at the center, and after 1775, having finally taken local administration into its own hands, it began to rule in the provinces.

~ VIII ~

Serfdom

The broad participation in local administration that opened up to the gentry in Catherine's reign was a consequence of its landowning significance, and its landowning significance rested on serfdom. The gentry directed the local administration because, apart from its role in government, almost half the local population, the serfs, was in its hands, living on its land. The connection between serfdom and the structure of local administration compels us to dwell on the fate of that institution.

A legend exists that, after issuing the charters on the rights of two of the estates, Catherine contemplated a third charter in which she intended to define the rights of the free rural inhabitants, the state peasants, but this intention was not carried out.[1] The free rural population under Catherine formed a minority of the rural population as a whole; a decided majority of the rural population in Great Russia consisted of serfs.

A change had been made in the position of the bound population during the reign of Peter I. The decrees on the first "revision" juridically merged two categories of bondsmen that had previously been distinguished in law: bond slaves and bond peasants. A bond peasant was tied to the person of the landowner, but he was still attached to a category from which even the landowner could not remove him: he was a permanently obligated state taxpayer. The bond slave, like the bond peasant, was personally tied to his master, but he did not bear the

---

[1]Catherine did draft what amounted to a charter to the state peasants, similar to the charters to the nobility and the towns, but it was never promulgated.

state tax that fell on the bond peasant. Peter's legislation extended the state tax on the bond peasants to the bond slaves as well. Thus the source of bondage changed. Previously, it had been a personal agreement between the bondsman, or peasant, and the master; now it became a governmental act—the revision. A person was considered bound not because he had entered into bondage by agreement but because he was registered to a certain individual on the revision rolls. This new source, which replaced the former agreement, made the serf category highly elastic. Once there were no longer either bond slaves or bond peasants, both of those categories having been replaced by the single category of serfs, or "souls," it became possible, as a matter of discretion, to contract or expand both the size of the serf population and the boundaries of serf dependence. After Peter's death, the serf category expanded both quantitatively and qualitatively: a growing number of individuals became serfs, and at the same time the boundaries of the owner's power over his serf souls expanded. We need to trace both of these processes.

The serf category proliferated in two ways: by registration and by awards of land. Registration affected those individuals who had failed to join one of the basic classes of society after choosing a permanent way of life. By a decree of Peter I, they were required to find themselves a master and a position, that is, to register for the soul tax with some individual or community. Otherwise, they were registered by a simple police order. Thus, after the second and third revisions (of 1742 and 1762), various minor categories of previously free individuals gradually sank into serfdom: illegitimates, freedmen, persons of unknown ancestry and other vagrants, children of soldiers, supernumerary church servants, foster children, non-Russian prisoners of war, and so forth. In this respect, both revisions continued the refinement and simplification of the social structure that had begun in the seventeenth century. Since registration was sometimes carried out against the will of those being registered, it permitted a number of abuses. Subsequently, the law recognized all those abuses and forcibly deprived people who had been registered of the right to lodge complaints about the illegality of their registration. The gentry Senate, acting in the interests of the dominant estate, shut its eyes to these violations, so that registration, which had been undertaken for police purposes—to eliminate vagrancy—now assumed the character of a plundering of society by the upper class. The size of the serf population increased even more, however, through awards of land, which I will now discuss.

Awards developed out of the old conditional or service grants. An award differed from a conditional grant, however, in regard both to the purpose of ownership and to the extent of the owner's rights. Until the Code of Laws of 1649, a conditional grant conferred on the serviceman only the use of state land. From the time the enserfment of the peasants was confirmed, that is, after the mid-seventeenth century, a conditional grant conferred on the landlord the use of the compulsory labor of the serfs settled on the estate. The landlord was the temporary owner of the estate, which was under contract to him; the serf registered to him in the cadastre was bound to him and all his successors because he was attached to the peasant taxpaying association, or commune, on the landlord's land. Since he was attached to that taxpaying commune, the serf was required to work for any landlord who came into possession of the land. Thus, I repeat, it was through the land that the landlord acquired the right to part of the serf's compulsory agricultural labor.

As conditional estates merged with hereditary estates, the landlord acquired the same right to the serf's compulsory labor that he had to the land—the right of full hereditary ownership. As a result, after Peter I, conditional estates were replaced by awards of land. The sum total of the obligations that fell by law on the serf, both to the master and to the state (for which the master was responsible), constituted what was called after the first revision a "serf soul."

A conditional estate had conferred on the landowner only the temporary use of state land and peasant labor, but an award gave him ownership of state land together with the peasant souls registered on it. A conditional estate also differed from an award in respect to the extent of the owner's rights. In the seventeenth century, a service estate gave a landlord conditional and temporary ownership of state land, that is, ownership on the condition of service and continuing to the death of the owner, with a limited right of disposal—he could neither give the land away, nor bequeath it, nor relinquish it at will. After the law of March 17, 1731, however, which definitively merged service and hereditary estates, an award conferred state lands and their serfs as full and hereditary property, with no such limitations.

In the eighteenth century, awards were the most widely used and effective method of increasing the serf population. From Peter's time, populated state and court lands were given to private owners on various occasions. An award sometimes had the significance of a payment or pension for service, thus retaining the characteristics of the old conditional grant. In 1737, for example, noble officers serving at state mining works were each awarded ten households in court and state villages as a supplement to their salary; non-noble officers were awarded half as many. At that time, four was considered the average number of revision souls in a household. These forty (or twenty) souls were given to the officers as hereditary property, but on the condition that not only they but their children had to serve at the state mines. By the middle of the eighteenth century, even such conditional awards bearing the characteristics of a service grant had ceased, and only outright distributions of populated land as full property continued to be made on various occasions: peasants and land were awarded to generals for a victory or the successful completion of a campaign, or merely "for enjoyment," on receiving a decoration or as a present for a newborn child. Every important event at court, every coup d'état, every feat of Russian arms was accompanied by the transformation of hundreds or thousands of peasants into private property. The greatest landowning fortunes of the eighteenth century were created by means of awards. Prince Menshikov, the son of a palace stablehand, was said to have had a fortune after Peter's death that amounted to 100,000 souls. In the same way, the Razumovskys became great landowners during Elizabeth's reign; through awards, Count Kirill Razumovsky, too, acquired about 100,000 souls. Not only the Razumovskys themselves, who were simple Cossacks by origin, but their sisters' husbands rose to noble rank and received rich awards of souls—the tailor Zakrevsky, for example, the weaver Budliansky, and the Cossack Daragan. In 1783, Budliansky's son had more than 3,000 peasant souls. Thanks to registration and awards, a considerable number of formerly free members of the rural population, like the court and state peasants, sank to the status of serfs, and by the middle of the eighteenth century, Russia had undoubtedly become much more enserfed than it was at the beginning of the century.

At the same time, the boundaries of serf dependence were being enlarged. The juridical content of serfdom was the power of the landowner over the person and labor of the serf soul within the limits indicated by law. But what were those limits? What did serfdom mean in the mid-eighteenth century? This is one of the most difficult questions in the history of Russian law. To this day, legal scholars have not attempted to formulate precisely the composition and extent of serf dependence. The essential feature of serfdom, as people in the eighteenth century understood it, was the view of the serf as the complete personal property of his owner. It is difficult to trace the development of this view, but there is no doubt that it was not entirely in accord with the legislation that had established the bondage of the peasants. In the seventeenth century, when that bondage was established, a peasant who accepted a loan fell into a dependence on an owner similar to that of an indentured bondsman. The indentured bondsman, however, was the temporary but complete property of the owner, and the owner regarded the bond peasant in the same way.

This view found its limit only in the state tax that fell on the bond peasant. It was a view that could be maintained only as long as the law allowed the free man the unlimited disposal of his person, of his freedom. The free man had been able to turn himself into someone else's bondsman by agreement, but the Code of Laws of 1649 abolished the right to dispose of one's personal freedom. According to the Code of Laws, the free man was required to serve the state through personal service or taxes and could not turn himself into private property by personal agreement. This legislation transformed the bondage of the peasant from dependence by *agreement* into dependence by *law*. Bondage did not free the peasant from state taxes, as it did the bondsman. The first revision definitively erased that distinction by imposing the same state taxes on bondsmen as on peasants. By law, the two together formed the single category of serfs, or serf souls. According to the law, the power of the owner over the serf soul was composed of two elements, corresponding to the dual significance that the owner had for the serf. First, the landowner was the immediate administrator of the serf, to whom the state entrusted supervision of the serf's husbandry and behavior along with responsibility for the strict fulfillment of his state obligations. Second, the landowner had a right to the peasant's labor as owner of the land that the peasant used and as his creditor who supplied the loan with the help of which the peasant worked. As governmental agent, the landlord collected state taxes from his serfs, supervised their behavior and their husbandry, and judged and punished them for their offenses—those were the landlord's police powers over the person of the peasant on behalf of the state. As landowner and creditor, the landlord assessed the peasant labor service or quitrent for his own benefit—that was his economic power over the labor of the peasant on the basis of civil, land obligations. This is how the limits of the landlord's power may be defined according to law up to the end of Peter's reign.

Even in old Rus, however, both sets of rights, police and economic—that is, the right to supervise and judge, and the right to assess labor service or quitrent—had certain limits placed on them. For example, the landlord's jurisdiction in the seventeenth century was confined to "peasant matters," that is, matters arising from land relations, the civil and other petty lawsuits that are now conducted in a peace court. The landlord did not have the right to try his peasants' criminal offenses. Kotoshikhin says bluntly that in serious criminal cases "owners of hereditary and conditional estates are forbidden to investigate or to issue edicts." The Code of Laws of 1649 contains a provision that the owner of a service estate who punishes a serf for robbery himself, without presenting him to a district [guba] court, is to be deprived of his estate, and if the owner of the serf robber does not have a service estate, he is to be subjected to knouting for the unauthorized punishment. There were also customs or laws that protected peasant labor from a landowner's arbitrariness. A landowner who ruined his peasants with his exactions was to have his land and peasants confiscated and turned over to his relatives, if it was hereditary or purchased land. Finally, in the seventeenth century, the right of the peasants to bring complaints before the government against their owners was recognized.

After Peter's death, these limitations on serfdom gradually faded away as a result of omissions and inconsistencies in the law. The legislation of the eighteenth century did not try to mark out the boundaries of the landlord's power more precisely and in some respects even enlarged them and strengthened his power. These legislative gaps gave the landlords broad latitude to develop the same attitude toward their serfs that the landowners of the sixteenth and seventeenth centuries had had toward their bondsmen.

The meager legislation of Peter's successors on the relations between serfs and landowners considered those relations only from two angles: it defined, first, the power of the landowner over the person of the peasant and, second, the master's right to the economic disposal of peasant labor. According to the legislation of the eighteenth century, the landlord remained a governmental agent, the supervisor of peasant husbandry and collector of state taxes. His jurisdiction, inadequately defined even before, now began to broaden, sometimes even beyond the law. Thus, in the first half of the eighteenth century, landlords began to appropriate to themselves criminal jurisdiction over their peasants, with the right to subject them to punishment corresponding to their guilt. During Elizabeth's reign, the landlord's right to punish his serfs was broadened by law: a decree of 1760 allowed landowners to exile their peasants to settlement in Siberia "for particularly insolent behavior." The landowners were given this right in the interests of increasing the colonization of Siberia, where there was a great deal of empty land suitable for cultivation. It was restricted by certain conditions, however: a landowner could exile a peasant only to settlement, and the peasant had to be healthy, fit for work, and no older than forty-five. A wife by law followed an exile, but the landowner could retain minor children; if he let them go with their parents, the treasury reimbursed him at a fixed price.

The right to the economic disposal of peasant labor also remained undefined. Even in the seventeenth century, the landowner had freely transferred his peasants from plot to plot, sold them with land and without land, exchanged them, and bequeathed them. The right of transfer and the right of sale were not revoked under Peter, but he did try to restrict the right of transfer by imposing certain conditions. For example, a landowner who wished to transfer his peasant from one village to another had to submit a request to the College of Revenue and was required to pay the soul tax owed for the transferred peasant in his old place of residence. This complicated procedure inhibited landowners from transferring peasants. During the reign of Peter III, the restriction was rescinded by a senatorial decree in January 1762. The Senate, "choosing the easiest method to satisfy the landowners," granted them the right to transfer peasants merely by making a declaration to the local regimental collectors of the soul tax.

Similarly, the law did not restrict the sale of peasants in whole families or individually, with land and without land. The landless and individual sale of peasants had troubled Peter, but he had not hoped for success in his struggle with this custom. In a decree to the Senate in 1721, he expressed only the irresolute wish that the future Code of Laws then in preparation include an article prohibiting the individual sale of people "like cattle, which is not done in all the world." This remained just a good intention on the part of the Reformer.

Finally, the legislation of the eighteenth century failed to touch at all on the important question of the boundaries of the landowner's power over the property of the peasant as well as his labor. In the seventeenth century, the law would seem to have defined clearly the "goods and chattels" of the peasant, that is, his working stock, as the joint property of the peasant and the landowner. Those goods and chattels were created by the peasant's labor but with the help of a loan from the landlord. The joint ownership was expressed in the fact that the landlord could not deprive the peasants of their movable property, while the peasant, without the agreement of the landowner, could not alienate his goods and chattels to individuals who were not serfs of the landowner. In practice, in the seventeenth century, the view of peasant property as the joint possession of both parties was maintained by custom and was not secured by a precise law. In the eighteenth century, the custom began to waver, and legislation should have defined the limits to which the power of the landowner over the property of the peasant extended and beyond which the latter's rights began. Legislation did not fill this gap, however. Instead, two laws helped the landlords adopt a view of the peasant's property as entirely their own. Peter had required landowners to feed their destitute serfs by imposing a special levy on their well-to-do peasants for this purpose. A law of Empress Anna, issued in 1734, required landowners to feed their peasants in famine years and to provide them with grain to plant their fields, "so the land does not lie idle." As a result of this new obligation imposed on the landlords, the view took hold among them that the state recognized only labor as belonging to the peasant, while the peasant's property was created and maintained by the landowner.

Nor do we encounter in the course of the first half of the eighteenth century any statute regarding the amount of labor service and quitrent payments that the landowner had the right to levy on his serfs. In old Rus there was obviously no incentive to establish such norms by means of legislation, for at that time the economic relations between landowner and peasant were determined by the struggle of supply and demand. The more a landowner demanded from his peasant, the sooner the peasant might leave him for another landowner who offered more advantageous conditions. In the eighteenth century, when all the peasants were bound either to individuals or to communes, defining norms of peasant labor service and payments to the landlords became an essential issue of state organization, but no such norms were established.

On the whole, there are more gaps and omissions than clear and precise definitions in the legislation regarding the serfs in the first half of the eighteenth century. Those gaps and omissions actually made it possible for the view of the peasant as the complete property of his owner to take root. Remember that the landowning concepts and habits of old Rus developed on the basis of slaveholding; the old landowners had worked their hereditary estates predominantly with the help of slaves. Making use of omissions in the law, they gradually began to transfer those concepts and habits onto the serfs—despite the law, which regarded the peasants as state taxpayers. By the middle of the eighteenth century, this view had fully developed, and government officials were beginning to adopt it. In the instruction of one governmental institution to its deputy to the Commission of 1767, we encounter the desire for the establishment of a law to deal with a landlord whose blows caused the death of a peasant. This desire is striking in its oddity: how could the seventeenth-century law that resolved precisely such cases have been forgotten? According to the Code of Laws of 1649, a landlord who tortured a peasant to death was himself subject to the death penalty, while the peasant's orphaned family was provided for from the property of the murderer. Catherine in her *Instruction* expressed the wish that the laws do something useful "for the private property of the slaves." How could it have entered Catherine's mind that the serf was a slave, when she knew that he bore a state tax, while slaves were not subject to taxation? In the *Instruction*, Catherine also expressed the thought that agriculture cannot flourish where "no one has any property"—obviously a reference to the serfs. But did the law really declare the belongings of the peasant to be the full property of his owner? No such law existed. On the contrary, it is well known that under Peter the state entered into business transactions with serfs, who took on state contracts and answered in court for the obligations they assumed. Thus, government officials themselves in the second half of the eighteenth century were acknowledging the well-known consequences of the view of the serfs that had imperceptibly taken root in the first half of the century.

Now it is easy for us to understand the task that lay before Catherine's legislation in regard to regulating the relations between landowners and serfs: it consisted of filling the gaps that had been permitted in the laws concerning the land relations between the two parties. It was a matter of proclaiming the general principles that should underlie those relations and, in accordance with them, of indicating the precise limits to which the power of the landowner over his peasants extended and beyond which the power of the state began. The definition of those limits evidently engaged the empress at the beginning of her reign. In the Commission of 1767, bold claims to serf labor were heard from several quarters: the classes that did not have the right to own serfs demanded its extension—the merchants; the Cossacks; and even, to their shame, the clergy. These slaveholding pretensions exasperated the empress, and, as we saw previously, she expressed her exasperation in a brief note that has come down to us from that time: "If the serf cannot be considered a person, it follows that he is not a human being; let him be considered a brute, then, for which the whole world will ascribe to us considerable glory and love for mankind." But this remained a passing, abnormal outburst by a humane ruler. Influential intimates who were acquainted with the state of affairs also advised her to intervene in the relations between peasants and landlords. It may be assumed that emancipation, the complete abolition of serfdom, was not yet within the power of the government at this time. The idea might have been implanted, however, in people's minds and in legislation, of curbing its arbitrariness by establishing mutually inoffensive norms of landlord–serf relations.

Statesmen advised Catherine to define by law the amount of peasant dues and labor that landowners had the right to demand. Peter Panin, one of the best statesmen of Catherine's time, in a memorandum of 1763 wrote of the necessity of limiting the unbounded power of the landlord over his peasants and establishing norms for the labor and dues the peasants paid him. Panin proposed a norm of no more than four days of labor service a week and no more than two rubles in quitrent per soul, which comes to fourteen to sixteen of our rubles. It is characteristic that Panin considered it dangerous to publish such a law. He advised that it be communicated confidentially to the governors, who would secretly transmit it to the landlords for their information and guidance. Another statesman, the exemplary administrator of Catherine's time Jakob Sievers, the governor of Novgorod, also found that the landlords' exactions from the peasants "exceeded all probability." In his opinion, too, it was essential to define by law the amount of dues and labor paid to the landlord and to grant peasants the right to purchase their freedom for a certain sum.

Peter III's law of February 18, 1762, added another substantial inducement to resolve the issue one way or another. Serfdom had had as one of its supports the obligatory service of the nobility; now, when that obligation had been removed and serfdom in its old form had lost its meaning, its chief political justification, it had become a means without an end. Given such a variety of incentives, it is interesting to see how Catherine approached the difficult question left to her by her predecessors.

From what we have said, the legislative tasks regarding the issue of relations between the serf population and the landowning class are evident. Serf labor had been the means by which the nobility bore its obligatory military service; consequently, once that obligation ceased, the distribution of populated state lands to private owners should of itself have ceased. Furthermore, not all of the serf's labor had been granted to the nobility as private property; part of it was taxed by the state, so that serf labor was the joint property of the landowners and the state. Therefore, legislation needed to set precise boundaries between the rights of the owners and the power of the state.

Catherine, however, did not end the distribution of state lands and peasants to private owners. On the contrary, she distributed them with an even more lavish hand than her predecessors. Her accession to the throne was accompanied by the award of almost 18,000 souls to 26 of her accomplices. These awards continued throughout the reign, sometimes on a mass scale that rapidly created enormous landowning fortunes. Potemkin, a petty Smolensk noble by origin, ended his career as the owner, it was said, of some 200,000 peasant souls. Without enumerating all the separate awards, I will limit myself just to their grand total: up to now, documents have brought to light 400,000 revision souls dispensed to private owners from state and court lands under Catherine. Four hundred thousand revision souls—that is almost a million actual souls.

Under Catherine, serfdom proliferated by yet another means: the legislative abolition of free peasant movement. In the eighteenth century, free movement was still allowed by law in the Ukrainian provinces. Here the "common" peasants, as they were called, entered into short-term agreements with landowners that they could break freely, moving to land where they were received on more profitable terms. The Cossack senior officers had long endeavored to end this mobility by enserfing not only the peasants but the free Cossacks as well. Kirill Razumovsky, the former hetman of Ukraine from 1750 to 1764, had assisted the efforts of the senior officers with particular vigor. He was the first to begin distributing state lands and peasants as full hereditary property instead of a temporary possession similar to our old conditional grant. These distributions were carried out on such a broad scale that shortly after Razumovsky's retirement, in all the territories of Ukraine belonging to the Russian state, the number of peasant households that had not been dispensed to private owners came to no more than 2,000.

From the very start of her reign, Catherine began to take measures to end the free movement of the Ukrainian peasants. Under a decree of 1763, peasants could quit their landowners only after receiving departure authorizations from them. The landowners, of course, in order to keep the peasants on their land, made it difficult to acquire these authorizations. Finally, right after the completion of the fourth revision, the law of May 3, 1783, was published, according to which all the common peasants in the governor-generalships or gubernias of Kiev, Chernigov (which also included present-day Poltava), and Novgorod-Seversky had to remain in the locations and with the owners where the just-completed revision had found and registered them. Soon this order was extended to Kharkov Gubernia and parts of Kursk and Voronezh Gubernias. In this way more than a million peasants registered in the designated gubernias according to the fourth revision found themselves under private ownership and were soon on a par with the serfs of central Great Russia. The success of this enserfment was aided by the fact that Catherine extended the rights of the Russian nobility to the Cossack senior officers.

Thus, the size of the serf population increased under Catherine in two ways: by awards and by the abolition of free peasant movement where it still existed. As a result, by the end of Catherine's reign Russia had undoubtedly become much more enserfed than it had been previously. At the end of Elizabeth's reign, according to the second and third revisions, the court peasants in Russia had numbered about half a million revision souls; by the end of Catherine's reign, in the same gubernias, according to the fourth and fifth revisions, the number of court peasants that remained was far fewer.

Catherine's legislation on the landowners' power over the serfs is distinguished by the same indefiniteness and incompleteness as the legislation of her predecessors. On the whole, it tended to benefit the landowners. We saw that Elizabeth, in the interests of settling Siberia, by the law of 1760 granted landowners the right "for particularly insolent behavior" to exile healthy serf workers to settlement in Siberia without the right of return. Catherine, by a law of 1765, turned this limited right of exile to settlement into an unlimited right to exile serfs to hard labor for any length of time, with the exile to be returned to his former owner whenever the latter wished. Furthermore, in the seventeenth century the government had accepted petitions against landowners for their cruel behavior, conducted investigations of those complaints, and punished the guilty. During Peter's reign, a series of decrees was issued that prohibited individuals of all ranks from submitting petitions to the sovereign, bypassing governmental institutions. These decrees were confirmed by Peter's successors. The government, however, continued to accept peasant complaints against landlords from rural communes. These complaints greatly troubled the Senate. At the beginning of Catherine's reign, it proposed measures for the complete prohibition of peasant complaints against landlords. Catherine confirmed this report, and on August 22, 1767, at the very time that the deputies to the commission were listening to the articles of the *Instruction* on freedom and equality, a decree was published stating that, if any persons "dare to deliver unlawful petitions against their landowners into Her Majesty's own hands," the petitioners and the compilers of the petitions would be punished with the knout and exiled to permanent hard labor in Nerchinsk, with their landowners to receive recruit quittances for the exiles. It was ordered that this decree be read on Sundays and holidays in all rural churches for a month. The Senate's proposal, confirmed by the empress, was so worded as to eliminate all possibility for peasants to lodge a complaint against a landlord.

Nor were the limits of patrimonial jurisdiction precisely defined under Catherine. A decree of October 18, 1770, stated that a landowner could judge peasants only for those offenses that according to the law did not entail deprivation of all the rights of the offender's status; the extent of the punishment that the landowner could impose for those crimes, however, was not indicated. Taking advantage of this, landowners imposed punishments on serfs for petty offenses that were supposed to apply only to the most serious crimes. In 1771, to put an end to unseemly public commerce in peasants, a law was issued prohibiting the sale, for payment of landlords' debts, of peasants without land by public auction, "under the hammer." The law remained without effect, and the Senate did not insist on its implementation. In 1792, a new decree restored the right of landless sale, for payment of landlords' debts, of peasants by public auction—but without the use of the hammer. In her *Instruction*, Catherine recalls that under Peter a decree had been issued according to which mad or brutal landowners were to be placed "under the supervision of guardians." Catherine says that this decree was implemented insofar as mad landowners were concerned, but its provision regarding brutal landowners was not being carried out, and she expresses bewilderment as to why the operation of the decree had been curtailed. She did not restore it in full force, however. Finally, in the Charter to the Nobility of 1785, when enumerating the nobility's personal and property rights, she failed to separate the peasants from the general category of the nobility's immovable property, that is, she tacitly recognized them as part of the landlord's agricultural stock. Thus the landlord's power, while divested of its former political justification, acquired broader juridical limits under Catherine.

Those are all of Catherine's directives concerning the serfs that are important enough to merit attention. Their incompleteness confirmed the view of the serfs that had taken hold within the gentry in the middle of the eighteenth century, outside the law and even despite the law— the view that recognized the serfs as the private property of the land-owners. Catherine's legislation confirmed this view not so much by what it said outright as by its silences, that is, by what it tacitly acknowledged.

What were the possible ways of defining the relations of the serf population in Catherine's reign? We saw that the serfs were attached to the person of the landowner as permanently obligated state farmers. The law defined their bondage to the person of the landowner but not their relationship to the land, which they worked to pay their state taxes. There were three possible ways of regulating the relations between the serfs and the landowners. First, the serfs could be freed from the person of the landowner but without binding them to the land; this would have meant a landless emancipation of the peasants. Liberal gentry in Catherine's time dreamed of such an emancipation, but it was scarcely a possibility; at the very least it would have plunged the national economy into utter chaos and perhaps led to a terrible political catastrophe. On the other hand, the serfs could be freed from the person of the landowner while bound to the land, that is, made independent of their masters but tied to land to be redeemed by the state. That would have placed the peasants in a position very close to the one that was first created for them on February 19, 1861: it would have turned the peasants into state taxpayers bound to the land. In the eighteenth century, however, it would hardly have been possible to carry out such an emancipation combined with the complex financial operation of a redemption of the land. Finally, the peasants could be bound to the land without freeing them from the person of the landowner, that is, the peasants would be placed in the position of state farmers bound to the land while the landowner retained certain powers over them. This would have created a relationship in which the peasants were temporarily obligated to the landowners; in such a case, legislation would have had to define precisely the personal and land relations between the two parties. This was the most suitable way to regulate relations, and it was the one advocated by Alexis Polenov and the practical men close to Catherine, such as Peter Panin or Jakob Sievers, who knew the state of affairs in the countryside well.

Catherine did not choose any of these methods. She simply consolidated the domination of the owners over their peasants in the form that it had assumed in the middle of the eighteenth century, and in some respects even broadened that power. As a result, serfdom under Catherine II entered a third phase of its development; it took a third form. The first form of serfdom, up to the decree of 1646, was personal dependence of the serfs on the landowners by agreement. This was the form in which serfdom existed until the middle of the seventeenth century. Under the Code of Laws of 1649 and Peter's legislation, serfdom was transformed into the hereditary dependence of the serfs on the landowners by law, on condition of the landowners' compulsory service. Under Catherine, serfdom assumed a third form: it turned into the complete dependence of the serfs, who became the private property of the landowners, but no longer on condition of the latter's compulsory service, from which the nobility had been released. That is why Catherine can be called the perpetrator of serfdom—not in the sense that she created it, but in the sense that under her it was transformed from a variable fact, justified by the temporary needs of the state, into a right recognized by law but in no way justified.

Now let us examine the consequences of serfdom in this, its third and last form. Those consequences were extremely varied. Serfdom was the hidden spring that moved and gave direction to the most diverse spheres of national life. It not only shaped the course of the country's political and economic life but put a sharp stamp on its social, intellectual, and moral life. I will briefly enumerate some of the most notable consequences of serfdom and indicate first of all the effect it had on the landlords' agriculture. For an entire century, from the manifesto of February 18 to the manifesto of February 19,[2] our social, intellectual, and moral development proceeded under the weight of serfdom, and perhaps another whole century will elapse before our life and thought are freed from its traces.

Under the shelter of serfdom, distinctive relationships and procedures took root in the landlord's village in the second half of the eighteenth century. I will start with the methods by which landlords exploited serf labor.

Until the eighteenth century, a mixed quitrent and labor-service system predominated in the landowners' exploitation of their land and serf labor. In return for the plot of land granted to them for their own use, the peasants in part cultivated land for the landlord and in part paid him quitrent. In the first half of the eighteenth century, this mixed system began to divide: the gentry's compulsory service did not allow it to take an active and direct part in agricultural affairs, so some landlords turned over almost all of their land to the peasants and assessed them quitrent for it, while others distributed part of their own land to the peasants and cultivated the remainder with the use of labor service. We cannot say how widespread either of these two systems was; we can only surmise that the labor-service system was no less widespread than the quitrent system.

From the time it was emancipated from compulsory service, the gentry seemingly should have concerned itself more closely with its own agriculture. It now had greater leisure to do so, and since a vast amount of land, the most productive force in the national economy of Russia at the time, was concentrated in its hands, it had the prospect of becoming the leader of the entire national economy. When we examine agricultural life at the beginning of Catherine's reign, however, we find that what took place in the countryside was precisely the opposite of what might have been expected. Not only did the quitrent system fail to disappear from the landlords' agriculture, but it became more widespread. This is indicated both by the latest statistical research and by the testimony of contemporaries. Catherine complained in the *Instruction* that "almost all the villages are on quitrent" and referred to

---

[2]That is, from the emancipation of the nobility from compulsory service in 1762 to the emancipation of the serfs in 1861.

the quitrent system as a "newly invented method." At the end of Catherine's reign, the statistician Heinrich Storch and the agronomist Peter Rychkov were complaining with one voice of the harmful consequences for agriculture ensuing from the predominance of the quitrent system on the landlords' estates. Some contemporaries explained this unexpected development on the grounds that the majority of the gentry was engaged in service in the towns and could not always entrust a labor-service system to bailiffs. But this testimony is not borne out by the evidence collected by the government in 1777: the number of nobles in state service totaled about 10,000, a very insignificant part of that estate; a decided majority of the nobles, however, while not holding governmental posts, did not live in their villages either but were concentrated in the gubernia or district towns.

In seeking to explain this strange phenomenon, we find two causes, one political and the other economic. Catherine's reign had begun with a number of local peasant uprisings that soon merged into the single vast Pugachev Rebellion. Frightened by these uprisings, the gentry for a long time thereafter drew close to the towns and their authority-wielding brethren, the governors and land captains. That was one reason for the absentee landownership of the gentry. The other was purely economic. It was pointed out in Catherine's *Instruction*. We read there that "the proprietors (that is, the landlords), who seldom or never reside in their villages, levy on each soul one, two, or even five rubles without regard to the means by which their peasants are to raise this money." So the quitrent system was preferred as the most convenient and profitable one. First, it freed the landowners from petty agricultural concerns. Second, it gave the landlord, with his unlimited right to increase the quitrent, the opportunity to obtain the kind of income he would never have received if he had farmed in the village himself.

Thus, contrary to expectations, when the gentry acquired greater leisure in the eighteenth century, landlords employed the quitrent system even more than they had before, and the landowner became even more remote from his land and his "serf souls" than he had been previously. As a result, distinctive economic and juridical relationships, which I will now indicate, established themselves in the landlords' agriculture.

As a result of the vague legal definition of serfdom, the demands of the landowners in regard to serf labor increased in the course of Catherine's reign and found expression in the gradual growth of the quitrent. Quitrents varied greatly because of the diversity of local conditions. The following can be regarded as approximating the norm: two rubles (equal to fifteen today) per revision soul in the 1760s; three rubles in the 1770s; four rubles in the 1780s; and five rubles (twenty-five today) in the 1790s. The market value of these sums can be determined on the basis of grain prices. At the beginning of Catherine's reign, a ruble was equal to approximately seven or eight of our rubles; at the end of the reign, it was equal to approximately four or five of our rubles. Thus, the standard quitrent at the beginning of the reign equalled approximately fifteen of our rubles and at the end of the reign approximately twenty-seven. That was the quitrent per soul. Its economic significance can be determined if we transpose it to land. The usual land allotment at the end of Catherine's reign was six *desiatinas* of arable, in three fields, per *tiaglo*. (A *tiaglo* was the term for an adult worker with a wife and minor children not yet able to form a separate household.) Contemporaries assumed two and one-half revision souls per *tiaglo*.

Thus, each *tiaglo* at the end of Catherine's reign paid quitrent to the landlord of approximately twenty-seven rubles multiplied by two and a half, meaning a quitrent of about eleven rubles for each *desiatina* of the peasant's land allotment. That was the quitrent in the central gubernias, the clay-soil regions of the upper Volga. In the southern black-earth regions, where the population was sparser, there was generally a little more land per *tiaglo*. Eleven rubles per *desiatina*—that is many times more than the present-day rent for land in the central Great Russian gubernias.

On some estates, the labor-service system prevailed. At the beginning of Catherine's reign, several highly placed individuals, headed by Gregory Orlov, formed a patriotic society with the objective of studying and fostering the development of agriculture in Russia. In 1765 Catherine approved this society under the name of the St. Petersburg Free Economic Society. It sent out questionnaires to the gubernia authorities on the condition of agriculture in the provinces. The replies that were sent back to the society are extremely interesting.

According to the information collected at the beginning of Catherine II's reign, the peasants in many gubernias gave the landlords half of their working time. In good weather, however, the peasants were forced to work for the landlord throughout the week, so that they were able to work for themselves only after finishing their toil for the lord.

In many localities, landlords demanded four or even five days of work from the peasants. Observers found the labor for the landlord in the Russian serf villages on the whole more onerous than in the neighboring countries of Western Europe. Peter Panin, a liberal to a very moderate degree, wrote that "the masters' requisitions and labor services in Russia not only exceed the examples of our closest foreign neighbors but often go beyond human endurance." Finally, the agronomist Rychkov has left us testimony that indicates the extreme consequences of the landlord's unlimited power to dispose of peasant labor. He complains of those landlords who "set their peasants to work for the master every day and give them monthly bread for their sustenance." Some landlords, then, taking advantage of the absence of a precise law defining the extent of the peasant's compulsory labor for the landowner, deprived their peasants of land completely and turned their villages into slave-owning plantations that are difficult to distinguish from the plantations of North America before the emancipation of the negroes.

On the other hand, the broad scope given to the landlord's powers fostered the proliferation of a class of house serfs that was a burden on the peasants. When the gentry bore compulsory service, a noble had to maintain a staff of domestics with whom he went on campaigns or to whom he entrusted the running of his estate in his absence. With the abolition of compulsory service, this staff should have diminished. From the mid-eighteenth century, however, it grew noticeably. Observers of gentry life under Catherine II attest that in the homes of Russian landowners there were generally three or even five times as many servants as in the homes of German proprietors of the same degree of wealth. As to the household servants of the magnates, Storch remarks, there is nothing to be said: in other countries such a quantity of domestics could not even be imagined. Some of them served the landlord as an instrument of peasant administration. The landlord was the complete master of the peasant world that was entrusted to his supervision: he administered justice there, maintained order and decorum, and organized all of the peasants' economic and social relations. For all their complexity, however, these administrative tasks did not require the multitude of domestics the landlords maintained. The extra ones served the capricious personal needs of the landowners, who showed little restraint in this respect since they imposed the upkeep of the house serfs on their peasants.

Some documents of manorial administration and justice in the eighteenth century have come down to us. Count Peter Rumiantsev drew up an instruction to his steward in 1751, when he was still a young officer. Accustomed to military discipline, Rumiantsev prescribed severe punishments for the offenses and crimes of his peasants. There were monetary fines from two kopecks to five rubles, shackles, beatings with rods, and whippings. (Rumiantsev did not care for the birch switch but preferred the rod, which made a stronger impression on the person being punished.) For failing to go to church without good reason, the guilty party paid ten kopecks to the church; for the smallest theft, a serf was to be punished by the confiscation of all his movable property and after corporal punishment was to be sent into the army without a report to the lord. In the *Russian Justice*[3] this sort of punishment bore the term "banishment and confiscation of property," but it was proposed for the most serious crimes: banditry, arson, and horse theft. Thus, a landlord of the eighteenth century managed to be stricter than the *Russian Justice* of the twelfth century. For insulting a nobleman, a serf was to be beaten with rods at the desire of the noble "until the latter is satisfied." He also paid a two-ruble fine to his landowner.

The severe punishments Rumiantsev stipulated, however, are sheer coddling compared to the penalties other landowners prescribed. A "Journal of Domestic Administration" from the 1760s has been preserved, a notebook containing the managerial instructions of one landowner. There, for every trifle, strokes of the lash rained down on the serfs by the hundreds, strokes of the birch switch by the thousands. (The relationship between a stroke of the lash and a stroke of the birch switch was calculated with mathematical precision: 1 stroke with the lash equaled 170 strokes with the switch.) The landlord lived in Moscow, where several of his house serfs resided, paying quitrent or learning crafts. On every holiday those house serfs had to appear at the master's house to pay their respects; a thousand birch strokes were stipulated for failure to do so. If a serf fasted but did not take communion, he was punished with 5,000 birch strokes. An individual who had been severely punished could go to the manorial hospital; it was precisely determined how many days he could stay there, however, the length of time depending on the number of strokes he had received. Someone who had been punished with 100 lashes or 17,000 birch strokes could remain

---

[3]The first Russian Code of Laws, compiled in the eleventh and twelfth centuries.

for a week; someone who had received no more than 10,000 birch strokes half a week. Anyone who stayed longer was deprived of bread and docked a corresponding portion of his monthly wages.

If only this savage document had come down to us from some Russian Don Quixote of landlord despotism, who was disposing not of living souls but of imaginary ones, the way Sobakevich[4] sold dead souls!

Landowners also developed broad powers to dispose of the person of the serf. They were helped by the law of 1765 on the landlord's right to exile serfs to hard labor in Siberia, with the exiles counting as army recruits. With the aid of this law, the landlords tried to reduce the losses that the peasants' military obligation entailed for them. Before each levy, landlords would exile their negligent or enfeebled peasants to Siberia and receive recruit quittances for them. Thus they saved their industrious and healthy workers from recruitment—to the great detriment of the Russian army, needless to say. Sievers, in a letter to Catherine, says that in the levy of 1771 the Russian army was deprived of at least 8,000 good soldiers as a result of this law. Sievers expresses doubt as to whether even a quarter of those exiled reached their destination. Academician Peter Pallas, on his travels in Siberia, saw a number of these exiles. Many of them were living without their wives and children, although Elizabeth's law prohibited the separation of wives and husbands. The exiles complained to Pallas, saying that they missed their abandoned children very much and that if they had been exiled with their families they would consider themselves more fortunate in exile than at home under the thumb of the landowners. In the 1770s, in Tobolsk and part of Yenisei Gubernias, the number of those exiled since 1765 came to more than 20,000.

Given the breadth of the landlords' powers, commerce in serf souls, with and without land, increased during Catherine's reign. Prices were established for them—"decreed," or state prices, and "free," or gentry prices. At the beginning of Catherine's reign, in purchases of whole villages, a peasant soul with land was usually valued at 30 rubles (225 current rubles). With the establishment of the Loan Bank in 1786,[5] the price of a soul rose to 80 rubles (more than 400 current rubles), al-

---

[4]The bearlike landowner in Gogol's *Dead Souls*, who extols the qualities of the deceased serfs he is "selling."

[5]A Nobles' Bank, which gave loans to nobles on the security of landed estates, had been established in 1754. In 1786 it became the State Loan Bank, which granted loans to the nobles and the towns.

though the bank issued mortgages on gentry estates at only 40 rubles per soul. At the end of Catherine's reign, it was generally difficult to buy an estate for less than 100 rubles per soul. In individual sales, a healthy worker purchased as an army recruit was valued at 120 rubles (about 850 current rubles) at the beginning of the reign and 400 rubles (about 2,000 current rubles) at the end of it.

Now we can see the impact serfdom had on the landlords' agriculture and the gentry's landholding position. Once emancipated from compulsory service, the nobles should have become a class of rural proprietors and the leaders of the Russian national economy; thanks to serfdom, they became neither one nor the other. In the countryside, they should have occupied themselves not so much with agricultural operations as with instructions for the administration of the peasants. Concerns about standards of cultivation, agronomy, and the application of new farming methods and improved implements gradually receded to the background, however, and yielded to concerns about the exploitation of peasant labor and arrangements for ruling peasant souls. Thus the proprietors were gradually transformed from landowners into serf owners policing their peasants. That is the way some judicious landlords began to regard themselves in the second half of the eighteenth century. One of them wrote that he viewed the landlords as "hereditary officials to whom the government, having given populated land, thereby entrusted guardianship of the people living on it and responsibility for them in all instances."

The effect of serfdom on the landholding position of the gentry, then, was to turn gentry landowning into gentry soul owning and the landlord himself from an agronomist into a police official. Serfdom gave a wrong direction to agriculture on the gentry estates and inculcated bad economic habits. The landlord satisfied his every new economic demand by imposing a new tax on his serfs. Free peasant labor deprived the noble of any desire to accumulate working capital. Serfdom was the hidden source of the chief shortcomings that marked gentry agriculture until recent times. It explains the lack of foresight, enterprise, and thrift, the aversion to improved farming methods, and the indifference to the technical inventions that have been applied to agriculture in other countries. The boundless expanse of power, the opportunity to get everything for free just by issuing an order from one's office, substituted for working capital and agricultural knowledge.

Finally, serfdom also left the peasants without manorial leadership and without sufficient working stock. Given his relations with the land-owner, the serf was deprived of demonstrations of technical knowl-edge, which the landlord himself did not have, and of adequate working stock, which the landlord did not accumulate. He had to work the land the only way he knew how, that is, the way he was accus-tomed to working it. Moreover, to pay the heavy quitrent, he had to resort to outside work, to migratory labor by which he made up the shortfall from his farming at home. This forced the separation of peas-ants from their families. Hence, the peasants acquired shortcomings similar to those from which their owners suffered: an inability to shift from old, customary methods of cultivation to new ones required by changing economic conditions; an inclination to till as much land as possible and an inability to till it better; and a lack of understanding of the advantages of intensive cultivation.

Serfdom had harmful effects not only on the landlords' agriculture but on the national economy as a whole by hindering the natural geo-graphical distribution of agrarian labor. Because of the circumstances of our external history, the agrarian population from time immemorial was concentrated particularly in the central regions, on less productive soil; it had been driven from the black-soil area of southern Russia by foreign enemies. Thus the national economy for centuries suffered from a disparity between the distribution of the agrarian population and the quality of the soil. From the time the black-soil regions were acquired, two or three generations would have sufficed to eliminate this disparity if peasant labor had been allowed free movement. But serfdom held back the natural dispersal of peasant labor to the southern Russian plain. It is sufficient to note that around the middle of the eighteenth century, according to the third revision, more than a third of the entire serf population of the state was concentrated in the old Moscow Gubernia (which before the "Statute" of 1775 corresponded to the present-day gubernia of Moscow and all those adjacent to it except Smolensk and Tver, but with the addition of Yaroslavl and part of Kostroma). With the annexation of New Russia under Catherine, a very weak influx of the agrarian population (and predominantly of nonserfs, at that) into the southern Russian steppes began. Even in the middle of the nineteenth century, traces of that disparity, created by history and maintained by the government, could still be detected. According to the last revision (the tenth), in 1858–59, serfs comprised 62 percent of the total population in the non–black-soil gubernia of

Kaluga and 69 percent in the even less fertile gubernia of Smolensk, while they comprised 30 percent in the black-soil gubernia of Kharkov and 27 percent in the black-soil gubernia of Voronezh. Such were the obstacles that the distribution of agrarian labor encountered in serfdom.

Furthermore, serfdom impeded the growth of the Russian towns, the progress of urban trades, and manufacturing. The urban population was very slow to develop after Peter. According to the first revision, it constituted less than 3 percent of the taxed population of the state; according to the third revision, at the beginning of Catherine's reign, it constituted just 3 percent, so that its growth in the course of almost half a century was barely perceptible. Catherine went to great pains to develop what was then called the "middling sort of people," the urban artisan and commercial class. According to her economic textbooks, this middle estate was the chief transmitter of popular well-being and enlightenment. Without noticing the elements of this class that already existed in the country, Catherine thought of all kinds of new elements from which it might be constructed; it was even proposed to include in it the entire population of the foundling homes. Catherine expressed her aspirations in her correspondence with her Parisian friend, Madame Geoffrin. Madame Geoffrin was very insistent that Catherine create a third estate in Russia. Catherine promised to do so: "Again, madame, I promise you," she wrote in 1766, "to introduce a third estate; but how difficult it will be to create it!" Her efforts were not very successful, however; the urban population was slow to develop in Catherine's reign, too. According to the fifth revision, which was carried out in the last years of the reign, of the 16.5 million souls in the taxed population, those in the urban categories numbered a little over 700,000, or less than 5 percent. Moreover, some of the increase in the percentage of the urban population must be attributed not so much to natural growth in the central regions as to the southwestern gubernias annexed in the three partitions of Poland, where the urban population was more developed than in the Great Russian regions.

The chief reason for the sluggish growth of the urban population was serfdom. It affected urban trades and manufacturing in a twofold manner. Every well-to-do landowner tried to provide himself with skilled house serfs in his own village, beginning with a blacksmith and ending with a musician, an artist, and even an actor. Thus, serf craftsmen represented dangerous competitors of urban craftsmen and manufacturers. The landowner tried to satisfy his everyday needs from domestic resources, and for more refined needs he turned to foreign shops. Native urban craftsmen and traders were thereby deprived of their most profitable buyers and consumers, the landlords. On the other hand, the ever-increasing power of the landlord over the property of the serfs curtailed the latter's disposal of their earnings—the peasants bought less and less in the towns. Urban labor was thereby deprived of its more modest but more numerous buyers and consumers, too. Contemporaries saw serfdom as the principal reason for the slow development of Russia's urban industry. The Russian ambassador in Paris, Prince Dmitry Golitsyn, wrote in 1766 that internal trade would not flourish in Russia "unless we introduce the right of the peasants to own their movable property."

Finally, serfdom also weighed down the state economy. This can be seen in the published financial registers of Catherine's reign, which reveal some interesting facts. The soul tax in the eighteenth century grew extremely slowly. Set at 70 kopecks under Catherine I, it had risen only to a ruble in 1794. By contrast, the quitrent collected from the state peasants grew significantly faster: under Peter I it had been set at 40 kopecks; in 1760 it had risen to a ruble, in 1768 to 2 rubles, and in 1783 to 3 rubles. What explains the difference in the growth of the soul tax and the quitrent? The soul tax rose more slowly than the quitrent because it fell also on the landlords' peasants, and they could not be burdened with taxes to the same degree as the state peasants because their surplus earnings, with which they might have paid a higher soul tax, went to the landlords—the landlord snatched away from the state any savings the peasant might amass. How much the treasury lost as a result can be judged from the fact that under Catherine the serf population made up almost half of the total population of the empire and more than half of the total taxed population.

Meanwhile, the state's needs were growing, and the government was forced to resort to indirect methods of satisfying them since it was unable to increase direct taxes. The financial registers reveal these methods. First, there was an increase in the proceeds from the tax farm on the sale of alcohol. The financial registers provide interesting evidence of the progress of this tax under Catherine. If we compare the growth of direct taxes with the rise in the state's proceeds from the indirect tax on alcohol, we see that the treasury did not have equal success with these two sources of revenue. All in all, direct taxes under Catherine increased less than threefold and the revenue from alcohol more than sixfold. If we divide the total sum of direct taxes, that is, from the soul tax and quitrent, by the number of revision souls at the beginning of Catherine's reign and at its end and then do the same for the total revenue from alcohol, we get the following results. At the beginning of Catherine's reign, a revision soul paid the state 1 ruble and 23 kopecks from his labor and at the end of the reign 1 ruble and 59 kopecks—meaning that direct taxes rose less than 50 percent. On the other hand, the alcohol revenue per revision soul at the beginning of the reign came to 19 kopecks and at the end of the reign to 61 kopecks—meaning that each soul had begun to drink more than three times as much for the benefit of the state, thereby becoming three times less capable of working and paying taxes.

The other method was state credit. In 1768 the Assignat Bank was founded with an exchange fund of a million rubles; an equal sum of bank notes was issued. At first the assignats enjoyed confidence and circulated on a par with metallic currency, but the second Turkish war, which drastically increased the expenditures of the treasury, forced the government to expand the issue of paper money beyond the dimensions of the exchange fund, so that by the end of the war there were 150 million rubles' worth of paper money in circulation. At the same time, the rate of exchange of the assignat ruble was falling: at the end of the second Turkish war, in 1791, it was worth only 50 metal kopecks on the market. In addition, Catherine had to resort to loans from abroad. By the end of the reign, the foreign debt had mounted to 44 million rubles and the domestic debt to 82.5 million, while the state budget was 68 million rubles. If we add in the assignat debt of 150 million rubles, we find that Catherine borrowed from posterity nearly four years' budgets.

Thus, by drying up the sources of revenue that the state received through direct taxes, serfdom forced the treasury to turn to indirect methods that either weakened the productive forces of the country or imposed a heavy burden on future generations.

These were the most appreciable juridical and economic consequences of serfdom in its third phase.

~ IX ~

The Gentry and the Impact of Western Culture

We have examined the consequences of serfdom for the national economy and the state economy. Serfdom extended its influence far beyond the material relations of Russian society, however; it profoundly affected its intellectual and moral life. I will touch on the most general features of that influence.

At first glance what I have just said may seem incomprehensible: How could a historical and juridical fact such as serfdom influence such an intimate aspect of the nation's existence as its moral and intellectual life? The transmitter of serfdom's influence on minds and manners was the gentry. Serfdom placed this estate in a quite abnormal position in Russian society, an abnormality first perceived from below, by the lower classes. If you recall the structure of Russian society in pre-Petrine times, then, too, the gentry, or the numerous class of servicemen, stood at its pinnacle. These servicemen enjoyed significant advantages, but they paid for them with a heavy service obligation: the gentry defended the country, served as its chief instrument of administration, and from Peter's time also became the obligatory transmitter of education to Russian society. Seeing the sacrifices this estate bore for the country, the lower classes reconciled themselves to the advantages it enjoyed.

After the middle of the eighteenth century, the balance of rights and obligations on which the Russian political order rested was upset. One estate continued to enjoy all of its previous advantages and received

174

some new ones while shedding its previous obligations one after the other. The lower classes felt this imbalance keenly, all the more so as its tangible expression was serfdom, which concerned them most intimately.

Now the vague idea began to arise in the lower strata of our society that the political order in Russia rested on injustice. This vague sentiment found a distinctive form of expression. The masses rebelled frequently, and they did so both in the seventeenth and in the eighteenth centuries, but the revolts of the eighteenth century were called forth by entirely different motives from those of the preceding one. In the seventeenth century, popular uprisings were usually directed against the organs of administration—the authorities and officials. It is extremely difficult to detect any social impulse behind these uprisings; they were uprisings of the governed against the governors. The reign of Catherine II, primarily its first half, also abounded in peasant uprisings, but now they assumed a different character. They took on a social coloration; they were uprisings not of the governed against the administration but of the lower classes against the upper, ruling class, against the gentry. Thus serfdom, in the phase of development that it entered in the latter half of the eighteenth century, first of all changed the mood of the lower classes, their relationship to the existing order.

Furthermore, serfdom gave the intellectual and moral life of the highest stratum of society a peculiar bent, which was a direct and natural consequence of the strange position in which serfdom placed the gentry. The gentry was the most privileged estate: it directed the entire local administration and concentrated in its hands a vast quantity of the country's basic capital and the people's labor. But the very privileges that raised the gentry to immeasurable heights above the rest of society to an even greater degree cut it off from this society, isolating it and alienating it still further not only from the rural world of the serfs but from the other free social classes as well. Meanwhile, thanks to serfdom, the privileged estate had nothing to do. Broad participation in local administration did not give it a serious public occupation. Noble self-government, even in Catherine's reign, managed to lose any serious significance and became a caricature mocked by the other classes of society and in literature. Noble elections became an arena for intrigues among relatives and friends, and noble assemblies, a school for idle talk and rhetoric. Nor did agriculture seriously occupy the noble. Enjoying unpaid labor, he did not involve himself in economic matters, did not introduce effective improvements in agriculture, did not try to take a productive part in the people's labor. He did not manage; he ruled peasant souls and gave orders.

Thus the gentry, freed from compulsory service, felt itself to be without any real, serious occupation. The gentry's idleness, political and economic, was an extremely important factor in the history of our educated society, and consequently in the history of our culture. It served as fertile soil from which a deformed way of life grew in the second half of the century, with strange ideas, tastes, and attitudes. When people of a certain class are cut off from reality, from the life of the society around them, they create an artificial way of life for themselves, filled with illusory interests. They ignore real interests as though they were other people's dreams, while taking their own reveries for reality. They fill the emptiness of their lives with fine-sounding foreign words, and they populate the emptiness of their souls with capricious and useless fancies; putting the two together, they create a noisy but illusory and purposeless existence. This was precisely the way of life that took shape within gentry society from the middle of the eighteenth century. The ground had been prepared for it even earlier, however. I will outline the two main phases of that society's development.

The first phase dates to the middle of the eighteenth century, the reign of Empress Elizabeth. Once the nobility was freed from compulsory service and felt itself at leisure, it began trying to fill its spare time, to occupy its boring indolence with the fruits of foreign intellectual and moral endeavors, the flower of a borrowed culture. Hence a strong demand arose for the elegant adornments of life, for esthetic diversions. Elizabeth's accession to the throne marked the end of German dominance at the Russian court, but the German dominance was replaced by another influence, equally foreign but now French. During Elizabeth's reign, French tastes, fashions, clothes, and manners began to install themselves at the Petersburg court and in the upper stratum of Russian society. Among those French styles and diversions, the theater became a serious matter of everyday life, and a passion for theatrical performances grew both at court and in society. The strong demand for dramatic entertainments called forth, alongside the French and German theaters, a Russian theater as well, which was first established in Petersburg at that time. Remember that this was the era of the first Russian dramatists and actors, the era of Alexander Sumarokov and Ivan Dmitrevsky. Following the capital, the provinces, too, began to acquire Russian theaters.

The progress of these tastes increased the demand for a kind of education adapted to them. Borrowed esthetic pleasures are peculiar in that they require a certain preparation before a real taste for them makes itself felt, the cultivation of a certain esthetic sense, or at least impressionability. This had a decided effect on the program of gentry education.

Under Peter, a noble was required to study; he studied "by order" and according to a "decreed" curriculum. He was under the obligation to acquire certain mathematical, artillery, and navigational skills, which military service demanded, and certain political, juridical, and economic skills, which civil service required. The educational obligations of the gentry began to decline with Peter's death. The technical education Peter had imposed on this estate as a mandatory requirement began to be replaced by another, voluntary kind of education. An interesting document has come down to us that attests to the rapidity with which the old technical education declined—a report by the College of the Admiralty submitted to the Senate in 1750. Two naval academies, or, more accurately, two navigational schools, came under the administration of this college, one in Petersburg and the other in Moscow (at the Sukharev Tower). The enrollment norms for these academies had been set in 1731: the academy in Petersburg was assigned 150 students and the one in Moscow 100 students. Neither academy, however, was able to recruit its allotted number of students. Under Peter, aristocratic and well-to-do gentry had sent their sons to these academies; in Elizabeth's reign they could entice only the sons of petty landowners or landless gentry. These poor gentry children, who received a meager award (or stipend) of one ruble a month, could not even attend the academy "because of barefootedness" and according to the report were forced to devote themselves not to the sciences but to their own sustenance, to obtaining outside means of support. Thus Peter's favorite child, navigational science, sadly declined. After this report, the Naval Corps of Cadets on Vasilevsky Island was established.[1]

Artillery and navigational education was replaced by schooling in genteel social life, the teaching of what was called under Peter "French and German courtesies." In 1717 a little book appeared in Russian translation, *An Honest Mirror for Youth*, which became the guide to polite behavior, a kind of textbook of refined manners. After the alpha-

---

[1] In St. Petersburg.

bet and "ciphers" (counting), the book laid out the rules of conduct in society: how to sit at table and handle a knife and fork, how to deal with one's nose and handkerchief, at what distance to take off one's hat upon meeting acquaintances, and the posture to assume in making a bow. This book was issued in a second "writing" in 1740, "by decree of Her Imperial Majesty," according to the title page, and was subsequently reprinted several more times, which means that it responded to a strong market demand.

The change in the program of gentry education had a grievous impact on the institutions of general education then in existence. They were headed by the two universities—first the university of the Academy of Sciences in Petersburg, then also Moscow University. During his stay in France, Peter had been made a member of the French Academy and had been so captivated by that institution that he decided to start one like it in Petersburg. He wanted to put the Russian Academy of Sciences on a firm scholarly footing right away and brought in a number of foreign scholars, assigning 25,000 rubles for the Academy's support, which equals almost 200,000 of our rubles. The Academy was adorned with some of the brilliant names in European science of the day, such as the two Bernoullis (a mechanics specialist and a mathematician), the astronomer Delisle, the physicist Bilfinger, the scholar of "Greek and other antiquities" Bayer, and others.[2] To satisfy the everyday needs of Russian society, however, two educational institutions, a gymnasium and a university, were founded and attached to the Academy. Graduates of the gymnasium were supposed to take the courses of the academicians, who formed a university with three faculties. The courses given there encompassed a range of sciences, which included mathematics (*mathesios sublimioris*, in the expression of the time), physics, philosophy, and *humaniora* (eloquence, *studium antiquitatis*, history, and law). Information has been preserved that depicts the teaching at the Academy's university in the most dismal terms. Lomonosov said that "neither the form nor the likeness of a university was in evidence" there. The professors usually gave no lectures; the students were rounded up like army recruits, primarily from other educational institutions, and for the most part were "in a far from good position to take the professors' courses." Even though no lectures

---

[2]After Bayer, the text lists "de Ligny," but no one by this name seems to have been a member of the Academy of Sciences in the eighteenth century.

were given, students were still whipped with birch switches for rudeness. In 1736, several students lodged a complaint with the Senate that the professors were not giving lectures. The Senate proposed to the professors that they give lectures; the professors gave a few, examined the students, and awarded them "good diplomas for show," and with that the affair ended.

Meanwhile, by the 1730s the Academy had managed to accumulate debts of 30,000 rubles beyond its regular income; Empress Anna paid them. By Elizabeth's reign, the Academy had run up new debts of almost the same amount; Elizabeth paid these, too. A contemporary, Münnich's adjutant Christof Manstein, claimed that the total benefit Russian education had received from the Academy in the twenty years of its existence (it was founded just after Peter's death) consisted of the following: it issued a calendar; it published the Academy's *Gazette* in Latin and Russian; and it recruited a few German scientific assistants at a salary of 600–700 rubles, that is, about 5,000 rubles in our money. In their scientific research, the academicians occupied themselves with higher mathematics, the study of "the structure of the body, human and animal," as Manstein put it, and investigations of the language and dwellings of "ancient, immemorial peoples."

Moscow University, founded in 1755, was in no better shape. When it opened, it had 100 students; thirty years later, it had only 82. In 1765, one student was enrolled in the whole juridical faculty; a few years later, one remained in the medical faculty. In Catherine's entire reign, not one physician received a scholarly diploma, that is, passed the examination. Lectures were given in French or Latin. The upper nobility was unwilling to attend the university. One contemporary says that, not only was it impossible to learn anything there, but one might even lose the respectable manners acquired at home. So Peter's goal was not achieved: to impart to the nobility "instruction in citizenship and economics."

Public education did, however, build itself a nest in a place where one would least have expected it—in the special institutions for military instruction. Two existed at the beginning of Elizabeth's reign: the Nobles' Infantry Corps of Cadets, established in Anna's reign in 1731 according to a plan of Münnich's, and the Naval Corps of Cadets, which appeared later, after the report of the College of the Admiralty in 1750. The first was not a specifically military institution. Military exercises occupied the students only one day a week, "so as not to impede instruction in other sciences." At the beginning of Catherine's reign, a new statute was issued for the Nobles' Infantry Corps of Cadets, dated September 11, 1766. This was an unusually well composed and elegant statute—elegant even in the literal sense, as it was gracefully printed and embellished with a number of superb vignettes. The program of instruction in this statute is interesting. The sciences were divided into those leading to a knowledge of subjects needed primarily for civil service and those that were useful or artistic. Then there were "those leading to a knowledge of other skills": logic, elementary mathematics, rhetoric, physics, sacred and secular history (again, no Russian history), geography, chronology, languages—Latin and French—and mechanics. The sciences needed primarily for civil service, which some of the students would be entering, were moral doctrine; natural, universal (international), and state law; and state economy. The useful sciences were general and experimental physics, astronomy, general geography, "nautics" (navigational science), natural history, military skills, fortification, and artillery. The "arts necessary for every individual" were drawing, engraving, architecture, music, dancing, fencing, and the making of statues.

Information has come down to us as to how this broad program was implemented. The Corps of Cadets accepted children at the age of five and no older than six. They were supposed to remain at the Corps for fifteen years and were divided into five age groups of three years each. The youngest class, from five to nine years of age, was assigned six hours of Russian language per week, the same number of hours of dancing, fourteen hours of French—and not a single hour of Scripture. The students in the third class, from twelve to fifteen years of age, were supposed to be taught chronology and history, among other things, but they did not study chronology because they did not know geography, which was supposed to have been taken up in the previous grade, but it had not been taken up in the previous grade because of the students' weak comprehension and in order to spend more time on languages. Thus, the change in the curriculum of gentry education also affected the curriculum of the state schools, which were forced to adapt themselves to the tastes and demands of gentry society.

The curriculum of the state schools was adopted also by private educational institutions, the *pensions*, or boarding schools, which began to appear in Elizabeth's reign. The Smolensk noble Lev Engelhardt provides us with information about the *pension* in which he studied in the 1770s. The director of this *pension* was a certain Ellert. He was a total ignoramus in all the sciences. The school curriculum consisted of brief instruction in every conceivable subject: Scripture, mathematics, grammar, history, even mythology and heraldry. Ellert was a ferocious pedagogue, a real tyrant, as Engelhardt calls him. French was taught more successfully than anything else, because the students were strictly forbidden to speak Russian. For every Russian word a student uttered, he was punished with a strap made of shoe leather. There were always a number of maimed students at the *pension*, but the institution was always full, despite the fact that the tuition was 100 rubles, the equivalent of 700 of ours. Twice a week there were dancing classes at the *pension*, to which noble girls from the town came to learn the minuet and the contradance. Ellert did not stand on ceremony even with the fair sex: once, in front of everyone, he rapped a grown girl's knuckles on the back of a chair because she was slow-witted. All these features of the education that was spreading in gentry circles had a strong impact on the habits of gentry society.

The upper nobility educated their children at home. At first, the teachers were German, then, from Elizabeth's reign, French. These Frenchmen were the "governors," or tutors, who are so well known in our educational history. They were first imported into Russia under Elizabeth. The tutors in this first consignment were very unsophisticated pedagogues. The decree of January 12, 1755, on the founding of Moscow University complained about them bitterly. It read: "Among the gentry in Moscow there are a great number of teachers on a high salary, the larger part of whom are not only unable to teach the sciences but are themselves lacking in the basic elements of the sciences. Many people, instead of seeking out good teachers, take individuals who have spent their whole lives as valets, barbers, and in other such trades." The decree speaks of the need to replace these unfit imported pedagogues with worthy "national" men who are well versed in the sciences. It was difficult to obtain "national" men, however, in view of the condition of the two universities we have described.

Under these educational influences, two curious representatives of the way of life of gentry society had emerged by the middle of the eighteenth century and shone forth in Elizabeth's reign. They received the generic names of the *petit-maître* and the coquette. The *petit-maître* was a fashionable cavalier, educated in French. Things Russian did not exist for him or existed only as objects of derision and contempt; he scorned the Russian language as much as he did German. He did not want to know anything about Russia. Eighteenth-century comedy and satire depict these social types with unusual vividness. In Sumarokov's comedy *The Monsters*,[3] one of the *petit-maîtres*, at the mention of Tsar Alexis's *Ulozhenie* [Code of Laws], exclaims with astonishment: "*Ulozhenie*? What kind of beast is that? Not only do I not want to know Russian law, I wish I did not know the Russian language, either. A stingy language! Why was I born a Russian? To learn how to dress, how to don a hat, how to open a snuff box, and how to take snuff requires a whole lifetime, and I have studied these things formally so that I might thereby serve my fatherland." "Truly, this is a monkey," another character remarks. "But an imported one," adds a third. The coquette was a fashionable lady, educated in French, who might have been called the *petit-maître*'s sister if distinctly nonfraternal relations had not frequently arisen between them. She felt at home everywhere except at home. Her entire catechism of life consisted of dressing tastefully, going out gracefully, greeting others pleasantly, and smiling decorously.

There was a good deal of both the tragic and the comic in the oppressive emptiness of this way of life, but gradually the emptiness began to fill up, thanks to a developing propensity for reading. At first, reading was simply a way of passing the time, of occupying a boring idleness, but then, as often happens, an involuntary inclination turned into a fashion, a requirement of genteel propriety, a condition of good breeding. People read indiscriminately, whatever came to hand: the history of Alexander of Macedon according to Quintus Curtius, *The Rock of Faith* by Stefan Yavorsky, and the novel *Gil Blas*.[4] But then their reading took a more definite direction. Summoned to assist in the struggle against spare time, when people did not know what to do with themselves, reading inclined the tastes of educated society toward belles lettres and sensitive poetry. It was the time when the first tragedies of Sumarokov began to appear, among them one borrowed from Russian history, *Khorev*.[5] A curious society fell avidly upon these tragedies and learned Sumarokov's dialogues and monologues by

---

[3]Written in 1750.

[4]*Gil Blas*, a picaresque novel by Alain-René Lesage, was written between 1715–35 and translated into Russian in 1754.

[5]Sumarokov's first tragedy, *Khorev*, was written in 1747. It was set in Kievan times.

heart, despite his ponderous style. The comedies and tragedies were followed by a whole series of sentimental Russian novels, not a few of which were written by the same Sumarokov. These novels were also learned by heart and never left the lips of clever young ladies and gentlemen. Andrei Bolotov, an amiable observer of contemporary society, a man of both halves of the century, attests in his memoirs that the middle of the century was precisely the time when "genteel life received its foundation." As soon as this new educational element gained currency in fashionable society, refined reading, and the stock of social types, grew more complex. The author of these memoirs of the first and second halves of the century depicts those types for us in their successive historical development.

In the depths of society, at its very bottom, lay a stratum largely untouched by the new influence. It consisted of the petty rural gentry. Major Michael Danilov, a man of the first half of the century, gives a vivid description of it in his memoirs. He tells of his aunt, a widowed Tula landowner. She was illiterate, but every day she would open a book—it did not matter which one—and read by heart, from memory, the acathistus to the Mother of God. She loved cabbage soup and mutton, and when she ate them, she ordered the cook who had prepared them to be flogged before her—not because the cook had prepared them badly but to whet her appetite.

On this rural cultural substratum rested the fashionable gentry world of the capitals and the gubernia seats. It was a world of the French language and the light novel, and it consisted, to use the language of the day, of "stylish dandies and fashionable scatterbrains"—that is, of *petit-maîtres* and coquettes. This society (to employ its own jargon) would peruse a fashionable book "without any distraction" and draw from this reading "unbuttoned speech and vaulting thoughts." A satirical journal of Catherine's time, the *Painter*,[6] parodied the love language of this society with great success, reproducing a note from a fashionable lady to her cavalier: "My man! Bring yourself to me: I am eager for you, oh, how glorious you are!"

These refined amusements, gradually growing in complexity, profoundly affected the nerves of educated Russian society. The effect vividly manifested itself in people who had already reached maturity at the beginning of Catherine's reign. Within this society, refined amuse-

---

[6]A satirical weekly published in the early 1770s by Nicholas Novikov.

ments cultivated an esthetic impressionability, a nervous susceptibility. The educated Russian, it seems, had never had such weak nerves as at this time. Highly placed men, like men who had barely tasted education, wept on every occasion that affected them keenly. The deputies to the Commission of 1767 wept at the reading of the *Instruction*. The adroit court politician Chernyshev wept tears of joy at a nobles' dinner in Kostroma, touched by the decorum with which the nobility received the empress. He could not reminisce about Peter the Great without tears, calling him "the true God of Russia." All these influences left strong traces on the ideas and manners that characterize the Elizabethan phase of development of gentry society. Those traces consisted of a fashionable appearance, a predilection for esthetic enjoyments, and a nervous sensitivity.

The second phase may be called the Catherinian. It was complicated by a new and very important educational element: the desire to embellish life was joined by a desire to embellish the mind. A good preparation for this new phase had been made in Elizabeth's reign— familiarity with the French language and the propensity for refined reading.

As it happened, France became the model of good breeding and social intercourse for Russian society just at the time when French literature was taking a particular direction. Prepared under Elizabeth, Russian society began to absorb with avidity the new ideas then being developed in that literature. It was in France, from the middle of the eighteenth century, that the most outstanding works with the strongest impact on the educated intellects of Europe began to appear. The assimilation of those ideas in Russia was facilitated by various means. First of all, the court encouraged the study of French Enlightenment literature. Some relations between the court and the kings of French literature had already arisen under Elizabeth. That was when Voltaire was made an honorary member of the Russian Academy of Sciences and received a commission to write a history of Peter the Great. Voltaire was assisted in this by the ardent adherent of French styles and literature Ivan Shuvalov, an influential figure at Elizabeth's court and the curator of Moscow University.[7] Catherine, as we know, had been

---

[7]Through Ivan Shuvalov, with whom he had corresponded, Voltaire was commissioned by Elizabeth in 1757 to write his *History of the Empire of Russia under Peter the Great*. It was published in 1760–63.

enthralled by French literature in her youth; upon coming to the throne, she hastened to establish direct relations with the leaders of the literary movement. In part enthralled by the general trend, Catherine was also guided by certain diplomatic considerations: she endeavored to ingratiate herself with the French men of letters, for she set great store by Parisian opinions of her and her deeds. Her interesting correspondence with Voltaire, beginning in 1763 and continuing until 1778, when Voltaire died, has come down to us. Both correspondents were unstinting in the compliments they paid to each other. Catherine even proposed to d'Alembert, Diderot's collaborator in the publication of the *Encyclopedia*, that he take upon himself the education of the heir to the Russian throne, Grand Duke Paul, and she reproached d'Alembert long and hard for declining this proposition. Nor did she overlook Diderot himself in her benefactions. When she learned that the editor of the *Encyclopedia* was in need of funds, she bought his enormous library from him for 15,000 francs and left it in his possession,[8] appointing him its librarian at a salary of 1,000 francs a year.

These ties with the French literary world found reflection in the educational aspirations of the upper educated nobility. In aristocratic homes, the French tutor retained a pedagogical monopoly under Catherine, but this was a new tutor, unlike his predecessor—he came from a second consignment of tutors. Some of them, equal to their calling, were acquainted with the latest word in French literature and even belonged to the extreme wing of the contemporary political movement. The court itself by its bold example supported that movement within the nobility: we saw that d'Alembert nearly became the tutor of the heir to the Russian throne. Catherine was undeterred by her initial failure and wanted to educate at least her grandson in the spirit of the age. With this objective, she invited the Swiss Frédéric La Harpe, who openly professed his republican convictions, to tutor Grand Duke Alexander. Aristocratic homes imitated the court. Count Paul Stroganov, a prominent figure at the beginning of Alexander I's reign, was tutored by the Frenchman Gilbert Romme, a true republican who later became a prominent member of the Party of the Mountain in the National Convention. Nicholas Saltykov's children were educated under the supervision of Marat's brother. This tutor also did not hide his republican convictions, although he did not share his brother's extremism, and

---

[8]The text erroneously reads "left it with d'Alembert."

with his pupils he more than once appeared at court in the company of Grand Duke Alexander. The upper nobility paid generously for the pedagogical labors of imported tutors. One of them, Brückner, received 35,000 rubles (more than 150,000 rubles in our money) for his fourteen years of pedagogical effort in the home of Prince Kurakin.

Such exalted pedagogical instruments as well-educated tutors were utilized only by the upper nobility, but even the rank-and-file reading gentry was not lacking in the means to assimilate the new ideas. French literary works, in the original and in translation, began to circulate freely in Russian society during Catherine's reign. Here, too, Catherine set the example for her subjects: she solemnly recognized the works of French literature as not only harmless but even useful and took upon herself the work of propagandizing them in her *Instruction*. Thanks to her patronage, the works of the French began to circulate briskly even in remote corners of Russia. It is hard for us to imagine now what a multitude of French works were translated into Russian during Catherine's reign and found their way into the bookstores. A Ukrainian noble, Gregory Vinsky, who served in the Guards, reports in his memoirs some interesting facts from the history of the circulation of liberal ideas in Russian society of the time. When he lived in Petersburg, he found in the libraries of his young friends in military and state service nearly all the best works of contemporary French literature. He was brought to trial for his disorderly way of life and exiled to Orenburg, where he found the same works of Rousseau, Montesquieu, and Voltaire. Out of boredom he began to read and translate these works and circulate them in manuscript form. The translations were actively disseminated among his acquaintances and earned praises for the translator. A few years later, Vinsky had the satisfaction of receiving as an interesting novelty his own translations, which had been brought from the depths of Siberia. In Kazan and Simbirsk, he adds, they were known to a great many people.

Under the influence of the new literary demands, the travels of young Russian nobles abroad took on a new purpose. Under Peter, the noble went abroad in order to study artillery and navigation. After Peter, he went there to acquire polite manners. Now, under Catherine, he went to pay his respects to the philosophes. Russian travelers from time to time turned up at "the coaching inn of Europe," as Voltaire called his house at Ferney. Catherine says in one of her letters to Voltaire: Many of our officers, whom you received so indulgently at

Ferney, have returned crazy about you and your reception. Our young people long to see you and to hear your conversation.

By all these highly varied routes, the influence of French Enlightenment literature, along with French styles and manners, flowed into Russian gentry society in a broad stream throughout Catherine's reign. It is difficult to imagine how painstakingly that influence was assimilated; some people achieved a colossally useless virtuosity in this respect. A well-educated Russian grandee, Dmitry Buturlin, conversing with a visiting Frenchman, a Parisian, surprised him with the accuracy with which he discoursed about the streets, hotels, theaters, and monuments of Paris. The foreigner's surprise turned to utter amazement when he learned that Buturlin had never been to Paris and knew all these things only from books. So, there were people in Petersburg who were better acquainted with the French capital than its old inhabitants were. Around the same time, the French literary world of Paris and Petersburg was enthralled by an anonymous play, *Epistle to Ninon*, which was written in such superb French verse that many people attributed it to the pen of Voltaire himself. It turned out that the author of this play was none other than actual state councillor Andrei Shuvalov, the son of the well-known diplomat of Elizabeth's reign. French travelers visiting Petersburg at the end of Catherine's reign affirmed that "the educated youth here are the most enlightened and philosophical in Europe" and that they knew more than the graduates of German universities.

The influence of French Enlightenment literature was the last phase of a process that had been taking place in the intellectual and moral life of Russian society since the death of Peter. What traces did this influence leave? The question is of some value in the history of our society. To explain the nature of those traces, we must have a knowledge of the influence itself. I ask you to remember the significance of French Enlightenment literature of the eighteenth century. As is well known, this was the first quite bold and headlong revolt against the existing order, based on tradition, and against the customary moral outlook then prevailing in Europe. The social order rested on feudalism, and the moral outlook was nurtured by Catholicism; thus French Enlightenment literature was a revolt against feudalism on the one hand and against Catholicism on the other. The meaning of this literature was of quite local origin: it was called forth by interests quite alien to Eastern Europe, which had known neither feudalism nor Catholicism. As he rained down blows on feudalism and Catholicism, however, the French man of letters of the eighteenth century accompanied them with a whole deluge of commonplaces and abstract ideas. The men of Eastern Europe, unfamiliar with feudalism and Catholicism, could assimilate only the commonplaces and abstract ideas. It must be supposed that in the place of their birth those terms and ideas had a rather conditional meaning; men who were contending with Catholicism and feudalism attached practical, everyday significance to abstract terms like political freedom and equality. With these terms, they masked the vital, often even base interests for which the offended classes of society were struggling. The conditional meaning of these abstract terms was unfamiliar to the men of Eastern Europe who were assimilating them. They took them literally, so that commonplaces and conditional, abstract terms became for them unconditional political and religious-moral dogmas. They assimilated these dogmas without reflection, and, once assimilated, these dogmas severed their intellects all the more from the reality around them, which had nothing in common with those ideas.

As a result of the influence of Enlightenment literature, Russian society from Catherine's time on, like Russian letters of the eighteenth century, displayed two peculiarities: first, loss of the habit of reflection, or, indeed, of any desire for reflection; and, second, loss of any understanding of the reality around it. Each of these traits made itself felt with equal force in educated society and in literature under Catherine. Without doubt, the highly talented and greatly successful Fonvizin stood first in the ranks of men of letters in the latter half of the century, but his comedies are either tracts on virtue as personified in character types like Pravdin and Starodum, plucked from who knows what actual soil, or caricatures like the Minor and the Brigadier, who are not lifelike individuals but amusing jokes.[9]

The impact of Enlightenment literature manifested itself also in the appearance of new types of people in Russian society that had not been noticeable under Elizabeth. The abstract ideas, commonplaces, and fine-sounding words that embellished the minds of the men of Catherine's time had no effect at all on their feelings. Underneath these embellishments, an astonishing callousness persisted, the absence of a sense of moral aspiration.

---

[9]The Minor and the Brigadier are the title characters of Fonvizin's two best-known plays. Pravdin and Starodum are characters in *The Minor*. See chapter VI, note 2.

A few exemplars of that society will suffice to enable us to see this perhaps unexpected effect of Enlightenment literature. Princess Catherine Dashkova was in the vanguard of the enlightened ladies of her time, and it was not for nothing that she occupied the president's chair at the Russian Academy of Sciences. While still in her youth, at fifteen or sixteen, she had immersed herself to the point of nervous exhaustion in the works of Bayle, Voltaire, and Rousseau. Upon the completion of her brilliant career, she withdrew to Moscow, and there she revealed herself as she really was: she received almost no one, reacted with indifference to the fate of her children, and unceremoniously fought with her servants. She concentrated all her maternal feelings and civic impulses on the rats she succeeded in taming. Her son's death did not grieve her, but a misfortune that befell her rat moved her to the depths of her soul. Only people of Catherine's time could have begun with Voltaire and ended with a pet rat.

In Penza Gubernia there lived a rich landlord by the name of Nicholas Struisky.[10] He had been governor of Vladimir; then he retired and settled on his Penza estate. He was a great versifier and printed his poems on his own printing press, one of the best in Russia at the time, on which he lavished enormous sums of money. He loved to read his works to his friends, and in his enthusiasm, without being aware of it, he would start to pinch his listener black and blue. Struisky's poems are notable, perhaps, only in that they surpass even the poems of Trediakovsky in their lack of talent. This great lover of the muses, however, was also a great jurist by passion, and in his village he instituted a system of jurisprudence that followed all the rules of European juridical science. He judged his peasants himself, drew up the indictments, and delivered defense speeches on their behalf. Worst of all, however, this civilized judicial procedure was combined with the barbaric method of investigation of old Rus—torture. The cellars in Struisky's house were filled with instruments of torture. Struisky was fully a man of Catherine's time—so much so that he was unable to outlive it. When he received the news of Catherine's death, he had a stroke and soon died.

* * *

---

[10]Nicholas Yeremeyevich Struisky: the text erroneously reads Nikita Yermilovich.

Now that we have set forth the principal developments of Catherine II's reign, let us attempt a historical evaluation of her based on the results of her activity. The significance of a certain historical era or historical figure can best be evaluated by examining the extent to which a nation's resources increased or decreased in that era or under the influence of that historical figure. The resources a nation has at its disposal are either material or moral. The question that needs to be determined, then, is the following: To what extent did the material and moral resources of the Russian state increase or decrease in Catherine's reign?

First, the material resources grew enormously. During Catherine's reign, the territory of the state almost reached its natural frontiers, both in the south and in the west. Three gubernias were formed out of the acquisitions made in the south: Taurida, Kherson, and Yekaterinoslav, not counting the lands of the Black Sea Cossack Host, which originated at the same time.[11] Eight gubernias were formed out of the acquisitions made in the west, from Poland, which I shall list in order from north to south: Vitebsk, Courland, Mogilev, Vilna, Minsk, Grodno, Volynia, and Bratslav (now Podolia). Thus, of the fifty gubernias into which Russia was divided, a total of eleven were acquired in Catherine's reign. This material progress appears in an even more tangible form if we compare the country's population at the beginning of the reign and at its end. At the beginning of Catherine's reign, in 1762 and 1763, the third revision was carried out. On the basis of the proportion of revision souls to total population, the latter, according to the third revision, came to 19 or 20 million souls of both sexes and all categories. At the end of Catherine's reign, in 1796, the fifth revision, completed by Catherine's successor, was undertaken. On the same basis of the relationship of revision souls to total population, there were, according to the fifth revision, no fewer than 34 million inhabitants of the empire.

Thus the size of the population increased by three-quarters during Catherine's reign. At the same time, the state's financial resources also grew. The pace of that growth is graphically reflected in the annual financial registers for the whole period of the reign. In 1762, the trea-

---

[11]The Black Sea Cossack Host was organized in 1787 as the successor to the disbanded Zaporozhian Host and was settled on lands along the northern coast of the Black Sea to provide military defense against the Turks.

sury calculated total state revenue at 16 million rubles. According to the financial register of 1796, total state revenue had risen to 68.5 million. So, the population of the state in the course of the reign nearly doubled, while total state revenue more than quadrupled. This means that not only did the number of taxpayers increase but their payments to the state also rose, which is usually taken as a sign of the increased productivity of the people's labor. Material resources in Catherine's reign, then, grew to an extraordinary degree.

On the other hand, moral resources grew weaker. The moral resources a state has at its disposal can be reduced to two sets of relationships. They consist, first, of the unity of interests that bind the different ethnic and social components of the state to each other and, second, of the capacity of the leading class to lead the society. That capacity in turn depends on the juridical position of the leading class in the society, the degree to which it understands the society's situation, and the degree to which it is politically prepared to lead the society. Those moral resources of the state declined significantly during Catherine's reign. First of all, the conflict of interests among the ethnic components of the state intensified. The Polish partitions introduced into the variegated composition of the population a new, extremely hostile element, which not only failed to strengthen or enhance the ready forces of the state but significantly hampered them. Previously, one element had existed, in the western borderlands, on which Russian society had to expend considerable effort; that element was the German population of the Baltic provinces conquered by Peter. Now that element, which with difficulty was being chemically absorbed into the Russian population, was joined by another, perhaps equally intractable one—the Polish population of the Republic's conquered provinces. The Polish element in the ancient Russian territories would not have constituted the slightest difficulty for the Russian state; it would have disappeared under the influence of the first favorable breeze from the east. But that element became a force as a result of the fact that, besides the southwestern regions, some parts of Poland itself were also added to the territory of the Russian state. On the other hand, one of the important regions of southwestern Rus, organically connected with the rest—Galicia—found itself outside the borders of the Russian state, intensifying the disarray introduced into our international relations in the west.

Furthermore, discord among the social components of the indigenous Russian society intensified. This was a consequence of the relationship between the two basic classes of Russian society, the gentry and the serfs, which Catherine's legislation had created. In order to explain the origins and significance of this discord, we must remember the course our domestic political life took after Peter. Peter had resolved one set of questions of domestic policy, all of which came down to a single question: the organization of the state economy with regard to raising the productivity of the people's labor. All of Peter's domestic activity had an economic character; he left the basic foundations of the juridical order untouched. Peter's legislation, however, while organizing the life of the people and the state, left one important political lacuna: the old order of succession to the throne, established by custom, had been abolished. According to the law of 1722, the designation of an heir was left to the personal discretion of the reigning sovereign. Since no customary heir remained after Peter, this law abandoned the throne to the free play of chance. As a result, for several decades the arbitrariness of individuals, the sway of accident—or, to put it a better way, the will of accidental individuals—established itself in the state administration. Amid this struggle of accidents, the state order Peter had completed was ruined. As we know, that order consisted of the compulsory allocation of state obligations among all the classes of society—the state's binding of the social estates. Thanks to the effect of chance, one estate had the opportunity several times to dispose of the throne and began to transform itself from a simple governmental instrument into a ruling class, casting off its former state obligations one after the other but without losing its former rights and even acquiring new ones. One estate was thus unbound from the state; it acquired the opportunity to live for itself, guided by estate or personal interests. Subsequently, another estate, the commercial and industrial one, was also unbound. The two classes together made up an insignificant part of the population as a whole, but they now came to occupy an exclusive position.

The logical consequence of unbinding these two estates should have been to lighten the state obligations of the other classes as well, that is, to distribute those obligations more equally. The unbinding of the other classes, however, would have to have been accomplished in a different way from that of the nobility. The new position of the noble was recognized by law, but the ground had been prepared for it in a manner that was not fully legal, by revolutionary means. The emancipation of the nobility from compulsory service would not have been accomplished so easily and quickly if that estate had not happened to take an active part in the creation of supreme governments, that is, in the palace coups d'état after Peter's death. Those palace coups paved the way for the legislative emancipation of the nobility from compulsory service.

The serf population intended to unbind itself in precisely the same way: following the nobility, it too wanted to attain freedom through a series of illegal uprisings. That was the meaning of the numerous peasant disturbances that began in the reign of Catherine II and, gradually spreading, merged into the vast Pugachev Rebellion. In the name of public order, such a forcible unbinding could not be allowed; the position of the serfs had to be determined in a lawful manner, by means of a legal definition of their relationship to the land. Catherine's government failed to make that legal definition. Hence, by the end of Catherine's reign, relations between the two basic classes of Russian society were even less harmonious than they had been before; social disunity had become even more acute. Thus, in Catherine's reign, discord intensified in both the ethnic and the social structure of the state.

On the other hand, the ability of the leading class to lead society diminished. In the second half of the eighteenth century, the leading class was still the gentry. Its moral and political resources had gradually been created by compulsory service, which was a political and social school for this estate. Let us recall how that service evolved in the course of the eighteenth century. Under Peter, the noble had undergone obligatory military and technical instruction. Under Peter's successors, that kind of instruction was replaced by drilling in etiquette, which differed from drilling in the Guards or instruction in navigation in that it was unnecessary for service itself but was required for success in service. Under Catherine II, neither form of instruction was required—neither navigational science nor drilling in etiquette—because compulsory service itself was not required. From the two schools it had passed through, however, despite the differences between them, the gentry drew, if not a recognition that it was essential to get an education, at least some skill in learning, a certain instinctive impulse toward education (or breeding), a memory of the learning it had experienced.

With this skill, or this memory, the gentry took up the position created for it by the law of February 18, 1762, on the freedom of the nobility, the gubernia institutions of 1775, and the Charter to the Nobility of 1785. The tastes acquired in service now developed freely, and willy-nilly they began to seek suitably nourishing fare. In Catherine's reign, under the influence of the examples coming from the court, the requirement of a certain literary polish was added to the previous drilling in etiquette. The extensive leisure that became available to the gentry with its emancipation from compulsory service afforded it the opportunity to acquire this polish. The propensity for reading, aimless and unsystematic under Elizabeth, assumed a more definite direction under Catherine. To enliven minds grown drowsy and sluggish from idleness, to arouse somnolent thought, the upper stratum of the nobility began avidly borrowing the bold and provocative ideas that were being disseminated in foreign literature.

Thus, we can designate the principal phases the nobility passed through in its educational development: the Petrine artillerist and navigator after a while turned into the Elizabethan *petit-maître*, and under Catherine II the *petit-maître* in turn became an *homme de lettres*, who by the end of the century had become a freethinker, a Mason, or a Voltairean. And that upper stratum of the nobility, having passed through those phases of development in the course of the eighteenth century, was supposed to lead society after Catherine.

We can readily perceive the meagerness of the political and moral resources this class had at its disposal for the exercise of its leadership. We must picture the situation of this stratum at the end of the century without reference to individuals, for in their fundamental characteristics all the individuals who served as its representatives were alike. The position of this class in society was based on political injustice and was crowned by social idleness. From the hands of the sexton who was his first teacher, a man of this class passed into the hands of a French tutor, completed his education at the Italian theater or in a French restaurant, applied the ideas he had acquired in the drawing rooms of the capitals, and ended his days in his Moscow or country study, Voltaire in hand. Clutching one of Voltaire's books, somewhere on Povarskaia Street or in a Tula village, this nobleman was a very strange phenomenon: the manners he had adopted, his habits, ideas, and sentiments, and the very language in which he thought were all foreign, all imported, while at home he had no vital, organic ties with his surroundings and no serious occupation, for, as we know, neither participation in local administration nor agriculture provided him with serious work. Therefore, no vital, everyday interests bound him to reality. A foreigner at home, he tried to make himself at home among foreigners, and, needless to say, he failed: abroad, in the West, he was viewed as a Tatar in disguise, while in Russia he was regarded as a Frenchman who had accidentally been born in Russia. Thus he ended up neither fish nor fowl, a historically useless creature.

Seeing him in this position, we are inclined to feel sorry for him, on the assumption that he must have been unbearably melancholy at times. There were occasions when he did display such melancholy, or despair, at the thought that he could not possibly reconcile himself with the reality around him. An example of such despair is a Yaroslavl landlord named Opochinin. He had been brought up on ideas and sentiments at the highest level of the contemporary intellectual and moral movement in Europe. Needless to say, the ideals he absorbed made him irreconcilably hostile to the reality around him. Unable to come to terms with it, Opochinin, more sincere than other men of the same cast of mind, in 1793 killed himself. In his will he wrote in explanation of his action: "Disgust at our Russian life is the motive that compels me to decide my fate by my own volition." Opochinin freed two families of house serfs in his will and ordered that the lord's grain be distributed to the peasants. (He did not free the peasants, for there was still a question as to whether a landlord had the right according to the laws at the time to emancipate his peasants and set them at liberty.) The most interesting lines in the will are those concerning the landowner's library. "Books," he wrote, "my beloved books! I do not know to whom I should leave them: I am sure no one needs them in this country. I humbly ask my heirs to consign them to the flames. They were my first treasure, they alone sustained me in life; but for them, my life would have been an uninterrupted affliction, and I would long since have abandoned this world with contempt." A few minutes before his death, Opochinin still had the spirit to begin a translation of Voltaire's poem "Oh, God, whom we do not know."

Opochinin was an exception, however. People of his cast of mind did not share his cosmopolitan chagrin, did not grow melancholy, and were not even bored; they began to grow melancholy somewhat later, in the reign of Alexander I, and to grow bored later still, in the reign of Nicholas I. The Voltairean of Catherine's day was cheerful, and that was all. He celebrated his retirement after his longtime compulsory service, and, like a graduate of the Corps of Cadets, he could not gaze fondly enough at the noble's uniform in which he had been freed from service. It would seem that the ideas that enthralled him, the books that he read, should have made him irreconcilably hostile to the reality around him, like Opochinin, but the Voltairean of the end of the eighteenth century was not hostile to anything and felt no contradiction in his situation. Books embellished his intellect, imparted luster to it, and even unsettled his nerves. It is well known that the educated Russian never wept so readily at fine words as in the eighteenth century. The impact of the ideas he absorbed went no further, however; without affecting his will, they served their bearer as an abnormal diversion, a nervous exercise. They softened the feelings without reforming relationships and embellished the mind without improving the existing order.

It should not be thought, however, that the generation of those Voltaireans was an entirely fruitless phenomenon in our history. It made no use of its ideas itself, but it served as an important transmission point. While it made no practical application of its intellectual stock, this generation preserved it for the time being and passed it on to the next generation, which made more serious use of it. Thus, the leading class, finding itself at the head of Russian society at the end of the eighteenth century, could not become its active leader. The greatest good it could do society could consist only of resolving to do it no harm.

~ Glossary of Names ~

ALEXANDER I, Emperor (1801–25), was the eldest son of Emperor Paul and the grandson of Catherine II.

ALEXIS, Tsar, ruled from 1645 to 1676. He was the father of Peter the Great.

ANNA, Empress (1730–40), was Duchess of Courland before her accession to the Russian throne. She was the daughter of Ivan V, Peter the Great's half-brother.

ANNA LEOPOLDOVNA was the granddaughter of Ivan V. She ruled as regent for her infant son, Ivan VI, from 1740 to 1741, that is, from the death of Anna to the coup d'état that placed Elizabeth on the throne.

BAYER, Gottlieb-Siegfried, an Orientalist, was one of the first members of the Academy of Sciences, where he served as professor of Greek and Roman antiquity.

BERNOULLI, Daniel, and his older brother, Nicolaus, both mathematicians, came to the Academy of Sciences in 1725. Nicolaus died in 1726, and Daniel served as professor of mathematics. Their family, settled in Basel, Switzerland, produced a long line of distinguished mathematicians.

BESSARABIA: a Romanian-speaking territory north of the Danube. It was under Turkish rule in the eighteenth century and subsequently changed hands several times between Russia and Romania. Today it is the Republic of Moldova.

BESTUZHEV-RIUMIN, Count Alexis Petrovich, served as chancellor, the equivalent of foreign minister, under Elizabeth from 1744 to 1758.

BETSKOI, Ivan Ivanovich, became Catherine's chief collaborator on educational matters and assisted in the establishment of foundling homes in Moscow and St. Petersburg and the Smolny Institute, a boarding school for noble girls in St. Petersburg.

BEZBORODKO, Count Alexander Andreyevich, was a leading military and diplomatic figure under both Catherine and Paul.

BIBIKOV, Alexander Ilich, was a general who had seen service in Prussia and Poland. He also served as marshal of the Commission of 1767. In 1773, Catherine appointed him head of an expedition to suppress the Pugachev Rebellion, but after some initial success he died suddenly in April 1774.

BIELFELD, Baron Jakob Friedrich von, was an eighteenth-century jurist best known for his work on political economy, *Institutions politiques*, which Catherine had translated into Russian. Along with Justi, he was a leading advocate of cameralism, an economic theory prevalent in the German states that assigned a prominent role to government in stimulating industrial activity.

BILFINGER (Bülfinger), Georg Bernhard, a philosopher, mathematician, and scientist, joined the Academy of Sciences at its inception in 1725.

BIRON, Count Ernst Johann, was Empress Anna's favorite and a powerful figure during her reign. His name became synonymous with the domination of Germans at Anna's court.

BOLOTOV, Andrei Timofeyevich, is best known for his extensive memoirs of Russian gentry life in the eighteenth century, *The Life and Adventures of Andrei Bolotov.*

BORIS GODUNOV, Tsar, ruled from 1598 to 1605.

BRETEUIL, Baron de (Louis Charles Auguste Le Tonnelier), became French ambassador to Russia in 1760.

BUTURLIN, Count Dmitry Petrovich, was famous for his encyclopedic knowledge and for the magnificent library he collected.

CATHERINE I, Empress, was the second wife of Peter the Great and the mother of Empress Elizabeth. Catherine succeeded Peter at his death in 1725 and ruled to 1727.

CHARLES XII was king of Sweden from 1697 to 1718 and Peter the Great's opponent in the Northern War.

CHEBOTAREV, Khariton Andreyevich, was a professor of Russian history. When the universities were reorganized under Alexander I in 1803, he was appointed the first rector of Moscow University.

CHERNYSHEV, Count Ivan Grigorevich, was a field marshal and president of the College of the Admiralty.

CHESME: a Turkish fortress on the Aegean Sea, the site of a naval battle in 1770 in which the Russians destroyed a Turkish fleet.

CHÉTARDIE, Jacques Joachim, Marquis de la Chétardie, the French envoy at Elizabeth's court, was expelled from Russia in June 1744.

CHOISEUL, Étienne François, Duc de Choiseul, served as French foreign minister from 1758 to 1770.

DANILOV, Michael Vasilevich, was the author of *Memoirs of Artillery Major Michael Vasilevich Danilov*, written in 1771.

DASHKOVA, Princess Catherine Romanovna, was a close friend of Catherine II's and a participant in the coup d'état of 1762. (Née Vorontsova, she was also the sister of Peter III's mistress.) She later served as president of the Academy of Sciences and was the author of *Memoirs*.

DELISLE, Joseph-Nicolas, a French astronomer and one of the original members of the Academy of Sciences, worked in Russia from 1725 to 1747.

DIMITRY (Sechenov), archbishop and then metropolitan of Novgorod, officiated at Catherine's coronation in September 1762.

DMITREVSKY, Ivan Afanasevich, was a leading actor in classical tragedy in St. Petersburg during the reigns of Elizabeth and Catherine.

ELIZABETH, Empress (1741–61), was the younger daughter of Peter the Great by his second wife, Catherine I.

ELPHINSTONE, John, a British naval officer, entered Russian service in 1768 as a rear admiral and commanded a squadron in the Aegean during the first Turkish war.

FONVIZIN, Denis Ivanovich (1745–1792), was the leading dramatist of the late eighteenth century. He was the author of two notable satirical comedies, *The Brigadier* and *The Minor*.

FREDERICK II (the Great) was king of Prussia from 1740 to 1786.

FYODOR, Tsar (1584–98), the son of Ivan IV (the Terrible), was the last ruler of the Rurik dynasty. His death marked the beginning of the Time of Troubles.

GALICIA: the southern part of Poland, annexed by Austria in the partitions. It had once been part of Kievan Rus.

GEOFFRIN, Marie-Thérèse, had been a friend of Catherine's mother's. She presided over one of the leading Paris literary salons.

GLEBOV, Alexander Ivanovich, was appointed procurator-general of the Senate by Peter III. He was suspected of corruption and was removed by Catherine.

GOLITSYN, Prince Dmitry Alekseyevich, was a diplomat and writer. He served at the Russian embassy in Paris in the 1750s and 1760s, becoming ambassador in 1762. He was friendly with Diderot, Voltaire, and other philosophes and was an adherent of their ideas. He became a member of the St. Petersburg Free Economic Society and published articles in its *Proceedings*.

GRIMM, Baron Friedrich Melchior, was a well-known commentator on literary matters during the Enlightenment and served as Catherine's European agent, purchasing art works and performing other commissions for her.

HERTZBERG, Count Ewald Friedrich von, served as Prussian foreign minister under Frederick II.

IMERITIA: an Eastern Orthodox kingdom in the Caucasus, closely related to Georgia, under Ottoman rule until 1774.

IVAN IV (the Terrible), Tsar, reigned from 1533 to 1584).

IVAN V was Peter the Great's half brother and ruled with him as co-tsar from 1682 to 1696.

IVAN VI, born in 1740, was the great-grandson of Ivan V. Named emperor by Anna in 1740, he was deposed by Elizabeth in 1741 and imprisoned for the rest of his life. Catherine issued a standing order that he be put to death in the event of any effort to free him, and the order was carried out during Mirovich's attempt in 1764.

JOSEPH II was emperor of Austria from 1780 to 1790.

JUSTI, Johann Heinrich Gottlob von, along with Bielfeld, was one of the leading eighteenth-century exponents of the economic theory of cameralism.

KABARDIA: a Moslem region in the north Caucasus, formerly under Ottoman and Crimean Tatar rule, annexed to Russia in 1774.

KAUNITZ, Prince Wenzel Anton von, was the chancellor, or foreign minister, of Austria in the second half of the eighteenth century.

KHITROVO, Fyodor, was a Guards officer who helped carry out the coup d'état of 1762. In the following year, however, he became involved in a vague plot against Catherine and was banished to his estates.

KHRAPOVITSKY, Alexander Vasilevich, served as Catherine's private secretary from 1782 to 1793. The diary he kept in those years is an important source for her reign.

KORFF, Baron Johann-Albrecht, was appointed Russian ambassador to Copenhagen in 1740. He had previously served as director of the Academy of Sciences.

KORFF, Baron Nicholas Andreyevich, as a cavalry major was dispatched to Kiel by Elizabeth in 1742 to convey the future Peter III to Russia. In 1760 he was appointed policemaster-general of St. Petersburg, and he retained his position under both Peter III and Catherine.

KOSCIUSZKO, Tadeusz, who had served as a general on the colonial side in the American Revolution, led an unsuccessful Polish uprising against the partitioning powers in 1794. He was imprisoned by Catherine but later released from arrest by Emperor Paul.

KOTOSHIKHIN, Gregory Karpovich, served as a clerk in the Ambassadorial Office (i.e., the office of foreign affairs) during the reign of Tsar Alexis. In 1664 he fled Russia, and eventually he took asylum in Sweden, where he wrote *On Russia in the Reign of Alexis Mikhailovich*, a detailed description of government and society in seventeenth-century Muscovy.

KOZITSKY, Gregory Vasilevich, was a leading literary figure and translator who served as Catherine's secretary from 1768 to 1775.

KRONSTADT: an island naval base just outside St. Petersburg, the home of Russia's Baltic Fleet.

LA HARPE, Frédéric-César, a Swiss lawyer, served as tutor to Catherine's two eldest grandsons, the future Alexander I and his brother Constantine.

LESTOCQ, Count Armand, the son of a French Huguenot physician, came to Russia under Peter the Great. He served as Elizabeth's personal physician and was an influential adviser until his arrest in 1748.

LOCATELLI, Giovanni Battista, was the founder of an Italian comic opera company and other theatrical enterprises in St. Petersburg and Moscow in the late 1750s.

LOMONOSOV, Michael Vasilevich (1711–1765) rose from peasant origins to become a distinguished scientist, poet, and scholar. He drew up the plan for the establishment of Moscow University in 1755.

MANSTEIN, Christof Hermann, served in the Russian military from 1736 to 1744 and subsequently in the Prussian military. He is best known for his memoirs, *Historical, Civil, and Military Notes on Russia from 1727 to 1744.*

MASLOV, Anisim, served as senior procurator of the Senate under Empress Anna. He advocated legislative regulation of the serfs' obligations to their masters.

MENSHIKOV, Prince Alexander Danilovich, rose from humble origins to become a favorite of Peter the Great's and one of the most powerful and spectacularly wealthy men in the Russian Empire. He died in Siberian exile in 1729.

MERCIER DE LA RIVIÈRE was a French jurist whom Catherine engaged to assist the work of the Legislative Commission of 1767. When she met him in Petersburg in 1768, however, his arrogance offended her and he soon left Russia.

MICHAEL, Tsar, was the first sovereign of the Romanov dynasty. He ruled from 1613 to 1645.

MIROVICH, Vasily Yakovlevich, was an army officer who made an abortive attempt to free Ivan VI from imprisonment in 1764.

MOLDAVIA: an Eastern Orthodox principality on the Danube, part of present-day Romania.

MÜNNICH, Field Marshal Burkhard Christoph von, entered Russian service in 1721. Exiled to Siberia by Elizabeth when she came to the throne in 1741, he was recalled by Peter III.

MUSIN-PUSHKIN, Count Alexis Ivanovich, was a noted collector of Russian historical manuscripts and books.

NICHOLAS I, Emperor (1825–55), was the brother of Alexander I and the third grandson of Catherine II. He succeeded the childless Alexander.

ORLOV, Count Alexis Grigorevich. the younger brother of Gregory Orlov, distinguished himself in the first Turkish war and subsequently retired from service.

ORLOV, Count Gregory Grigorevich, a Guards officer, became Catherine's lover in 1761; in April 1762 she bore a son by him, who was named Count Alexis Grigorevich Bobrinskoi. She broke with Orlov in 1772, and he died in 1783.

OSTERMANN, Count Andrei Ivanovich (Heinrich Johann Friedrich), a German-born statesman and diplomat, began his career in Russia under Peter the Great in 1704. Under Anna he served as vice-chancellor and directed Russia's foreign affairs. He was exiled by Elizabeth when she came to the throne.

PALLAS, Peter Simon, of German birth, became a member of the St. Petersburg Academy of Sciences in 1767. He directed scientific expeditions to study various parts of Russia, including Siberia, and collected scientific material in several scholarly fields.

PANIN, Count Nikita Ivanovich, under Elizabeth served as ambassador to Sweden and under Catherine managed Russia's foreign policy from 1763 to 1781 as senior member of the College of Foreign Affairs (though he was not named chancellor). He was also Grand Duke Paul's tutor until Paul reached his majority.

PANIN, Count Peter Ivanovich, the brother of Nikita Panin, was a general and an influential voice in political and military affairs in the early part of Catherine's reign.

PASSEK, Peter Bogdanovich, was an officer in the Preobrazhensky Guards and part of the conspiracy of 1762 that put Catherine on the throne. He became a provincial governor later in Catherine's reign.

PAUL, Emperor (1796–1801), born in 1754, was the son of Catherine and (presumably) Peter III.

PETER I (the Great) was the son of Tsar Alexis. He reigned with his half-brother Ivan V from 1682 to 1696, and as sole ruler from 1696 to 1725. He was the first Russian sovereign to adopt the title of Emperor.

PETER II, Emperor, was Peter the Great's grandson. His father was Peter the Great's son Alexis, who died under interrogation in 1718. Peter II succeeded Catherine I in 1727 and ruled until 1730.

PETER III was Russian emperor for six months in 1761–62. He was the son of Peter the Great's elder daughter Anna, who had married the Duke of Holstein-Gottorp.

PLATON (Levshin), Archbishop and then metropolitan of Moscow, was one of the most distinguished Russian churchmen of the latter eighteenth century, particularly notable for his familiarity with the literature of the Enlightenment.

POLENOV, Alexis Yakovlevich, a nobleman who had studied law at the universities of Strasbourg and Göttingen, submitted an essay critical of serfdom in a competition sponsored by the Free Economic Society in 1765. He urged that the peasants be given property rights to their land and that the dues and services they paid to the landlords be legally regulated.

PONIATOWSKI, Stanislas, was the last king of Poland. He had been Catherine's lover before she came to the throne, and she had him elected king in 1764. He reigned as Stanislas Augustus IV until the final partition of Poland, and abdicated in 1795. He died in St. Petersburg in 1798.

POSOSHKOV, Ivan Tikhonovich, a peasant merchant, was the author of *On Poverty and Wealth*, a treatise on Russian economic development completed in 1724. Among other things, he advocated legal protection of the serfs from the demands of the landlords.

POTEMKIN, Prince Gregory Aleksandrovich, first attracted Catherine's attention as a Guards officer; he later became her lover as well as the central military and administrative figure of her reign. She may possibly have married him in a secret ceremony. He died in 1791 in the south of Russia, where Catherine had put him in charge of developing the territories newly acquired from Turkey.

PUGACHEV, Yemelian, was a Cossack by origin. Claiming to be Peter III, who had escaped death at the hands of his assassins, he led the great peasant rebellion of 1773–74. He was executed in Moscow in January 1775.

PULASKI, Joseph, belonged to a family of Polish patriots. His son Casimir, after helping his father organize the Confederation of Bar, achieved renown as a military commander of the colonial forces in the American Revolution.

RASTRELLI, Bartolomeo, originally from Florence, was a prolific architect in the baroque style under Anna and Elizabeth. In addition to the Winter Palace in St. Petersburg, he built the Smolny Cathedral and the palace in Tsarskoe Selo.

RAZUMOVSKY, Count Alexis Grigorevich, became Elizabeth's favorite in the early years of her reign. He is reputed to have married her in a secret ceremony in 1742.

RAZUMOVSKY, Count Kirill Grigorevich, the younger brother of Alexis, was an influential figure at Elizabeth's court. He was the last hetman, or chief, of Ukraine, from 1751 to 1764, and also served as president of the Academy of Sciences.

RUMIANTSEV, Count Peter Aleksandrovich, was a military man whom Catherine appointed governor-general of Ukraine in 1764, after the abolition of the hetmanate, to integrate the region into the administration of the empire. He distinguished himself in the first Turkish war and was promoted to field marshal.

RURIK, the semilegendary Scandinavian prince, was regarded as the founder of the Kievan state in 862.

RYCHKOV, Peter Ivanovich, was a geographer, an economist, and a historian. His scholarly interests focused particularly on the southeastern regions of Russia.

ST. SERGIUS OF RADONEZH (d. 1392) was the most revered church figure of the fourteenth century and the founder of the Trinity Monastery outside Moscow.

SALTYKOV, Prince Nicholas Ivanovich, a field marshal, served in important military and political posts under Catherine, Paul, and Alexander.

SECHENOV, Dimitry. See DIMITRY.

SÉGUR, Louis Philippe, Comte de Ségur, was appointed French ambassador to Russia in 1783 and accompanied Catherine on her journey down the Volga in 1787.

SHCHERBATOV, Prince Michael Mikhailovich, is best known today for his essay "On the Corruption of Morals in Russia," which contained harsh criticism of Catherine for licentiousness and vainglory.

SHUVALOV, Count Alexander Ivanovich, the brother of Peter Shuvalov, in addition to being marshal of the court, was director of the Secret Chancery under Elizabeth. He was promoted to field marshal under Peter III.

SHUVALOV, Count Andrei Petrovich, was the son of Peter Ivanovich. He served in a variety of governmental capacities under Catherine. His "Épître à Ninon de Lenclos" was written in 1773–74.

SHUVALOV, Ivan Ivanovich, was Elizabeth's favorite in her last years and one of the sources of the Shuvalov party's influence at her court. He later served as the first curator of Moscow University and as president of the Academy of Arts.

SHUVALOV, Count Peter Ivanovich, a cousin of Ivan's, participated in the events that put Elizabeth on the throne in 1741. He remained an influential political and military figure during her reign and was the author of numerous reform projects.

SIEVERS, Count Jakob Johann, of Baltic German origin, served as governor of Novgorod Gubernia from 1764 and as governor-general of northwestern Russia from 1775 to 1781. He was Catherine's chief adviser on the administration and reform of Russia's provincial government.

SOPHIA, Tsarevna, was the daughter of Tsar Alexis. She ruled as regent for the co-tsars Ivan V and Peter I (her brother and half-brother, respectively) from 1682 to 1689.

SPERANSKY, Count Michael Mikhailovich, served as adviser to Alexander I until 1812 and was the author of a number of governmental and legal reforms.

SPIRIDOV, Gregory Andreyevich, was the admiral of the Russian fleet sent from the Baltic to the Aegean in the first Turkish war.

STANISLAS AUGUSTUS IV, King of Poland. See PONIATOWSKI, Stanislas.

STORCH, Heinrich Friedrich, a Baltic German, was a political economist and one of the first popularizers of Adam Smith in Russia. He was the author of a historical and statistical survey of Russia at the end of the eighteenth century.

STROGANOV, Paul Aleksandrovich, served as a member of Alexander I's so-called Unofficial Committee, an intimate group of advisers that drew up plans for eform in the early years of his reign.

STRUBE DE PIERMONT, Friedrich Henrich, a jurist, was born and educated in Germany. In 1738 he was appointed a professor of law in the St. Petersburg Academy of Sciences.

STRUISKY, Nicholas Yeremeyevich, served in the Guards before retiring to his Penza estate to devote himself to writing poetry. He died in 1796, the same year as Catherine. It is questionable whether he was ever governor of Vladimir.

SUMAROKOV, Alexander Petrovich (1717–1777), was a man of letters and Russia's first professional playwright, composing tragedies in the classical mode and comedies based on French models. He was appointed director of the public theater established in St. Petersburg by Elizabeth in 1756.

TIFLIS: present-day Tbilisi, the capital of the Republic of Georgia.

TODORSKY, Simon, a Ukrainian, was one of the most learned Orthodox theologians of the eighteenth century. Educated by Jesuits, he was also influenced by German Pietism.

TREDIAKOVSKY, Vasily Kirillovich (1703–1769), was a prolific poet of little talent, but he played an important role in the development of Russian literature as a translator and literary theorist.

TRUBETSKOI, Prince Nikita Yurevich, served as procurator-general of the Senate and then president of the College of War under Elizabeth.

USHAKOV, Fyodor Fyodorovich, Russian admiral, defeated a Turkish fleet just outside Constantinople on July 29, 1791.

VIAZEMSKY, Prince Alexander Alekseyevich, noted for his honesty, was appointed procurator-general of the Senate in 1763. He held that post for twenty-nine years, while also serving Catherine in several other important governmental capacities, especially in the financial realm.

VILBUA (Villebois), Alexander Nikitich, was the son of a French naval officer who had joined the service of Peter the Great. He was appointed master of ordnance by Peter III but played an important part in the conspiracy that brought Catherine to the throne.

VINSKY, Gregory Stepanovich, born in 1752 and educated in Ukraine, was the author of *My Times: Memoirs*.

VOCKERODT, Johann Gotthilf, was the secretary of the Prussian embassy to the court of Empress Anna. His *Russia under Peter the Great*, compiled in 1737, was published in Leipzig in 1872.

VORONTSOV, Count Michael Illarionovich, served as vice-chancellor and then chancellor (after the fall of Bestuzhev-Riumin) under Elizabeth and Peter III. His wife, Anna Karlovna, née Skavronskaia, was part of Elizabeth's inner circle.

WALLACHIA: an Eastern Orthodox principality on the Danube, part of present-day Romania.

YAGUZHINSKY, Count Paul Ivanovich, served as procurator-general of the Senate under Peter the Great and Catherine I.

YAVORSKY, Stefan, was an erudite Ukrainian monk who held a number of high ecclesiastical positions under Peter the Great, although he opposed Peter's encroachments on the independence of the church. In 1721, Peter appointed him the first president of the Holy Governing Synod. *The Rock of Faith*, written in 1718 but published only after Yavorsky's death, was a defense of Orthodoxy against Protestantism.

ZAPOROZHIAN COSSACKS: a Cossack host, or community, on the
Dnieper River in Ukraine, south of Kiev. The Zaporozhian Cossacks had spearheaded the Orthodox revolt against Polish rule in the
seventeenth century. Catherine abolished their autonomous organization in 1775.

ZORNDORF and KUNERSDORF: the sites of two major battles between
Russia and Prussia in the Seven Years' War, in 1758 and 1759,
respectively. The second was a particularly notable Russian victory.

~ Glossary of Terms ~

ASSEMBLY OF THE LAND: a body of elected representatives of the various estates and towns at the end of the sixteenth century and in the first half of the seventeenth. It brought an end to the Time of Troubles by electing Michael Romanov tsar in 1613 and continued for several decades to play a role in governing the country.

"BLACK CLERGY": the term for monks from whom the members of the hierarchy of the Russian Orthodox Church were drawn.

COLLEGES: created by Peter the Great, they were the central departments of the Russian government in the eighteenth century. Each was headed by a collective board rather than an individual minister.

DESIATINA: a unit of land measure equal to 2.7 acres.

ESTATES: the hereditary social groups into which Russian society was divided. The principal estates were the nobility, or gentry; the merchants and townsmen; the peasantry; and the clergy. Kliuchevsky often uses the term "class" interchangeably with "estate," but it should be kept in mind that the estates were legal and social categories rather than economic groups in the modern sense.

GUBERNIAS: the chief provincial units of the Russian Empire. They were first created by Peter the Great, who subdivided them into provinces and districts. Catherine the Great then subdivided them into new districts without provinces.

MARTINISTS: followers of the doctrines of Claude de Saint Martin (1743–1803), a mystical freemason.

OLD BELIEVERS: adherents of the Old Belief; those Russian Orthodox who opposed the ritual reforms of the mid-seventeenth century and broke away from the official church. They were severely persecuted, and many fled to remote areas of Russia as well as abroad.

OPRICHNINA: an administrative, police, and terror institution created by Ivan the Terrible. It functioned from 1564 to 1572.

PUD: a unit of weight equal to 36 pounds.

REVISION: a periodic census of the male tax-paying population, that is, peasants and townsmen, instituted by Peter the Great in 1718. Each individual listed in the census was termed a "revision soul."

SECRET CHANCERY: created by Peter the Great, the agency in charge of investigating political crimes.

SEJM: the lower house of the Polish diet, or parliament. The Senate was the upper house. One of the peculiarities of the Sejm was the *liberum veto*, under which a negative vote by a single deputy could not only defeat a specific piece of legislation but dissolve the Sejm and nullify all its previous decisions.

SINGLE HOMESTEADERS: originally, petty military servicemen who had been settled on the southern frontier of Russia as a defense against the Tatars. By the eighteenth century, they had become essentially a class of free peasants.

SOUL TAX: a head tax or poll tax, the state tax paid by each "revision soul."

STATE COUNCIL: a consultative body of officials established by Alexander I in 1810 to advise the sovereign on legislative matters.

SUPREME PRIVY COUNCIL: created in 1726, the council was a small body of important dignitaries that exercised considerable power in the years after Peter the Great's death. It was abolished in 1730 after its abortive effort to impose conditions on the new empress, Anna, under which she would have had to share her powers formally with the council.

SYNOD: the Most Holy Governing Synod was created by Peter the Great in 1721. Organized in the manner of one of the administrative "colleges," it was a board of clerics that replaced the patriarchate as the directing body of the Russian Orthodox Church.

TAX FARM: an exclusive right to a certain economic activity or to the collection of certain taxes or customs duties, purchased from the government for a fixed sum.

TIME OF TROUBLES: the period from 1598 to 1613 in which the extinction of the Rurik dynasty, social upheaval, and foreign invasion combined to reduce Russia to chaos. It came to an end with the election of Michael, the first ruler of the Romanov dynasty, to the Russian throne.

TSAREVICH: son of a tsar.

TSAREVNA: daughter of a tsar.

UNIATES: adherents of the Uniate (or Greek Catholic) Church, formed at the Union of Brest in 1596, which united the Orthodox in Poland with the Catholic Church. The Uniate Church recognized the pope as its head but retained Slavonic and Orthodox rites and customs.

VERST: a measure of length equal to two-thirds of a mile.

"WHITE CLERGY": the term for the secular clergy, or parish priests, who, in the Orthodox Church, married and had families.

⌒ Bibliography ⌒

Primary Sources

[Catherine the Great]. *The Memoirs of Catherine the Great*, ed. Dominique Maroger, trans. Moura Budberg. New York: Collier Books, 1961.

[Dashkova, E.R.]. *The Memoirs of Princess Dashkov*, trans. and ed. Kyril Fitzlyon. London: Calder, 1958.

Dukes, Paul, ed. *Russia under Catherine the Great*. 2 vols. Newtonville, MA: Oriental Research Partners, 1977–78.

Griffiths, David, and Munro, George E., trans. and eds. *Catherine II's Charters of 1785 to the Nobility and the Towns*. Bakersfield, CA: Charles Schlacks Jr., 1991.

Lentin, Antony, trans. and ed. *Voltaire and Catherine the Great: Selected Correspondence*. Cambridge: Oriental Research Partners, 1974.

Radishchev, Aleksandr N. *A Journey from St. Petersburg to Moscow*, trans. Leo Wiener, ed. Roderick Page Thaler. Cambridge, MA: Harvard University Press, 1958.

Raeff, Marc, ed. *Plans for Political Reform in Imperial Russia, 1730–1905*. Englewood Cliffs, NJ: Prentice-Hall, 1966.

Reddaway, W.F., ed. *Documents of Catherine the Great: The Correspondence with Voltaire and the Instruction of 1767, in the English Text of 1768*. Cambridge: Cambridge University Press, 1931.

Segel, Harold B., trans. and ed. *The Literature of Eighteenth-Century Russia*. 2 vols. New York: E.P. Dutton, 1967.

Shcherbatov, M.M. *On the Corruption of Morals in Russia*, trans. and ed. A. Lentin. London: Cambridge University Press, 1969.

Secondary Works

Alexander, John T. *Autocratic Politics in a National Crisis: The Imperial Russian Government and Pugachev's Revolt, 1773–1775*. Bloomington: Indiana University Press, 1969.

————. *Catherine the Great: Life and Legend.* New York and Oxford: Oxford University Press, 1989.

Black, J.L. *Citizens for the Fatherland: Education, Educators, and Pedagogical Ideals in Eighteenth Century Russia.* Boulder, CO: East European Quarterly, 1979.

————. *G.-F. Müller and the Imperial Russian Academy.* Kingston: McGill–Queen's University Press, 1986.

Byrnes, Robert F. *V.O. Kliuchevskii, Historian of Russia.* Bloomington and Indianapolis: Indiana University Press, 1995.

Canadian Slavic Studies 4, no. 3 (Fall 1970). Special issue: "The Reign of Catherine II."

Canadian-American Slavic Studies 20, nos. 3–4 (Fall–Winter 1986). "Kliuchevskii's Russia: Critical Studies," ed. Marc Raeff.

Daniel, Wallace L. *Grigorii Teplov: A Statesman at the Court of Catherine the Great.* Newtonville, MA: Oriental Research Partners, 1991.

Dukes, Paul. *Catherine the Great and the Russian Nobility: A Study Based on the Materials of the Legislative Commission of 1767.* Cambridge: Cambridge University Press, 1967.

Fisher, Alan W. *The Russian Annexation of the Crimea, 1772–1783.* Cambridge: Cambridge University Press, 1967.

Garrard, John G., ed. *The Eighteenth Century in Russia.* Oxford: Clarendon Press, 1973.

Gleason, Walter J. *Moral Idealists, Bureaucracy, and Catherine the Great.* New Brunswick, NJ: Rutgers University Press, 1981.

Hartley, Janet M., and Bartlett, Roger, eds. *Russia in the Age of the Enlightenment—Essays for Isabel de Madariaga.* London: Macmillan, 1990.

Jones, Robert E. *The Emancipation of the Russian Nobility, 1762–1785.* Princeton: Princeton University Press, 1973.

————. *Provincial Development in Russia: Catherine II and Jakob Sievers.* New Brunswick: Rutgers University Press, 1984.

Jones, W. Gareth. *Nikolay Novikov: Enlightener of Russia.* Cambridge and New York: Cambridge University Press, 1984.

Kahan, Arcadius. *The Plough, the Hammer, and the Knout: An Economic History of Eighteenth-Century Russia.* Chicago: University of Chicago Press, 1985.

Kaplan, Herbert H. *The First Partition of Poland.* New York: Columbia University Press, 1962.

LeDonne, John P. *Absolutism and Ruling Class: The Formation of the Russian Political Order.* New York: Oxford University Press, 1991.

————. *Ruling Russia: Politics and Administration in the Age of Absolutism, 1762–1796.* Princeton: Princeton University Press, 1984.

Leonard, Carol S. *Reform and Regicide: The Reign of Peter III of Russia.* Bloomington and Indianapolis: Indiana University Press, 1993.

Lord, Robert H. *The Second Partition of Poland.* Cambridge, MA: Harvard University Press, 1915.

McConnell, Allen. *A Russian Philosophe: Alexander Radishchev, 1749–1802.* The Hague: Martinus Nijhoff, 1964.

Madariaga, Isabel de. *Catherine the Great: A Short History.* New Haven and London: Yale University Press, 1990.

————. *Russia in the Age of Catherine the Great*. New Haven and London: Yale University Press, 1981.

Marker, Gary. *Publishing, Printing, and the Origins of Intellectual Life in Russia, 1700–1800*. Princeton: Princeton University Press, 1985.

Papmehl, K.A. *Freedom of Expression in Eighteenth Century Russia*. The Hague: Martinus Nijhoff, 1971.

Raeff, Marc, ed. *Catherine the Great: A Profile*. New York: Hill and Wang, 1972.

————. *Origins of the Russian Intelligentsia: The Eighteenth-Century Nobility*. New York: Harcourt, Brace & World, 1966.

————. *Political Ideas and Institutions in Imperial Russia*. Boulder, San Francisco, and Oxford: Westview Press, 1994.

————. *The Well-Ordered Police State: Social and Institutional Change through Law in the Germanies and Russia, 1600–1800*. New Haven and London: Yale University Press, 1983.

Raleigh, Donald J., ed. *The Emperors and Empresses of Russia: Rediscovering the Romanovs*. Armonk, NY: M.E. Sharpe, 1996.

Ransel, David L. *The Politics of Catherinian Russia: The Panin Party*. New Haven and London: Yale University Press, 1975.

Russian Studies in History: A Journal of Translations 33, no. 4 (Spring 1995). "Catherine the Great and the Search for a Usable Past," ed. Gary Marker.

Vucinich, Alexander. *Science in Russian Culture: A History to 1860*. Vol. 1. Stanford: Stanford University Press, 1963.

Wortman, Richard S. *Scenarios of Power: Myth and Ceremony in Russian Monarchy*. Vol. 1: *From Peter the Great to the Death of Nicholas I*. Princeton: Princeton University Press, 1995.

~ Index ~

A

Academy of Sciences, 89, 123, 178–79, 184

Alembert, Jean le Rond d', 96, 100, 185

Alexander I, Emperor, 185–86, 195, 197

Alexander, John, xix

Alexis, Tsar, 4, 197

Anna, Empress, 5, 14, 47, 73, 133, 134, 197
  and events of 1730, 10, 146, 210
  and serfdom, 155

Anna Leopoldovna, 28, 50, 134, 197

Assembly of the Land, 29, 110, 112, 128, 145, 209

Assignat Bank, 173

Augustus III, King, 64, 65, 79

B

Bar, Confederation of, 77–78, 79

Barre, Joseph, 45

Bayer, Gottlieb-Siegfried, 178, 197

Bayle, Pierre, 45, 189

Beccaria, Cesare, 138
  On Crimes and Punishments, 98–99, 100, 103, 104

Bender, conquest of, 72

Bernoulli brothers, 178, 197

Bessarabia, 72, 73, 197

Bestuzhev-Riumin, Alexis, 12, 13, 48, 65, 88, 197
  character of, 47

Betskoi, Ivan, 60, 198

Bezborodko, Alexander, 73, 198
  quoted, 87

Bibikov, Alexander, 113, 198

Bielfeld, Jakob Friedrich von, 99, 198

Bilfinger, Georg Bernhard, 178, 198

Biron, Ernst Johann, 12, 20, 47, 198

Black Sea Cossack Host, 190

Bolotov, Andrei, 19, 21, 198
  quoted, 18, 183

Boris Godunov, Tsar, 122, 198

Bredikhin, Guards officer, 22

Breteuil, Baron de, 60, 198
  quoted, 51

Buturlin, Dmitry, 187, 198

C

Catherine I, Empress, 5, 9, 11, 13,
    36, 133, 198
Catherine II (the Great), Empress
    character of, 39–57
    childhood of, 33–36, 40–41
    and cultural development of
        Russia, 184–89
    and d'Alembert, 96, 100, 185
    and Diderot, xvii, 185
    at Elizabeth's court, 36–51
    family background of, 32–33
    and Frederick II, 35, 40, 52, 59, 65,
        70, 99, 130
    and French Revolution, xix, 86
    to Grimm, 56
    historians' views of, xv–xx
    Instruction, 111, 112, 122, 123,
        126, 129–30, 138–39, 143,
        160, 184, 186
        composition of, 98–100
        contents of, 100–4
        quoted, 107, 113, 120, 156, 161,
            163–64
    to Madame Geoffrin, 98, 171
    and Montesquieu, 44, 45, 56, 97,
        98–99, 102, 104
    Oleg, 57
    Pushkin's view of, xvii
    quoted, 38–50, passim, 53, 54, 65,
        69–70, 71, 83, 86, 92, 95–100,
        passim, 126–27, 129, 130,
        131, 134
    and Peter III
        relations with, 21–22, 38–39, 50
        overthrow of, 24–28
        death of, 28
    and religion, 36, 41, 43, 51
    and serfdom, 156–62, 193
    and Voltaire, xvii, 45, 56, 69, 91,
        98, 185, 186–87

Catherine II (the Great) (continued)
    writings of, 56–57
Chaliapin, Boris, xiv
Charles XII, King, 15, 33, 198
Charter to the Nobility, 140–41, 144,
    145, 148, 161, 193–94
Charter to the Towns, 140–41, 144,
    148
Chebotarev, Khariton, 56, 198
Chernyshev, Ivan, 91, 184, 199
Chesme, battle of, 11, 71, 199
Chebotarev, Khariton, 56, 198
Chétardie, Jacques Joachim,
    Marquis de la Chétardie, 38, 199
Chicherin, Boris, xi
Choiseul: Étienne François, Duc de
    Choiseul, 85, 199
Code of Laws (Sudebnik) of 1550,
    105, 123
Code of Laws (Ulozhenie) of 1649,
    4, 105, 116, 128, 150, 152, 182
    and serfdom, 153, 156, 162
College of the Admiralty, 177, 179
College of Economy, 19, 107
College of Foreign Affairs, 39
College of Justice, 124, 133
College of Revenue, 154
Commission of 1754 on a New Code
    of Laws, 4–5, 14, 105–6, 108,
    123
Commission of 1767 on a New Code
    of Laws, xvii, 69, 184
    debates in, 115–21, 127, 129, 146,
        157
    elections to, 106–9, 140
    instructions to, 109–110, 111, 114,
        115, 118–19, 121, 124–26,
        129, 138–39, 156
    opening of, 113
    organization of, 111–12, 121–23
    and serfdom, 118–21
    termination of, 114–15

Commission on the Rights of the Nobility, 94
Commission on the State Land Survey, 92
Constantine, Grand Duke, 73–74
courts, 124–26
  conscience courts, 137, 139, 142–43, 145
  high (*nadvornye*) courts, 133
  reorganization of, in 1775, 137–45
Crimea, conquest of, 72–74, 84

D

d'Alembert: *See* Alembert, Jean le Rond d'
Danilov, Michael, 183, 199
Dashkova, Catherine, 53, 59, 189, 199
  and overthrow of Peter III, 22, 25
  quoted, 17, 60
Delisle, Joseph-Nicolas, 178, 199
de Madariaga, Isabel, xix
  quoted, xx
Diderot, Denis, xvii, 185
Dimitry (Sechenov), 19, 22, 121, 199
Dmitrevsky, Ivan, 176, 199
Dowe, pastor, 41
Dubiansky, Fyodor, 12, 49

E

eastern question, 63, 69, 74
Elizabeth, Empress, xxi, 4–5, 9, 33–35, 52, 88, 89, 93, 133, 199
  and Catherine, 34–36, 38–40, 48–50
  character of, 11–15, 50–51
  court of, 13–14, 36–51
  and cultural development of Russia, 176, 181–84
  on Peter III, 16–17, 50, 51

Elizabeth, Empress *(continued)*
  quoted, 49–50
  and serfdom, 154, 159, 168
  and Seven Years' War, 13, 21, 48, 64
Elphinstone, John, 71, 199
Encyclopedia (French), 99, 185
Engelhardt, Lev, 180–81

F

Fedotov, George
  quoted, x
Fonvizin, Denis, 199
  The Minor, 117, 188
  The Brigadier, 188
Frederick II (the Great), King, 34, 38, 72, 80, 82, 199
  and Catherine, 35, 40, 52, 59, 65, 70, 99, 130
  and Peter III, 16, 17, 19, 20, 21
  and Poland, 68–69, 76, 80–82
  quoted, 81
  and Russian alliance, 65–69, 73
  and Seven Years' War, 13, 20, 21, 48
Frederick William II, King, 83
Free Economic Society, 165
French Revolution, xix, 82, 85, 86
Fyodor, Tsar, 29, 199

G

Galicia, 81, 83, 191, 199
gentry, Russian. *See* nobility, Russian
Geoffrin, Marie-Thérèse, 98, 171, 200
Glebov, Alexander, 89, 200
Gogol, Nicholas
  Dead Souls, 66, 168

Golitsyn, Dmitry, 200
  quoted, 172
Gonta, Ivan, 79
Greek Project, 73–74
Grimm, Friedrich Melchior, 56, 200
gubernias, 209
  reorganization of, in 1775, 135–47
Gudovich, Andrei, 21–22

H

haydamak uprising, 79
Hertzberg, Ewald Friedrich von, 85,
  200
An Honest Mirror for Youth, 177–78

I

Imeritia, 70, 200
Ivan IV (the Terrible), Tsar, 30, 200,
  210
Ivan V, 197, 200, 203
Ivan VI, 31, 58–59, 200
  murder of, 59, 200

J

Jassy, Treaty of, 57
Jones, Robert
  quoted, xxvi*n.21*
Joseph II, Emperor, 68, 73, 200
Justi, Johann Heinrich Gottlob von,
  99, 200

K

Kabardia, 70, 74, 200
Kagul River, battle of, 72
Karpovich, Michael
  quoted, xiv
Kaunitz, Wenzel Anton von, 73, 85,
  200

Khitrovo, Fyodor, 22, 200
Khrapovitsky, Alexander, 56, 57,
  201
Kizevetter, Alexander, xv-xvii, 110
Kliuchevsky, Vasily
  birth and education, xi
  The Boyar Council of Old Rus,
    xi-xii, xiii
  and Chaliapin, xiv
  A Course in Russian History,
    xiv-xv
  origins and development of, ix-x,
    xiii, xx
  in post-Soviet period, xi
  in Soviet period, x, xiii
  translations of, xxiv*n.3*
  on eighteenth century, xv, xxii
  and Kadet Party, xvi, xx
  Soviet views of, x, xiii, xxv*n.6*,
    xxv*n.7*
  and "state school," xi-xii
  as teacher, ix-x, xi, xiii-xiv
Konissky, George, 75, 77
Korff, Nicholas, 15, 201
Korff, Johann-Albrecht, 66, 201
Kosciuszko, Tadeusz, 82, 201
Kotoshikhin, Gregory, 201
  quoted, 153
Kozitsky, Gregory, 99, 201
Kronstadt, 25, 71, 201
Krylov, Ivan, 67, 99
Kuchuk Kainarji, Treaty of, 75, 84
Kunersdorf, battle of, 13, 208

L

La Harpe, Frédéric-César, 185, 201
*Landrat*s, 9, 139, 146
Larga River, battle of, 72
Lasunsky, Guards officer, 22
Lestocq, Armand, 38, 201
Locatelli, Giovanni Battista, 14, 201

Lomonosov, Michael, 201
quoted, 178
Loran, schoolteacher, 41

M

Mainotes, 70
Manstein, Christof Hermann, 202
quoted, 179
Marat, Henri, 185–86
Martinists, 57, 209
Maslov, Anisim, 5, 202
Melgunov, Alexis, 37
Menshikov, Alexander, 151, 202
Mercier de la Rivière, 202
quoted, 143
Michael, Tsar, 29, 202, 209, 210
Miliukov, Paul, xv-xvi
Outlines of Russian Culture, xv
Mirovich, Vasily, 59, 200, 202
Moldavia, 72, 73, 75, 80, 82, 202
Montesquieu, Charles de Secondat,
Baron de, 44, 56, 97, 102
Spirit of the Laws, 45, 98–99, 104,
186
Moscow University
founding of, 13, 178–79, 181
Münnich, Burkhard Christoph von,
25, 179, 202
Musin-Pushkin, Alexis, 56, 202

N

Naryshkin, Lev, 37, 38
Naval Corps of Cadets, 177, 179
Nicholas I, Emperor, 139, 195, 202
nobility, Russian
education of, 177–89, 193–96
and emancipation from
compulsory service, 5, 7, 61,
118, 146, 157, 163, 192–93
estate institutions of, 138–47, 175

nobility, Russian *(continued)*
origins of, 116–17
See also Charter to the Nobility
Nobles' Infantry Corps of Cadets,
179–80
Northern System, 66–67, 69, 73, 77
Northern War, 8, 198
Novikov, Nicholas
The Painter, 183
Nystadt, Treaty of, 8, 63

O

Ochakov, conquest of, 74
Odoevsky, Ivan, 37
office of social welfare, 138, 139,
142, 145
Office of State Expenditure, 64
Old Believers, 18, 209
Opochinin, landowner, 196
quoted, 195
oprichnina, 30, 210
Orlov, Alexis, 22, 23, 70, 74, 107, 202
and death of Peter III, 27–28
and Free Economic Society, 165
quoted, 71, 72
Orlov, Gregory, 22, 70, 81, 115, 202
Ostermann, Andrei, 4, 134, 203

P

Pallas, Peter Simon, 168, 203
Panin, Nikita, 73, 74, 87, 100, 203
character of, 65–67
and Imperial Council plan, 93–94,
135
and Northern System, 66–67, 77
and overthrow of Peter III, 22, 23
and Poland, 68, 76–77, 79–81
quoted, 77
Panin, Peter, 157, 162, 203
quoted, 166

Passek, Peter, 22, 23–24, 203
Paul, Emperor, 17, 22, 51, 58–59,
    65, 203
  birth of, 46
Pérard, Father, 41
Peter I (the Great), Emperor, 17, 80,
    119, 203
  and army, 145–46
  and education of nobility, 177–78,
    179, 186
  and navy, 11, 64, 177
  and Northern War, 8, 198
  reforms of, 3, 5, 7–8, 10–11,
    29–30, 116, 128, 132–33,
    192
  and serfdom, 148–49, 152–53,
    154, 155, 156, 162
  succession law of, 31, 90, 192
Peter II, Emperor, 133, 203
Peter III, Emperor, xxi, 31, 35, 37,
    47, 61, 88, 133, 203
  character of, 15–17, 39
  death of, 27–28
  and emancipation of nobility, 5
  overthrow of, 23–26, 51
  quoted, 21, 46
  reign of, 17–20, 51
  and serfdom, 154
Platon (Levshin), 11, 203
Poland
  confederations in, 77, 82
    Confederation of Bar, 77–78, 79
    Confederation of Targowica, 82
  and Czartoryski princes, 68
  dissidents in, 76–79, 82
  government of, 64, 68, 76–77, 82,
    210
  and haydamak uprising, 79
  and Kosciuszko uprising, 82
  partitions of, 79–84, 171, 190–91
Polenov, Alexis, 162, 204
Poliansky, Alexander, 26

Poniatowski, Stanislas, 64–65, 79,
    204
  quoted, 76
Pososhkov, Ivan, 5, 204
Potemkin, Gregory, 22, 73, 158, 204
Pugachev, Yemelian, 130, 204
Pugachev Rebellion, xvii, xxi, 78,
    131, 135, 164, 193
Pulaski, Joseph, 77, 204

R

Raeff, Marc
  quoted, xix-xx
Rambour, Stephen, 12
Rastrelli, Bartolomeo, 14, 204
Razumovsky, Alexis, 11, 37, 204
Razumovsky, Kirill, 151, 204
  and overthrow of Peter III, 22, 24,
    48
  quoted, 11
  and serfdom in Ukraine, 158–59
Romme, Gilbert, 185
Roslavlev brothers, 22
Rousseau, Jean-Jacques, 186, 189
Rumiantsev, Peter, 167, 205
Rurik, Prince, 117, 205
Russian Justice, 167
Rychkov, Peter, 164, 205
  quoted, 166

S

St. Sergius, 56, 205
Saltykov, Nicholas, 185, 205
Secret Chancery, 18, 210
Ségur: Louis Philippe, Comte de
    Ségur, 59, 205
Semevsky, V.I., xvi
  quoted, xxvin.21
serfdom
  and agricultural life, 162–70

serfdom *(continued)*
and alcohol tax, 172–73
and Catherine, 156–62
and Commission of 1767, 118–21
and emancipation of 1861, 120,
161–62, 163
origins of, xxi, 148–56
and peasant disturbances, 7, 175,
193
and population distribution,
170–72
in Ukraine, 158–59
See also Elizabeth; Peter I;
Peter III
Seven Years' War, 13, 20, 47, 48,
63–64, 65, 67
Shcherbatov, Michael, 116–21, 126,
205
quoted, 119
Shuvalov, Alexander, 49, 205
Shuvalov, Andrei, 187, 205
Epistle to Ninon, 187
Shuvalov, Ivan, 4, 48, 50, 184, 205
Shuvalov, Peter, 4, 13, 37, 205
quoted, 10
Shuvalova, Mavra, 13
Sievers, Jakob Johann, 206
on serfdom, 157, 162, 168
single homesteaders, 106, 109, 113,
125, 210
Solovyov, Sergei, xi
Soltyk, Kajetan, 77–78
Sophia, Tsarevna, 13, 206
Speransky, Michael, 94, 206
Spiridov, Gregory, 71, 206
Stanislas Augustus IV, King. *See*
Poniatowski, Stanislas
State Council, 94, 210
State Loan Bank, 168–69
Statute for the Administration of the
Gubernias, 135–38, 170
See also gubernias

Storch, Heinrich, 164, 166,
206
Stroganov, Paul, 185, 206
Strube de Piermont, Friedrich
Henrich, 5, 206
Struisky, Nicholas, 189, 206
Sumarokov, Alexander, 176,
182–83, 206
The Monsters, 182
Khorev, 182
Supreme Privy Council, 5, 10, 93,
97, 133, 210
Synod, Most Holy Governing, 14,
19, 23, 24, 105, 106, 122, 210

T

Targowica, Confederation of, 82
Tiflis (Tbilisi), 70, 206
Time of Troubles, 28, 29, 210
Todorsky, Simon, 41, 206
towns
magistracies in, 133, 141
population growth of, 8, 171–72
*ratusha*s in, 133
self-government of, 141–42, 144,
145
see also Charter to the Towns
Trediakovsky, Vasily, 189, 207
Trubetskoi, Nikita, 19, 207
Turkish war, first, 66, 69–75, 80–81,
84, 94
Turkish war, second, 73–74, 84–85,
173, 190

U

Ulozhenie. See Code of Laws of
1649
Uman, massacre in, 79
Uniates, 76, 79, 211
Ushakov, Fyodor, 84–85, 207

V

Viazemsky, Alexander, 134, 207
Vilbua, Alexander, 94, 207
Vinsky, Gregory, 186, 207
Vockerodt, Johann Gotthilf, 6, 207
Volkov, Dmitry, 37
Voltaire (François-Marie Arouet), 38, 189, 194–96
 and Catherine, xvii, 45, 56, 69, 91, 98, 185, 186–87
 History of the Empire of Russia under Peter the Great, 184
Vorontsov, Michael, 21, 25, 207
Vorontsova, Anna, 13
Vorontsova, Elizabeth, 21, 23, 26, 47, 50, 199

W

Wallachia, 72, 73, 75, 80, 82, 207
Wagner, pastor, 41
West Russian question, 63, 75–76, 79–80, 83–84, 85

Y

Yaguzhinsky, Paul, 5, 134, 207
Yavorsky, Stefan, 207
 The Rock of Faith, 182

Z

Zaporozhian Cossacks, 79, 190, 208
Zhelezniak, Maxim, 79
Zorndorf, battle of, 13, 208

About the Author

Vasily O. Kliuchevsky (1841–1911) was the most eminent Russian historian of his day—a pathbreaking scholar, a spellbinding lecturer, an engaging stylist, and a great synthesizer whose works have stood the test of time. He was a long-time professor of Russian history at Moscow University before his death. His lectures, published as *A Course in Russian History*, have exerted a powerful influence on Russia's conception of its national history, not only before 1917 but in the Soviet period and to the present day. This is the first reliable translation of the section of the *Course* on Catherine the Great.

About the Translator and Editor

Marshall S. Shatz is Professor of History at the University of Massachusetts at Boston. He is the author of *Soviet Dissent in Historical Perspective* (1980) and *Jan Waclaw Machajski: A Radical Critic of the Russian Intelligentsia and Socialism* (1989). He has also edited and translated a number of works on Russian intellectual history, including (with Judith E. Zimmerman) *Vekhi (Landmarks)*, published by M.E. Sharpe in 1994.